THE VILLAGE OF VIRIATINO

THE VILLAGE OF
VIRIATINO

*An Ethnographic Study of a Russian Village
from before the Revolution to the Present*

Translated and Edited by
SULA BENET

ANCHOR BOOKS

*Doubleday & Company, Inc.
Garden City, New York*
1970

The Village of Viriatino was first published in Moscow in 1958. The Anchor Books edition is an original translation, published by agreement with Mezhkniga Moscow, USSR.

Anchor Books edition: 1970

309.147
V71
76394
Nov.1971

This book is dedicated to the people of Viriatino.

P. I. KUSHNER
Editor-in-Chief

CONTENTS

TRANSLATOR'S PREFACE

The Village of Viriatino is one of the first community studies undertaken in the Soviet Union. It traces the culture, family life, economy, and architecture of one Russian peasant village from before the Revolution to the present. It is impossible, of course, to find a "typical village" representative of Russian rural areas as a whole, and so the decision was made to select one typical of those in one province. Viriatino was selected. It is an ancient settlement approximately two hundred miles southeast of Moscow in the Sosnov region of Tambov province with deep historical roots in grain agriculture. The study was undertaken to reconstruct the prerevolutionary life, trace the processes of change to the period after the Revolution, and to study the influence of seasonal workers on the culture of the village.

The study was prepared under the direction of P. I. Kushner under the auspices of the Miklukho-Maklai Institute of Ethnography of the Academy of Sciences of the USSR. It was written by nine men, each a specialist within a particular field:

Chapter I—P. I. Kushner
Chapter II—L. N. Chizhikova
Chapter III—M. N. Shmeleva
Chapter IV—V. U. Krupianskaia
Chapters V and VI—L. A. Bushkarev
Chapter VII—P. I. Kushner, S. M. Ozhogin, and V. U. Krupianskaia
Chapter VIII—L. N. Chizhikova
Chapter IX—M. N. Shmeleva
Chapter X—V. U. Krupyanskaya
Chapters XI and XII—L. A. Pushkareva

L. V. Rulakovskii, a musicologist, and R. P. Aldoni-noia, an architect, also participated in the study. The authors used questionnaires extensively and collected a sizable amount of statistical data, keeping close ties with the village at all times to study the changes as they took place. A number of field trips were organized to verify all of the theoretical conclusions.

Since each author apparently worked independently in preparing their findings for publication, the Russian text contained a considerable amount of overlapping material. I have accordingly deleted repetitious material where it seemed unnecessary and shortened standard ideological formulas which seemed to me to relate to Russia as a whole and did not seem immediately pertinent to the village of Viriatino. Since this book is being published in this country as largely an ethnographic study I have also omitted a number of paragraphs which contained obscure local colloquialisms, such as the vocabulary used in peasant building trades. The transliteration of Russian orthography was done according to the standards set by the United States Library of Congress.

My warm thanks go to the late Carl Withers for advice and help in understanding some of the agricultural processes as well as his good editorial advice. I am also indebted to Madame Lilia Filippova, a candidate in Historical Sciences at the University of Moscow, for her interpretation of the many acronyms in the original text and for much information about the development of the collective farm in the Soviet Union; and especially to M. V. Krylov, an agricultural economist, for assistance in that area and for his invaluable help in the final states of preparation of this book. My thanks, too, to Maria Polushkin for her help in the translation of a portion of this book as well as her editorial assistance.

SULA BENET

1970

PART I

RUSSIAN VILLAGE LIFE
BEFORE THE REVOLUTION

CHAPTER I

THE ECONOMIC LIFE OF THE PREREVOLUTIONARY VILLAGE

Village Farming — Communal Landowning

At the middle of the nineteenth century the province of Tambov, together with other provinces of the Middle Black Belt (Ryazan, Voronezh, Orlov, Kursk, Penzensk), were considered the breadbasket of Russia. Its people had always been agricultural and were among the major suppliers of rye for the population of the cities and the earliest industrial regions.

On the eve of the abolition of serfdom, most of the farmland of Tambov province belonged to landowners, some of whom held quite large tracts of land which were counted in thousands of desiatins (each equivalent to 2.7 acres).

The ancestral manors in Tambov province had a corvée system. The basis of this agrarian economy of that period was as follows: The entire farming area of a given manor was divided into the lord's and the peasants' land; the latter was distributed in allotments among the peasants, who received other means as well, for example, timber, sometimes cattle, etc. The peasant worked the lord's land some days of the week, and on other days he worked his own. All the work was done with the implements provided by the peasants themselves. In this type of economy, their allotment served as wage payment in exchange for labor on the manor.

Besides the manor's serfs who worked the lord's land, the province of Tambov had other categories of peasant population. These included the descendants of freeholders who worked land originally earned through military service and were subject to the peasant poll tax and to the system of joint responsibility, and peasants who paid rent in addition to the poll tax for the use of land.

In the Morshansk district of Tambov province where the village of Viriatino is located, all these categories of peasants were represented, the number of freehold peasants and manor serfs being about equal. According to the Tenth Census, taken in 1857, there were 8403 homesteads of free peasants, numbering, together with their families, 82,765 people; 10,435 homesteads of manor serfs numbering 81,787 people; and 1378 households of wage earners numbering 9991 people. The last category of peasants received only a plot of land on which to build a house; the other categories had some farm land in addition to a building lot.

The land reform of 1861 gave the freehold peasants an inalienable right to the land that they had owned for a long time. The manor serfs, however, lost their right to use parts of those arable lands they had previously worked with their own equipment and the meadows where they had pastured their livestock. These "remnants" remained with the landowner. The loss of meadows for pastures created a difficult situation for the peasants, for henceforth they were obliged to lease from the landowner on terms dictated by him.

Since the landowners appropriated from the former peasant allotment lands without which the peasants could not sustain a self-supporting homestead, the landowners had a chance, even after the reform, to preserve the remnants of serfdom in the form of corvée labor.

The types of corvée were exceedingly varied. Sometimes the peasants undertook to cultivate the landowner's fields with their own implements for payment in money. Sometimes the peasant borrowed grain or money and undertook to work off either the entire loan or the interest due on it. Under this form of otrabotki,[1] its most characteristic feature became obvious, the usurious nature of this sort of hired labor amounting to bondage. Otrabotki became very widespread as either cropping or labor in exchange for land rented, etc. Otrabotki embraced the whole cycle of jobs in rural life; all operations related to field cultivation, the harvesting of grain and hay, the gathering and storing of firewood, carting, the repairing of roofs and chimneys, and the delivery of poultry and eggs were undertaken.[2]

The presence of this system of working to make up debts after the reform explained the economic backwardness of both the landlords' and the peasants' farms in those areas where it existed. One of these areas was the Tambov region, which Lenin called "a region with a very weak development of capitalism."

The basic factor that hastened the end of serfdom in Russia was the development of capitalistic industry which required freely hired labor. The Law of 1861 made it easier to recruit workers, although many difficulties remained; the preservation of communal land tenure, the difficulties entailed in leaving the village community, and the establishment of joint responsibility for taxes in great measure prevented the peasants from giving up an agricultural way of life. Moreover, many of them preferred seasonal labor to steady work in industry. But if the peasant reform did not fulfill the expectation of eager industrialists, and did not at once spur a flourishing growth of industrial enterprises (which came later), it did at least, without doubt, immediately facilitate the development of capitalistic relations in the village itself.

The political party of Narodniks thought that the preservation of the free landed community would prevent Russia from developing capitalism. But this belief proved

[1] *Otrabotki*—Paying rent by workdays (Tr.).

[2] Lenin, V., *Works*, vol. 3, pp. 163–65, in Russian.

to be erroneous; capitalism in farming, as it revealed itself, coexisted very nicely with the equalizing principles of rural community structure. As a matter of fact, capitalism found the most fitting conditions for its further development in this "equality." "Contrary to the theory which has governed our thinking in the last half century," wrote Lenin, "Russian communal peasants are not antagonistic toward capitalism, but represent the deepest and most solid basis for it. In spite of existing institutions which restricted the development of capitalism, the peasants represent the deepest factor for it because it is here in the community, isolated from any 'artificial' influences, that we see a steady formation of capitalistic elements. And the peasants are its most solid foundation because the village is based on agriculture in general and peasantry in particular. The old traditions weigh heaviest and most solidly on agricultural people, especially the peasants. The tradition of patriarchal structure was affected by the working of capitalism (development of production forces, changes in all social relations, etc.). The progress here is extremely slow and gradual."[3]

When studying the economic history of Viriatino, we first encounter a peculiarity in the village's economic development in the post land reform period, and a multitude of lingering survivals of serfdom such as otrabotki, equalization of land allotment, imposed rotation of seeds, and so on. But capitalism built itself a solid base in the village community and with the development of interdependent capitalistic relations, there was a reversal of the land equalizing principle.

In the second half of the nineteenth century, two categories of inhabitants survived in Viriatino: the State peasants (freeholders) and the serfs of the manor. The Emancipation Act of 1861 found a group of State peasants already progressing from individual land ownership to

[3] Lenin, V., *ibid.*, vol. 3, p. 141.

equalized communal parceling with specific parcels for each male "soul" regardless of age. Among the State peasants, there were those who had freed themselves by land redemption payment, and others who had previously owned individual parcels of land. Thus not long before the abandonment of serfdom a gardener of the landlord Davidov by the name of Zhdanov was received into the community after making the land redemption payment. Other families of former freehold peasants were also received into the land tenure community.

In Viriatino the State peasants formed a separate community which was part of Perkinsk county of Morshansk district. The former serfs of the estates formed another community in the village that was part of Kulevatovsk county of Morshansk district. In spite of the fact that the lands of the State peasants were surrounded on all sides by the lands of former serfs, the two peasant communities lived side by side in the same village, not merging under a unified administration until the October Revolution.

Communal land tenure existed among both categories of peasants in Viriatino, although the customs of the two groups differed.

In 1861, when former State peasants received 316.6 acres of land, they divided the land according to the number of registered "souls." Each "soul" received 5.3 desiatins of land, which included arable land, meadows, and pastures. National taxation and communal duties and obligations were divided among members of the community in proportion to the size of the family holdings and thereafter had to be fulfilled regardless of the expansion or diminution in the number of adult workers in a family or mouths to be fed. In the Viriatino community there was no new redistribution of land for the State peasant until 1872, and after that date even the faint possibility of such an event vanished. The communities by their own decision bound the existing allotments to the families that used them, thereby making them private property.

In 1870 the head official of Perkinsk county, who happened to be a rich timber merchant, began to agitate for the division of lands into private homestead property that would be inherited in the family. The rich peasants backed the proposal; for them the communal tenure and land redistribution with periodic equalization were not desirable. The great majority of peasants remained categorically opposed to permanent division of land into privately owned property, and the meetings in Viriatino and other villages of Perkinsk county at which the decisions about land division were taken. Those present gave "formal, although far from comprehensive, agreement to proposals for division." Ten years later, Romanov, a land statistician, wrote: "After personally interviewing the peasants of Perkinsk county, we were entirely convinced that the peasants have a far from exact understanding of the separate proprietorship established for them. Without exaggeration one can say that one could leave Perkinsk county without being aware that here the land was divided into private inheritable homesteads. At our investigation we avoided such misunderstandings only because we had the village foreman present while we spoke with the peasants. The peasants themselves were reluctant to admit that in their village private landownership is an established fact and that adjustment in land redistribution is not possible anymore. At the present time most of the peasants in all the communities in the district would like to have a redistribution of allotments according to the number of people in the household. The district officer, of course, does not allow such redistribution of land, pointing out that at the present time the land allotments have become private property. But the peasants are reproaching the officer for this situation, claiming that they never gave their approval to divide the land forever."[4]

[4] Romanov, N., Krestianskoe Khoziaistvo v Morshanskom uezdie. In *Sbornik Statisticheskikh Svedenii po Tambovskoi Gubernii*, vol. 3, Tambov, 1882, p. 59.

The new land was not fully acted upon immediately, however, and the old communal land tenure lingered for some time. But the practice of redistribution came to an end, with the exception of pastures, meadows, and haylofts.

In the meantime, the archaic system which provided allotments according to the number of "souls" in each family immediately after the reforms gradually created discrepancies because the number of people in families constantly changed. By the 1880s some families who had only a few adult workers were in possession of more land than they could possibly farm, and the poll taxes and other obligations they had to meet were in accordance with the size of the holdings, not the number of workers. For these people it became necessary to lease part of their holdings to others on the understanding that the one to whom the land was transferred would assume responsibility for the payment of taxes. On the other hand, there were families with a large number of adults capable of working who had allotments too small to make a living. These people were forced either to lease some land from their co-villagers or to leave the village for outside jobs. The system of equal tenure of land had turned into its opposite. Not only was it responsible for the practice of land leasing, it facilitated the development of capitalistic relations.

The former Viriatino manor serfs found themselves in a somewhat different situation but the results were the same. On February 19, 1861, the land allotment for manor serfs of Morshansk district was established at 3 desiatins a person. The measures taken in the agricultural reorganization deprived the former manor serfs of about one third of the land, and also of the pastures and haylofts they had used in the past. About 2016.7 desiatins (5500 acres) of farm land had to be redeemed from the landowner, Davidov. These redemption payments became a great burden to the newly freed serfs. Their community annually paid 4880 rubles to the landlord and another 2213 to the State.

According to an agreement of 1865, the allotted land was to be on the basis of a share for each of the 705 males who were considered former serfs as listed in the Tenth Census of 1857, and divided among the families. However, during the intervening years, the composition of the participating families changed somewhat and the number of males increased to 721. For this reason, when the communal lands were divided, those families with sons born after 1857 did not receive allotments, while other families in which the death of a male member or members had occurred, received a surplus of the allotted land. Thus at the very beginning of the agreement, the principle on the basis of which the land was to be divided did not indeed provide for an equitable distribution. Shortly afterward, when it became clear that the division of land among the families did not secure the projected schedule of payments, some families with few adult workers and many people to feed having defaulted in their payments, the community became concerned. In view of the collective responsibility for taxes and land redemption, the community as a whole was held responsible for delinquents. It collected payments from each of its members and the debt of the delinquent had to be divided among the rest. In order to avoid this kind of situation, the village assembly began on an annual basis to distribute the land more equitably by taking part of the allotment from peasant families with few working adults and giving it to those who were more "reliable in their payments." To the casual observer, it looked as if the mir[5] forced the well-to-do families to take upon themselves the additional allotments,

[5] *Mir*—The affairs of the community were conducted by an assembly of heads of households, and by the elder selected by the community. The Mir exercised self-government, bore joint responsibility for taxes, made periodic redistribution of land, and controlled common use of meadow and fisheries (Tr.).

releasing poorer households from the burden of unnecessary lands. Actually, things were quite different; in assembly, all members of the village community council were elected by the assembly starosta (head elder and scribe). In spite of the high price paid for redeemed land and the relatively low price paid for renting other people's allotments, well-to-do peasants who had started bakeries on a small scale considered it profitable to add to their communal land plots.

Partial redistribution of lands was practiced in Viriatino annually up to 1881. During the twenty years since the end of serfdom, the ratio of families with small labor force to the amount of allotted land changed importantly. Also, payments to the landlord for redeemed land were subject to annulment and only payments to the State were enforced. As a consequence the value of allotted land increased. Now it was possible to lease out allotted land on more favorable conditions than before and to use the rent money to pay the State. Some sectors of public opinion demanded a new overall redistribution according to actual numbers. In 1881 the village council decided to take that step and at this very year a new household census was taken. The new equalizing principle was not always, however, applied in full. Some well-to-do families had grabbed additional allotments of land when it was redistributed in the past and had held them for many years; they had already paid the greater part of the redemption on those allotments and did not want to pass them on to others. It was hard to convince such influential families to lease out the extra land, especially when the assembly wished to avoid an angry dispute with them. In consequence the rich usually kept all the land they had for their own use.

The next general redistribution of communal lands in Viriatino took place in 1894. By then, some allotments had been freed, mostly because people had left the community. In addition, the council had frequently cut up an owner's land, leased out plots from communal holdings, and re-distributed some small strips. All these actions required the setting up of a lottery and greatly complicated the actual farming of the land.

In part, the complication had to do with the quality of the communal lands in Viriatino. In both peasant communities, it was not very high; black earth plots were few since the majority were ashlike and sandy. In order to equalize the holdings of all kinds, fields were divided into a multitude of small strips. "The peasants," wrote N. Romanov, "did not hesitate to divide their land into the tiniest parcels if the land had parts that were not of equal quality, even if from this division there resulted tiny strips that were not only difficult but sometimes impossible to cultivate. Such narrow strips were always made, as far as we know, when the land of a given community consisted of parts of very good and parts of especially poor soil. The governing principle was to give everyone an equal share of good and poor land."[6] To insure fairness and avoid arguments between individual families over the quality of strips, the community of former manor serfs and the community of State peasants in Viriatino always accomplished the division of lands through a lottery.

The division of land into matching strips was most complicated in itself. The procedure was that, first of all, the village assembly elected a surveyor to determine the quantity and quality of land available. Then the parcels of land were divided into two categories, good and poor, and then matched up to form "pies." In the community of former manor serfs, the "pie" was equivalent to fifteen personal allotments. Each "pie" consisted of better and worse strips of land, some near and some at a distance from the village. The "pies" were then grouped into fields, and a lottery of "pies" was held, and the fields were raffled off. This was the traditional system of land division in Russian peasant communities.

[6] Romanov, N., *ibid.*, vol. 3, p. 33.

The land surveyor dug small holes in the ground on the edge of each field for the new owner to set up his property markers. Since roads led from one plot to another, the markers were placed near the road. When, as often happened, the strips of field and pastures belonging to a family were scattered in a multitude of different places the family would make its holdings more compact by exchanging them with other families who also had scattered lots. Families were pleased if they could group their land into fifteen to twenty pieces situated in far fields. As a result of this method of distribution, the tillable land of the community was transformed into a multitude of narrow patches in an open field.

In the second half of the nineteenth century, the peasants of both Viriatino communities organized their farming according to the three-field system. Each homestead trisected its land into winter, spring, and fallow fields. Whenever possible, the peasant planted the same grain as his neighbor because after harvesting the cattle were let out to graze on the stubble, and if one's crop ripened later than a neighbor's, cattle from the neighboring field would destroy the standing grain. From time immemorial winter rye had been the basic crop. Both winter and spring barley were also planted extensively, but after the end of serfdom, barley was replaced by spring crops, mostly millet. The sowing of oats and buckwheat was also curtailed.

The tools used in Viriatino for plowing included wooden double plows with a detachable share and a harrow. Wooden harrows were made with wooden teeth tied to them, not inserted, and because of this the harrow was called a "bound." Oak teeth were fastened with shoots from young oak and bird-cherry trees. Recently, one of these harrows was found in a neighboring village, Atmanov Ugol, where the same type was used almost up to the time of collectivization. The use of such harrows in Viriatino in the past is attested to by the old people and by a widely known refrain, "Harrow, harrow, harrow, The oak teeth, Bird-cherry tree points."

For tilling virgin land, a large wooden harrow drawn by six to eight horses was used. Door-to-door inquiry in 1881 established the fact that there were only a few of these larger harrows in the whole district. Their owners used them not only to work their own virgin lands, but also to rent out to neighboring villages. Sometimes the owners of such outfits, well-to-do peasants or families with only a few working men, would unite into an artel.[7] Together they would buy a plow and hire themselves out for work, each one using his own horses. One such plow in Viriatino for six horses was owned by Matrochin, who harrowed land for his co-villagers for a wage. Another was often brought into Viriatino from a neighboring village, Nizhnee Griaznoe.

The harvest was gathered with sickles, scythes, and rakes. In the 1870s the sickle was used mostly for harvesting rye and millet. It is possible that the choice between scythe and sickle for cutting grain was determined by the numbers of available workers in the household. When the family had enough men to work the fields, the scythe was used; women always reaped with a sickle. During serfdom men also reaped with sickles on the landlords' farms. The scythe was considered too difficult for a woman to handle, although it is hard to say whether handling a sickle was easier. Rye was threshed with chains on an open-air threshing floor, and millet, oats, and peas were threshed usually with detached cart wheels. Afterward the grain was winnowed (fanned) with a spade or put through a large sifter.

[7] The *artel* is an ancient Russian institution for cooperative work, but historical records of its existence go back only as far as the fourteenth century. Members of a Russian artel were of more or less equal class. They were often from the same village or locality. Each artel had an elected leader who acted as manager, making contracts with employers and handling finances for the group. Members were bound by the principle of collective responsibility, which was recognized by law. Earnings were shared equally, though younger workers got less for work requiring less skill (Tr.).

With the development of capitalistic relations in the village and the growth of income from non-agricultural occupations (which gave the seasonal workers an opportunity to improve their farms), farm tools changed. Beginning in the 1890s, a plow with a single iron share came to be used, and one with two shares appeared soon afterward. But these improved agricultural implements were used in few homesteads (only 11 percent) as late as 1917.

Some innovations in the technique of making wooden plows were introduced. At first only the well-to-do owned metal moldboards, which were made by smiths in the neighboring villages of Berezovka and Degtianka, but later almost all did. Often the peasant did not have to buy a new moldboard; a smith simply converted the old one by plating it with melted metal. Such a plow was more efficient in breaking up the soil. Yet if this new equipment were left in the field after work with tufts of dirt covering the surface, it would soon be covered with rust. The harrow also underwent a transformation; the oak teeth which were previously used gave way to iron teeth.

The first farm machines—horse-drawn threshers and reapers—appeared at the turn of the century. But only the rich and the kulaks[8] could afford them. For the majority in Viriatino, the low level of farm technology remained the same, as can be seen from the fact that during the fifty years

---

[8] *Kulak* literally means *fist*. The peasants call those rich men of the peasant class kulaks who practiced usury, who often rented land from other peasants who were then in the economic position of tenant farmers in the American South, and who dominated the village council because they had so many people in debt to them. They were also called "mir-eaters." As a result of the policy of expropriating the property of the kulaks, they were liquidated as a class between 1929–30. They were deprived of the right to the free use of land and implements, and of the right to lease land and hire labor. Many kulaks were exiled or tried and sentenced to forced labor. For the remainder, the only way to survive was to migrate to the cities or join collectives. On the other hand, many collectives voted against admitting kulaks into their midst (Tr.).

after the peasant reform of 1861, about 89 percent of peasant households continued to work the fields with wooden plows and harvest with the scythe and the sickle. These backward methods were very time-consuming and demanded more laborers, and the amount of effort exerted by the peasants did not correspond to the results since the primitive plows did not allow deep enough tillage. The fields were overgrown with weeds and land productivity fell lower from year to year.

In the fields in Viriatino work usually began at the beginning of May. First came the plowing and harrowing of spring crops, then the sowing of oats with a wooden plow. Next, after two preliminary plowings, buckwheat and millet were planted, also with a wooden plow. The first plowing of the field lying fallow began during the first weeks of July. The peasant did not rush with his work because the fallow field was frequently used as a pasture for cattle. A busy period followed; it was necessary to weed spring crops (oats were weeded only once, millet two to four times), to cut and harvest hay, to harvest grains, and sow rye in winter fields. Events rushed by one after another; harvesting demanded fair weather and the cycle of the work could be upset if it had to be put off.

Haying began shortly after the plowing of the fallow winter fields for the crops. As the men cut the hay, the women shook it, turning it over with rakes, and, when it was dry, helped to spread it out on carts. Part of the hay was stored in the hayloft; the rest was piled in stacks. The mowing and storing of hay took about two weeks. Afterward, while the weeding of spring crops was in progress, the second plowing of the fields for the winter crops took place. About the end of July, depending on the condition of the crops, the harvest began and the winter sowing was done sometime during the end of August.

In Viriatino during most of the nineteenth century women still harvested rye with sickles. By the nineties more and more rye was cut with scythes. Not long before the Revolution of 1905, the scythe hook had completely replaced the sickle. The men cut and the women bound the sheaves. During the harvesting all able-bodied members of the family were present, including the teenagers; all left the house at three or four in the morning and did not return until evening. Only old people and small children remained at home; mothers brought their nursing infants with them into the fields so that they would not have to return home during the day. When all the rye had been cut and bound into sheaves some of them transported the sheaves to the open threshing floor, while others began the work of threshing.

At the same time the spring crops ripened and people were busy harvesting them, interrupting the threshing of rye. It took about two days to cut the oats, bind them into sheaves, and fork the sheaves into carts. The peasants would bring a cart or two near home, empty the oats on the ground and drive the carts back and forth over them. Sometimes oats were left for the winter in storage bins. Rye was laid in stacks.

After the sowing of winter crops, millet was harvested with the hook. The last work to be done in the fields was the digging of potatoes. Cabbage was the last crop to be brought in from the gardens.

Flax and hemp were also sown, although the former was not widely cultivated. Hemp was grown mostly in the gardens, pulled out of the ground by hand, each blade separately, and bound together in bunches that were dried standing up. Besides serving as the raw material for cloth, hemp also provided an oil used in cooking.

All of the plowing, harrowing, and sowing were done by men. Tradition strictly regimented what work should be done by whom. Harvesting grain with the sickle was women's work; only men worked with the scythe and hook. The scattering of fertilizer on the fields and the binding of sheaves was also done by women, as was weeding, collecting the dug-up potatoes, and pulling hemp. Generally, when the sickle was no longer used in harvesting, basic work in the fields was performed by men; the women played a supporting role.

Until the 1890s, most if not the overwhelming majority of peasant fields were not fertilized. Manure was used only in the gardens that were part of every peasant household or for improving the landlords' fields—a form of payment made by the peasants of the landlords' pastures. As a result, peasant land became impoverished. At first, the peasants explained their unwillingness to fertilize it, saying that because of the frequent land redistribution there was no reason to be especially concerned about the quality of a field that might be owned by someone else the next year. But the small number of cattle the peasants owned also limited the amount of organic fertilizer. It was only in the 1880s that there began a more or less systematic fertilizing of some fields, mostly those that were sandy or in which millet was grown.

For the peasants of Viriatino rye at one time was the only winter crop. Their attempts to grow winter wheat did not give satisfactory results because the fields were too poorly fertilized. In dry years, however, they found that only millet brought a good harvest. According to the peasants it was better to plant millet than oats because while the cattle needed "oat straw, we need porridge even more." Whatever the reason, millet became the basic winter grain in the fields of Viriatino, but this was comparatively recent because porridge was a rarity during serfdom. Buckwheat porridge, formerly the staple food in Viriatino, almost entirely disappeared from peasant tables with the exception of those of the well-to-do peasants. In this way, millet replaced other grains in the winter fields. The sowing of peas gradually diminished because the harvest yield dropped. Potatoes, which in the first years after the peasant reform occupied a small part of the fields, were increasingly grown after a molasses factory was built in Sosnovka; but the people of Viriatino grew them more for personal than for commercial consumption.

A large proportion of the agricultural produce was kept by the peasants of Viriatino for their own needs. Millet was entirely set aside for their own use. The nearest market place usually received peas, buckwheat, and rye. The poorer people sold their rye in autumn when the taxes and levies were due. The more well-to-do took their rye to the markets in the winter and spring, in order to take advantage of the seasonal increase in prices. However, most peasants did not produce enough bread for the whole year. Romanov remarked about the Morshansk region that one could not survive on what one could grow and that most families had to buy bread to feed themselves, some having run out by Easter or Shrovetide, but others even by October 1 (old calendar). According to the agricultural statistics in the 1880s, three fourths of the peasant households in the district could not grow enough grain in their own fields for their personal needs and the payment of taxes. The only peasants who did not have to buy additional bread were those who rented land from villagers who did not have enough able-bodied people to work their allotments. Some of those who rented additional land needed their entire harvest for themselves; those who were somewhat richer sold the surplus bread at market or lent money on a high percentage to poorer households.

The community of former State peasants was in somewhat better circumstances in being assured of an allotment than the community of former manor serfs because their allotments consisted almost entirely of pasture land. Peasants who raised cattle could survive only by renting pasture lands from landowners. Therefore the purchase in the late 1880s of about 1700 desiatins (4600 acres) consisting of small parcels of peasant lands, which since the Reform of 1861 had become the property of the landlord Davidov, was a great event for the future of cattle raising. Part of this land was covered with forest which then represented a great value because of the demand for wood for railroad ties, telegraph poles, and the construction of railroad stations. On some plots unsuitable for agriculture there were excellent clay beds that could be used in the manufacturing of bricks. The purchase of these lands alleviated somewhat the shortage of land among the peasants but did not solve it entirely.

The shortage of land was acute for the peasant householders of the Middle Black Belt Region, where after the reform huge tracts were, as before, concentrated in the hands of large landowners. The peasants' communal holdings were so small that it was impossible to employ motorized machinery to farm the black earth strips. At the beginning of the twentieth century, when peasant farming in the Middle Black Belt provinces collapsed and the Tsar's government was forced to account for this agricultural catastrophe, the official statistician, A. Rittikh, offered the following explanation: "It is hardly necessary to prove that the small size of the allotment constitutes one of the main obstacles to sound economic conditions on the village homesteads. Of all the factors on which the operation of the peasant homestead depends, the size of the allotment is of the greatest importance. When the homestead allotment is below par, the full work potential of the farmer and his farm animals is not utilized. The amount of land set aside for grazing depends on the overall size of the allotment. It is known that the smaller the tillable area, the more land is given over to grazing. But on an extremely small farm the peasant must utilize part of the grazing land for grain production—in other words, the smaller the food-producing area, the fewer cattle, the less manure. On a very small homestead, keeping cattle becomes almost impossible. Such homesteads are deficient in horses, cows, and generally all farm animals. These conditions on undersized farms explain the peasants' shift from being independent owners of homesteads to being farm hands or wage laborers. The allotment is rented out and finally completely lost."[9] Rittikh was an important government official who worked hard to put Stolypin's agricultural measures into effect.[10] In his report he noted correctly the correspondence between the difficulties of cattle raising and the shortage of peasant land. Lenin, in his article "Stolypin and Revolution," noted that the land shortage among Russian peasants was nothing more than the natural result of the presence of large landowners, and that there existed a real possibility of ending the shortage by liquidating the landowners' estates and distributing their lands among the peasants. The proposed Stolypin's measure would immediately double the amount of land in the peasants' possession. Shortage of land among the peasants was not a product of the natural growth of population and subdivision of holdings (the picture presented by official statistics and liberal agrarian economists), but a direct result of land deprivation of the peasants caused by the Reform of 1861 and also by the preservation of landlords' huge estates.

The agrarian statistics of the Tambov province for 1881 established beyond a doubt that the possession of more than one cow in peasant homesteads was very rare in many districts there. In particular, in the Morshansk district, of every one hundred homesteads, ten were entirely without

[9] Rittikh, A., *Krestianskii pravoporiadok*, Petersburg, 1904, p. 232.

[10] *Stolypin Reform*—In the period preceding the Revolution of 1917, the Russian peasants were at an extremely low level of technical and agricultural development. An effort was made to do away with the traditional communal holding of land, since it was recognized by agrarian and sociopolitical reformers as an obstacle to increased productivity and a contributor to the continuing poverty of the peasants. A legislative program was introduced by Prime Minister Stolypin designed to encourage the development of a strong class of individual peasant proprietors by freeing them from the limitations imposed by the Mir system. This reform was finally passed in 1912 but took effect very gradually, and was accompanied by a great deal of agitation, anxiety, and confusion among the peasants (Tr.).

cattle, eighty-five had only one cow and only five had two or more cows. In Viriatino the number of cattle per homestead was slightly above that of the other villages of the district. Five percent of the homesteads in Viriatino were without cattle, 73 percent had one cow and 22 percent had two cows or more. The average homestead had six sheep.

One of the basic reasons preventing families including only a few working adults from taking care of their allotment was the lack of badly needed draft animals such as horses. In the 1880s, Viriatino possessed 484 horses for 252 households. The existing statistical data for 245 households point to extreme inequality in the distribution of horses; twenty-eight of the poorest homesteads (11 percent) had none at all and were forced to lease out their allotments or hire horses from neighbors. Seventy-one homesteads (28 percent) had only one horse to work with, a difficult situation considering the amount of work to be done on a farm. Eighty-eight homesteads had two horses each, and thirty-six had three each; all these (about 50 percent of the total) were of a middle class or well-to-do peasantry. For the most part, they worked their own allotments, but they also often worked part of an allotment that they rented from poorer peasants or, owning horses, worked another man's allotment for payment. Such agreements were made with horseless families. There were also nineteen homesteads (8 percent) that owned four or five horses, and three (1.2 percent) that owned six or seven; these belonged to rich kulaks. At the turn of the century most of the horseless homesteads, numbering about fifty, belonged to migrant miners' families.

When leaving for the mines a peasant usually asked his relatives or neighbors to work his land either for a payment in money or for a share of the harvest. Thus, for instance, Neverov, one of the peasants, worked the land of his son-in-law, a miner. This arrangement produced arguments, however. Neverov relates: "First they make an agreement as to who is going to plow, but later, being dissatisfied, they curse the whole summer. Our daughter cursed her own father daily because he worked his field first and hers after, and also accused him of taking better care of his field than hers. It was bad when the arguments started, but when the agreement was made with strangers, it was even worse."

Widows and poor people without horses got someone else to plow their allotments in return for one half or one third of their whole harvest. Some made agreements to complete work already half-done; others hired help for specific kinds of field work like plowing, sowing, clearing, etc. Widows usually paid for clearing with spring straw or hay for use as feed, as winter straw was set aside for heating the owner's house. Sometimes even a man who did all of the work in the fields was paid only in fodder crops. In the 1880s, almost 60 percent of all homesteads in the community of former serfs and over 20 percent in the community of state peasants had to resort to leasing out their allotments. The amount of land rented out in Viriatino was equivalent to 267 desiatins (716 acres) which according to official statistics averaged 1.8 desiatins (5 acres) for each lease. These figures point to a wide distribution of small rentings, which for middle-class peasants and kulaks was the way to enlarge their allotments. True, the kulaks usually preferred to rent land in other ways, either directly from the village communal reserve or from private landlords. The business of renting small parcels of land within the community was intertwined with the still lively survivals of serfdom like paying rent by workdays instead of money. The slow development of capitalism and the old system of serfdom in land tenure on many estates of the Middle Black Belt was responsible for these backward conditions.

As late as 1881, twenty years after the abolition of serfdom, the peasants of the Viriatino mir retained the old bondage-serfdom relationship with the local landlord family, whose name was Davidov. For the privilege of grazing their livestock in the Davidov meadows, the peasants of the community were obliged to perform the following duties: "On 11 desiatins (270 acres) of the fallow field to sow and till rye, to harvest 100 desiatins (270 acres) of buckwheat and 50 desiatins (135 acres) of other grains." In addition to those services, the peasants were to construct a fence and to cart brushwood to the road. Although the conditions of the land lease in return for rendered services were extremely hard and demanding, the peasants had really no choice but to accept them since their livestock had to be grazed and they had no pastures of their own. Besides giving their own services to work the fields of the landowner, the peasants also had to use their own tools and horses for the job. Duties were specified by the landowner always to his own advantage, with the result that peasants were very often late with work on their own fields. The leasing of communal lands by the rich peasants played an important part in village affairs. The kulaks often leased from the community such virgin lands as hay meadows which they plowed and planted with sunflower, millet, and other crops. The kulak Makarov leased pasture land from the community and made the peasants pay him for each head of cattle that used the pasture. Kulaks and middle-class peasants also rented shrub-covered corner plots on river banks from the county office of forestry. These corners were the result of the border lines of the communal lands running parallel to the river in a straight line and the uneven lines where the pockets were formed extending into the river, the land which belonged to the forestry. Direct ownership of these corners went to the foresters (employees of the Office of Forestry), who received 8 desiatins of this land and leased it out for eight rubles a desiatin. It was difficult for one family to prepare this virgin land for the first sowing—to root out the underbrush and break up the virgin soil. For this kind of work a few families pooled their resources, worked together and divided the grain after threshing. Middle-class peasants according to their economic capacity could lease from 1 to 4 desiatins (2.7–10.8 acres) from their priest (who received an allotment in the general distribution but did not work it himself). The cost was around ten to twelve rubles per desiatin. The poor peasants rented out part of their allotment for livestock enclosures at three rubles per year for an enclosure. The kulaks grabbed the best plots of communal land not earmarked for subdivision. For example, the kulak Kabanov rented a plot from the mir that previously had served as a threshing floor for the community. The peasants had to move their threshing into their homesteads and Kabanov raised a rich harvest of millet for a few years on the fertile soil they had left.

Gradually resentment against the rich began to ferment. A peasant by the name of Diakov, now in his eighties, remarked: "They [the rich] were purchasing land when they had enough of everything. Except for them, no one could buy land. They would get other people to work for them, paying fifteen kopecks a day and, during the season, twenty kopecks. They were really skinning us—making us work from dawn to dusk. And with all this they even laughed at us."[11]

Diakov's use of "purchasing" instead of "renting" was not an accidental lapse. In the beginning of the twentieth century, those who rented allotted lands usually said they were purchasing land; the terminology sharply pointed up the existing state of affairs.

During the first years after the abolition of serfdom, renting agreements were made for one to two years. Later the terms were lengthened because it was not profitable to take land for such a short period of time, work it, and then return it to its owner. The terms of the general redistribution of communal lands were not established by law, but it was assumed that redistribution should coincide

[11] *Arkhiv Instituta Etnografii Akademii Nauk SSSR, fond Russkoi Etnograficheskoi Ekspeditzii, Tombovskovo Otdela,* 1953, folder 245/4.

with the census, which took place every twelve years. This was the reason why people were eager to make leasing agreements for allotted land for a twelve-year period. After the redistribution in 1894, the rich members of the community started to demand even longer periods between redistributions. The result was that the rented land gradually became the property of the one who rented it.

House plots were not inheritable but were considered communal property and therefore subject to redistribution under the same terms as arable land. However, to implement this principle was most difficult because it was impossible at the time of redistribution to move the structures (houses, etc.) of the villagers. It was therefore traditional practice that house plots were not divided according to the number of individuals but remained at the disposal of those households which owned it already. Some had larger plots than others. If families separated, this event brought about even greater inequality in respect to the amount of land; but if fire should happen to destroy a few households, regrouping on the empty space took place. In the latter case the size of households was equalized and each household received an equal amount of land for housing, averaging half a desiatin (1.4 acres). On the land of the homestead many peasants cultivated orchards; in 1881 there were fifty-two peasant orchards with 1654 trees in the village. Two homesteads also had beehives, 416 in all; one of these homesteads belonged to the Krikow family who dealt in honey and especially in wax, which went to the factory and was manufactured into church candles.

As for the plots of arable land adjoining the house which included hemp plots, orchards, and threshing floors, these should have been divided equally with the rest of the communal land according to the number of people. But these "equalizers" were seldom handed over to the other communal members because they were the most valuable, fertilized part of the land; they remained with the previous owners.

Besides peasants who received allotted land, there were also landless peasants in the village. Former serfs of landlord Davidov, about ten families, received only household plots on which to build a house for themselves. The landlord said that "this is all you get—there are no fields for you." And so, these people worked as shoemakers, stonemasons, or stovemakers. Since there was no land, they had to buy for cash whatever they needed.

Later, landlessness came about also in other ways. After the eighties, when, as a result of family division, the lack of land became acute, families owning less than enough land to support one "soul" appeared in Viriatino. In the next ten years many families had no land to divide; the little they had remained in the hands of the old people. Those married children who separated did receive land for a farmstead outside the village, but they usually preferred to build their houses in the courtyard of their parents' house in order to stay in the village.

During the first 10 years after the abolition of serfdom some peasants attempted to go to Siberia and settle on new lands there, but moving presented great economic and legal difficulties. When the intended settler belonged to the commune of former landlords' peasants, he had to obtain the consent of the mir for his move, find a buyer for his house and farmstead, and find someone who would take over the redemption payments for the allotment and taxes. The law said that up to the time of the next redivision of the communal lands, the emigrant was responsible for the taxes and other payments due on his allotment. If he had outstanding debts, he had to make them good before departure. The other alternative was to get the mir to consent to be responsible for his debt.

While kulaks like Zhdanov or Starodubov bought and rented land from others, increased the production of grain for sale, bought farm animals and farm machinery, employed day workers on a large scale, and generally speaking, prospered, the peasants of Viriatino hardly could make ends meet. Impoverished by improper rotation of crops, without fertilizers and proper plowing, the land produced less and less; the villagers' need for grain increased as a result of the growth of population. The peasant's commercial output of grain for sale became smaller with every year. This change in the economy was true not only of Viriatino and the whole Tambov province but also throughout the Middle Black Belt provinces in the 1880s. In the 1860s and 1870s the Middle Black Belt provinces had held first place in grain production; a decade later they lost it to the Steppe and Lower Volga province.

Non-Agricultural Occupations

The central provinces were genuine Russian lands since ancient times. Survivals of the old feudal system prevented the peasants from permanently leaving their small allotments, so small in fact that they could not make a living from agriculture alone. Consequently seasonal migrations into other industries assumed greater proportions from year to year. Farming remained the basic occupation, and the seasonal loss of manpower had a detrimental effect on the non-agrarian productivity of the village. Since all field work took place only during the warm weather, taking care of the varied and multiple other chores during this short period was most difficult. One job was hardly finished before another demanded attention. But with the first frost work in the fields stopped altogether, even if, as sometimes happened, part of the grain remained in the fields unharvested. The better situated peasants with more grain continued threshing; the poor people in contrast did not need much time for their modest harvest. With cold weather other chores awaited them, chopping wood for fuel, collecting the manure, feeding the farm animals, repairing the farm tools. Other winter chores were done by women, who processed hemp, combed wool, wove, spun, and made clothes at home to take care of the needs of the family and household but did not bring in additional income. Nonetheless, the need for money became increasingly sharp.

Acute shortage of land invariably plagued the mir from the end of serfdom until the Revolution. Unless they were able to enlarge their holdings by renting additional plots, a large part of the Viriatino peasantry was forced to look for supplementary jobs. During the first years after the peasant reform of 1861, there was a notable increase in part-time occupations that did not take time away from farming.

Not all types of work were equally available to every homestead. Those with a sufficient number of horses would work as teamsters transporting goods or a variety of other jobs (for instance, carting building materials). Those with only one horse or none at all could help herd cattle to market or hire themselves out as woodcutters, carpenters, sowers, or coal miners. With every year the non-agricultural occupations became more important in sustaining the economy of small and even middle-sized homesteads in Viriatino.

The first of these occupations to become widespread, as it was by the sixties and continued to be until the beginning of the eighties, was the carter's trade. Viriatino's peasants carted grain and other farm products from the landlord's manor to the city markets—to Tambov, Morshansk, and other cities. They were hired by middlemen to move merchandise to and from neighboring markets. Hired by the landlord's administrators, they moved in a caravan to Astrakhan for fish. Their activities usually started when the snow on the roads was packed hard enough to use sledges. United into artels, Viriatino peasants traveled in caravans led by an elder across many hundreds of kilometers, sleeping and eating in inns and taverns en route. In the spring they returned to the village.

The development of the carting trade required a corresponding development in other trades. Large numbers of carts and sledges were needed and required constant repair. The horses had to be shoed often and fitted with four strong harnesses. Therefore in the village there were not only artisans who specialized in the making of sledges, wheels, and shafts, but also blacksmiths and harness makers. Some of the carts and sledges were made in Viriatino itself and some were bought from peasants in Atmanov Ugol and Vikhlyaika where the local artisans were considered the best in the field.

The development of railroads changed the flow of bulk merchandise. Trains took over the most profitable cross-country loads and so undercut cart and sledge transport that toward the end of the eighties it was reduced to almost a trickle in the Morshansk district. Only cart and sledge transport of a purely local character remained.

The second most important seasonal occupation which had great influence on the economic life of the village and which the old people remember was the large-scale transport of livestock from the Caspian steppes. From the end of serfdom, cattle, horses, and, later, sheep herds were moved into Tambov province. The business of buying livestock in Southern Russia and moving flocks of sheep to Central Russia was carried on by landlords and Viriatino's rich peasants like Sarapin, Makorov, and Toukinin. In the sixties and seventies, the Makorov, Sarapin, and other families obtained money from a Morshansk merchant, Plotitzin, who did much of this kind of business, to buy and move livestock and to hire shepherds from the same village. They went to Astrakhan province, where they bought sheep and drove them during the summer and autumn (up to the middle of October) to the Tambov province.

The wholesale trading of meat became so widespread in the Morshansk district that in the village there appeared people who specialized in butchering and in packaging cut-up meat. In the eighties in the neighboring village

called Novoye Griaznoe, there were about a hundred
butchers, and these men sometimes worked part-time in
Viriatino.

Viriatino was situated on the edge of a forest and steppe
area and had developed a timber industry. The exploitation
of the forest in a densely populated province made very
good business. The peasants from neighboring villages
needed logs, planks, and fuel for their households. The
exploitation of the forest, which began during the period
of serfdom, was especially widespread during the eighties,
the period of railroad building. The building of railroads,
especially the one that ran through the neighboring village
of Sosnovka, put an end to the carrier trade and the wholesale business in Viriatino but accelerated the exploitation
of the forest. Close to Viriatino was a large forest which
belonged to the State and from which parcels were sold
at auction. The auctioneer generally informed the peasants
at the village meeting where the next auction was to take
place, and the rich and the middle class would go to examine the parcels beforehand. The parcels went from two
hundred to six hundred rubles; the price of a small "orphan's parcel" was twenty-five to thirty rubles. Kulaks
would get larger plots at four hundred to six hundred rubles and would hire artels of carpenters for the work in
the forest, working alongside them to bring in the wood,
sort it, saw it, and remove the bark for the wood-tar factories. The carpenters' artel prepared the logs for building
cabins, sledges, carts, and so on. Middle-class peasant
families who bought small parcels did all the work on the
timber themselves, cutting down trees and sorting out
wood used for firing bricks and making plows; only for
the preparation of logs for building cabins would they
sometimes bring in the carpenters' artel.

However, their lack of business connections meant that
peasant woodcutters did not derive worthwhile profits from
forestry because all wood usually wound up in the hands

of wholesalers. An older Viriatino carpenter sadly remarked, "Our only profit was in doing the work."

The Viriatino kulaks, on the other hand, smartly organized a whole system that exploited their co-villagers, becoming extraordinarily rich in the forestry business and gradually developing into industrialists. For instance, Sarapin systematically bought parcels of forest land from the landlord, Davidov, and so successfully conducted his affair that when he died his son inherited a huge timber business.

Many peasants from the village were day laborers in the timber industry in which they were organized into artels. Artels of sawmen were usually composed of peasants from the neighboring village Atmanov Ugol, while the artels of carpenters were made up of Viriatino peasants. Peasants who were not qualified carpenters hired themselves out for work on small parcels where they cut down trees, trimmed away the branches and chopped them up for firewood.

A team of carpenters consisted of four to six people. The membership of an artel was not stable. The earnings were divided equally between the members except for the apprentices, who received 10 percent less than the others. Apprenticeship lasted a year or two, depending on the abilities of the pupil. Neverov relates that he and his brothers were apprentices for one year, "while others suffered for two years, and there were some who worked all their lives and somehow could not become masters." The artel spent a whole week working in the woods, and the horses of the members were used for transportation in strict rotation. Sometimes the owner of the parcel of land drove his artel to the woods. Each member took along with him a pillow, blankets, and beddings, ten to twelve pounds of wheat, the same amount of baked bread, and enough potatoes to last a week. Salt pork and butter were bought for the whole artel. Those who did the sawing ate meat every day because their work was considered very hard and required good nourishment. In wintertime the workers dug underground huts to live in, or the owner of the artel would find a dugout from the previous year. Sometimes they lived in tents. Food was cooked over an open fire next to the hut by the youngest member. In the dugout the logs were turned into planks. During the summer the men wore sweaters, and covered their faces with towels in order to escape the mosquitoes.

In the summer the worker got up at dawn, breakfasted at 8 A.M., and after a short rest worked until dinner, which took about two hours, and then on until dark. During winter they worked without stopping all during the daylight. Carpenters' work was considered the best paid in the timber industry, but it was scarce and the carpenters often went to work in woods at tasks that did not require their skills. The timber industry employed about 20–25 percent of the male population of Viriatino, among them many well-to-do peasants.

Other work in the woods was paid poorly, and the working conditions were difficult, but peasants had to be content with them. Diakov, who had worked previously in the mines, later worked a few seasons for a landlord and considered himself underpaid. Most workers, however, did not understand the exploitation to which they were subjected. They saw, of course, that Sarapin was getting rich, but they interpreted this in their own way: "He lives well from fooling counts and princes; on the peasant one does not get rich." Sarapin appeared to them as a generous, kindly, and affable man. For each piece of work, he paid on-the-spot. Sometimes he gave treats to those who worked for him, as when, on the day of the burial of one of the members of his family, he brought a few buckets of vodka and a few carts of rolls into the village for the peasants "to remember the soul." All this tended to hide class contradictions and prevented the peasants from clearly understanding that they gave their own labor to build Sarapin's riches.

The Viriatino peasants considered the seasonal timber

work of considerable importance because it did not take them away long from farming and it provided additional work for horses as well as for the people who owned harnesses. According to Diakov, during the first decade of the twentieth century his father and brother, before making hay and plowing the fields for winter crops, would go to the forest for ten days to prepare wood for the winter. They hired themselves out to industrialists and provided their own food, earning seventy-five kopeks a day. When they banded together with some other men into an artel they could move up to twenty carts of timber from the woods in two or three days and earn up to two rubles a cart. While working in the forest a man could prepare enough wood for his own homestead and sell the rest on the market.

There was also occasionally some other work in the village, as when in the spring the miller hired workers to close the dam in order to keep water in his pond.

With the beginning of the seventies, most of Viriatino's peasants began seasonal migrations to jobs that could be combined with the seasonal work in other provinces, especially in the South where large landowners' and kulaks' estates were in need of workers. In the eighties many peasants left for the construction of railroads. But soon after that, the most common employment was seasonal, and later steady, work in Donet's coal-mining industry.

Usually the coal miners chose to leave for the mines on a church holiday, the fifteenth of August, and returned the twenty-fifth of March (both dates according to the old Gregorian calendar). Because of the technology of the times, mining was usually halted during the spring when flooding raised the level of subterranean waters. Many workers who were not occupied in the draining of water and the reinforcement of the mines left for home. During the summertime the seasonal coal miners were busy in the fields, and when they departed for the mines in autumn they left the final harvesting to their families. "In those settlements where the coal-mining industry was especially well developed," wrote N. Romanov, "many homesteads during the winter were left in the care of women because most of the men in small families and all the able workers of large families went to the mines."[12] In Viriatino, as a rule, one working man always stayed behind.

Miners' artels were formed ahead of time, usually organized by an experienced coal miner who selected twelve or more men (a full artel might include as many as twenty-four people). Each new member presented the artel with a bucket of vodka. After an artel had been formed, the leader went in July to Donbass and made an agreement there with the current administration about the working conditions and housing of his people. The members were called upon to appear at the mine at a certain time and had to find money for their journey. Some migrants were obliged to sell sheep or part of the harvest; others resorted to loans from priests, who sometimes played the village usurers, or from kulaks. In some instances, artels as a unit took a loan for all their members under a common voucher. When they arrived at the mines, members of an artel occupied one dormitory. Sometimes a man would go to the mines ahead of time to prepare an artel and upon his return would organize it. After he collected the members' identification papers he would give each of them an advance on future earnings.

Working conditions in the mines in the seventies were exceptionally hard. A workday lasted up to fourteen hours, including going down and coming up the shaft, and was divided into two shifts. The first one began about midnight and ended at dawn; the second started after the noon break for dinner and lasted until dusk. The time from the end of the second shift to midnight was used for rest and sleep; in winter months this period was only six hours long. A full artel, consisting of twenty-five people, per-

[12] Romanov, N., p. 250.

formed all the basic and secondary operations in extracting coal. At the back of the mine about twenty people worked at breaking the rock and carrying away excavated coal on sleds up to the elevators. The rest remained at the gate of the elevator or worked on the surface. The sleds had to pull up to six hundred pounds while the men crawled often on all fours into difficult places. This kind of work sometimes was given to youngsters of fifteen and sixteen, and they also drove the horses that moved the gates. After ten years of heavy labor, very few miners could continue to work underground.

Arrangements for rest breaks actually did not exist. The dorms were filled to capacity, the air in them was always thick, the people slept in their clothing, removing only their boots. The unsanitary state of housing, the absence of good drinking water, a multitude of vermin disturbing normal sleep, the lack of steam baths or other facilities for bathing—all this exhausted the workers and facilitated the spread of dysentery, smallpox, and other diseases. The migrant workers often contracted tuberculosis and venereal diseases. All this they would bring home with them to the village.

Earnings in the seventies were not high. After food expenses only a rare miner could bring home seventy to seventy-five rubles saved from seven months' work. Most did not save as much in spite of the strict economy, almost stinginess, that marked the migrant miners. If a man started to drink, he would return home without any savings. There were enough bar owners who would let him drink on credit, getting him into debt.

Organizers played an important role in the migrant miners' artels; they did the accounting with the administration of the mines, they held the artel's money, they paid for food, they determined what work was done by every man in the group and also what he earned. Large artels divided workers into a number of teams and the organizer received his part from each team. It was more profitable for him to have a larger artel, and so began the transformation of organizers into entrepreneurs who were interested in recruiting larger numbers of workers. As time went on, the organizers ceased to work underground themselves, and they were not seen even above the ground; they devoted themselves exclusively to the management of the artel, still taking a whole share of the money earned. It is necessary to note that the personal characteristics of the organizer were important for the success of the enterprise. The organizers were older, experienced people; often they came from better situated families, which added to their authority in the artel.

In the eighties the miners worked as they had before they formed artels, but the general earnings of an artel were counted not according to the number of teams but according to the weight or measurement (of 19.8 cubic feet) of excavated coal. Although the work of cutters, those who tugged the sleds, those at the wagons and others was not equal and required different skills and different amounts of physical strength, the members of an artel divided the earnings equally. Meanwhile, the regular miners who were not members of artels were receiving differential pay according to their work.

The migrants accepted the hard work and bad living conditions in the mines as part and parcel of their job. The regular miners who worked side by side with the migrants did not. Their class consciousness was awakened much sooner and they rebelled. Under pressures of protest and unrest which developed into general strikes, the owners of the mines were forced to reduce the workday, to raise the pay, and to better somewhat the living conditions of the miners. In the nineties the twelve-hour working day was established, including trips up and down the shaft. The earnings of the migratory miners were also increased. As a result of this general improvement, migration to the mines from the many villages of Tambov province, including Viriatino, assumed the nature of a mass exodus. The number of migrants who left the villages of Morshansk district in the nineties grew to fifteen hundred. In Viriatino alone in 1881, sets of identification papers for leaving the village were issued to one hundred and fifty-six men and two women. These were full-time coal miners. After 1905 it was a rare peasant homestead that did not have at least one worker in the mines, and in some villages there were two or three such migrants in every homestead.

The economic importance of seasonal migrations into the Donbass varied with the economic level of the families to which these people belonged. For the middle-class homesteads, the earnings of the migrant represented a supplementary income, for the poor it was the basic source of their existence. Large families and those economically better off, often sent one or two of their men to do seasonal work in the mines. Their income was fully invested in the homestead. From this money cattle were bought, better clothes purchased, buildings enlarged. Many advantaged families looked upon this source of income as the only possibility of establishing a new homestead when a large family had to be divided, or as a means of support for the parents' home, which might be declining. The family reconciled themselves to more farm labor for the remaining members so that the earnings of the migrants could be used to improve the economic conditions of the homestead.

Here are some data regarding one of Viriatino's middle-class families who regularly dispatched their men to the mines. When Diakov and his family separated from his brother in 1886, he received a log cabin, one horse, one cow, five sheep and an allotment of 6 desiatins. The family consisted of eleven persons. In order to make ends meet they were forced to look for additional income. Soon after the division, Diakov sent his two oldest sons to the mines in Donbass. In 1895 Diakov's oldest son separated from the family; then the three younger sons were sent to the mines.

The average monthly earnings of a seasonal miner in

the eighties and nineties was eighteen to twenty-five rubles. Out of this money the worker spent ten to twelve rubles monthly on his personal needs and the rest was sent home. With three seasonal miners in his family, Diakov was able to improve his homestead. At the time of a new family division, which took place in 1900, the family had three horses, two cows, one bull, one calf, and ten sheep. The family at that time numbered twenty people. It also had some savings for building new homes in anticipation of more sons marrying and moving out. Four brick buildings were built and the family separated in 1900. One son, Prokofiy, received at the separation about four desiatins of land, one horse, one calf, and one sheep. His family consisted of a wife and seven children, too many to live on the income from farming alone, and therefore until the children grew up he went yearly to the mines for the winter season. In 1906 his oldest son, Grigoriy, and in 1913 the second son went away to the mines. The father then remained at home to do the farming full-time and with the money coming from his sons' earnings managed to raise somewhat the family's standard of living. During the winter of 1907–8, Grigoriy sent his father one hundred and twenty rubles. New furnishings were bought, and wooden beds appeared, along with iron pots and pans, tea cups, and plates. All these items were the result of new tastes and new needs acquired during stays at Donbass. But for the family of Diakov, middle-class peasants though they no doubt were, the yearly seasonal earnings of the two sons could not advance it into the category of the well-to-do. Under the most favorable conditions around 1900 the seasonal miner could not save more than one hundred to one hundred and fifty rubles. Not until the First World War did the miners begin to earn up to seventy-five rubles per month. Viriatino workers then sent their families "big money," the value of which the war inflation greatly reduced.

Income from seasonal work in the mines thus played a

large part in the budget of peasant households. Mining also had first class importance for other non-farming occupations. Parallel with migration there existed also local industries. Some Viriatino peasants specialized in the production and firing of bricks. Before the end of serfdom, the landlord had a few brick buildings, and the church in Viriatino had been built of brick. Clay suitable for making bricks was available on the landlord's land. The landlord's bricks were called "heels" or "sticks" because serfs mixed the clay with their feet, and the overseer prodded them with sticks to hurry them. The clay formed in a mold was then fired in a horizontal kiln.

After serfdom ended the manufacture of bricks continued, since the landlord and the wealthier peasants needed them for building. The brick industry reached its peak in the nineties when individual lots where layers of clay were discovered were added to the Viriatino communal lands. At that time the peasants were engaged in building and repairing housing; two or three families would unite to prepare the bricks and fire them in kilns of the same kind as the landlord's. During this period, the brickmaker's occupation was established. Later, building of brick houses ceased but skilled workers remained in the village and from time to time made bricks for co-villagers and for neighbors. The technique was never perfected, however.

Besides the occupations mentioned there were other skills that had not at that time developed into independent crafts. There were a few sheet-metal workers, housepainters, and tailors, but since there was no great demand for their work, they had to combine farming with the occasional practice of their trade. In most cases, these trades belonged to small families who were too poor to own horses. In their efforts to retain their allotments of land, they accepted any odd job to keep their homestead from falling into decay. The sheet-metal workers made roofing for the houses, and repaired pails, mugs, and other utensils.

There was always one family in the village which took in linen and woolen homespun for dyeing. The methods of dyeing and the making of dyes were kept secret. It was known only that the colors were fast. The tailors who made mainly topcoats of fur and wool were, as a rule, men. Some of them were local people; others would come temporarily from neighboring villages.

From ancient times the technique of bleaching linen had been known in the village, but in the nineties this industry assumed a different character. The intensified desire of peasant women to earn independent incomes resulted in their getting orders from customers. Viriatino's location on the bend of a large river, Chernovaya, and a stream, called Pishlyaika, flowing through the village helped to develop this trade. The grass on the banks provided a convenient surface for bleaching materials. The customers, peasants from surrounding villages, sometimes brought over to Viriatino the linen to be bleached, but generally the Viriatino women went out to collect it. Bleaching was done from May to October. The price for thirty arshins (one arshin equals twenty-eight inches) was fifteen to twenty kopeks. During the summer a woman bleached an average of one hundred and fifty pieces. When the tradition of home spinning gradually ceased, the bleaching of linen as a trade also disappeared.

Economic Situation of the Viriatino Peasantry

The agrarian structure of Russia was clearly a hindrance to the country's needs for industrial development; a change in this structure could be accomplished only by revolutionary means, since the class of serf-holding landlords not only dominated Russian agriculture, but was also the ruling class. This was the setting for the first Russian Revolution of 1905–7. The statistical data of 1905 concerning land holdings in Morshansk district, Tambov province, demonstrates the extent to which the agrarian structure in the central regions of European Russia remained archaic and the important role the great landlords' patrimonial estates continued to play in it.

Between 1877 and 1905, almost 40 percent of landowners' holdings consisted of forests and barren land. In this same period, merchants, industrialists, and some peasant communities had already bought from the owners of latifundia almost fifty thousand desiatins of timber forest. In 1905 in Morshansk district, the average allotment for one peasant homestead was fourteen and a half acres for the former serf communities and thirty-five acres for the communities of former crown peasants. But at the same time forty-three large landowners, each owning at least a thousand desiatins of land, possessed altogether 136,000 desiatins, 50 percent of which were never plowed and consisted of forests. Borderline categories of wooded lands were rented from the landlord by the neighboring peasants for pastures in exchange for days of work, but the forests were gradually sold to industrialists for timber. The size of peasant holdings did not change, however, during the twenty years before the Revolution in spite of the diminishing fertility of the land and the increase of population.

How to solve the agrarian problem was one of the most important tasks of the Revolution of 1905–7, but not the only one. The abolition of an absolute monarchy and the establishment of a democratic republic was the foremost problem, because unless that were done, it would be impossible to liquidate the landlords' estates. As the revolution progressed the working class became the main functioning force, ahead of all other social classes of Russian people. "The peasants also took part in the struggle against the landlords and against the government during the revolution, but their struggle was much weaker. The peasants fought with less determination, more disorganization, less consciously, often still hanging onto their hopes of the goodness of their little father—the Tsar. In 1905–6, the peasants intimidated the Tsar and the landlords. But it was not intimidation that was needed; they had to be eliminated; their government—the tsarist government—had to be removed from the face of the earth,"[13] wrote Lenin. The Tsar's government was able to break the workers' uprising and the rule of landlords over the peasants was re-established. The landlords' ownership was preserved and, therefore, "it was inevitable that the peasantry remained for long, long years poor, hungry, suppressed, downtrodden masses."

After suppressing the revolution, the Tsar's government made an attempt to create for itself some support among the "strong" peasant-landholders, by giving them an option to separate themselves from the community, while keeping their original allotments, and to buy additional land from the community in order to become independent farmers. This was the basic idea of the Stolypin Reform. But little resulted from it, especially in those provinces where communal landownership was most widespread. However strange it may appear, it was specifically this level of peasantry, who would seem to be the most interested in separating the village bourgeoisie who remained indifferent to the opening opportunities from the communal organization —the kulaks. Only a negligible number of homesteads, in Viriatino only four, actually separated. The largest entrepreneurs of other people's allotments and other communal lands did not want to break with the communal organization because it insured their further enrichment and the enlargement of their land.

To make clear the basic reasons for this phenomenon, a few words should be said about the distribution of land in the community at this time. At the head of both village communities (the state peasants and the former manor serfs) was a "mir," that assembly of representatives made up of all peasant homesteads who received allotted land.

[13] Lenin, V., *Works*, v. 16, p. 276.

This assembly elected functionaries for the village; that is, the village headman and the village scribe. Both received a salary, but usually not a large one; at the end of the 1890s, the headman, for instance, received sixty rubles yearly. The scribe kept records of all communal business, and as it often happened that the headman was illiterate, he played a decisive role in the village. Bribery and extortion, widespread among all the Tsar's officials, also flourished within the village administration.

The village council decided on the basic economic and legal questions involving its members—the peasants. The council established the order in which land was used, added to, redistributed, and rented from communal holdings, designated taxes and services, took "necessary measures" against tax delinquents, accepted new members or allowed others to leave, etc. There was also a multitude of other business, large and small, which the council had to decide upon. According to the memories of old people in Viriatino, business at the council used to be voted on by "voice" (that is, "shouting"). A few older peasants from local well-to-do families systematically used the council for their own personal interests and frequently obtained decisions in their favor. Among the poorer peasants, there were always enough bawlers who were deep in debt to the kulaks. These people made proposals in their own names which were in reality favorable to the kulaks. The poor peasants seldom dared to oppose the rich on the council. Not until the 1900s, when the migrant miners increased in number, did the rich encounter any restraints on their demands. This state of affairs could be partially explained by the fact that the most active group in the village—the young men—could not take part in the village council; the homesteads were represented by the heads of the families, that is, most of the time by old people who were not inclined to strain relations with influential members. A. S. Matrochin, when he returned in 1911 from army service, spoke once at the council, but this was met with general condemnation. "Your place is not here," he was told, "your old father is still alive." Women generally were not allowed to take part in the council, even when they became widows and heads of households.

There were many instances in communal assemblies when, in anticipation of an offering of wine, the council became a blind executor of somebody's revenge or pronounced measures that were directly adverse to the interest of the community.[14]

The council had the duty to watch over the regular payments for allotments and land taxes. As long as the law of collective responsibility existed, and it was abolished only in the 1900s, all possible measures were taken to influence the delinquent to pay his share. In questions of nonpayment, the council did not hesitate to demand that those in arrears sell cattle, draft animals, or their harvests to profiteers at very low prices, or rent out their allotments on exceedingly bad conditions, to the ruin of the delinquents. These were common occurrences, the results of which were precisely recorded in 1903 in the meetings of local committees' special sessions.[15] One of the notations, for example, reads: "There are no cases in which the community should take upon itself the payment of a delinquent taxpayer, no matter how difficult his situation may be . . . Usually such delinquents, because of the indif-

[14] Rittikh, p. 262.

[15] In the former state peasant community, a tragic occurrence took place. A member of the community named Lysov decided to bring his son-in-law into the community of Viriatino as a member, the kulak Sleptsov, who was a peasant in another village. The heads of the households were offered some vodka, and were half-drunk when they were ready to accept Sleptsov as a member. However, a peasant named Zhdanov was against it. No conclusion was reached at the meeting. Zhdanov was invited to come along to the tavern, and there he was beaten half-dead. Selptsov was then unanimously accepted into the community. (*Arkhiv Instituta Etnografii Akademii Nauk SSSR, fond Russkoi Etnograficheskoi Ekspeditzii, Tombovskovo Otdela,* 1954, folder 280.

ference of the community to them, never raised themselves above the position of laborers, once they had fallen . . . The ways and means which the community used against delinquent taxpayers brought many peasants to a disastrous position, taking away from them all possibility of starting an independent farm again. In such a way, the number of impoverished peasants removed from agriculture grew, as can be seen from the increasing number of homeowners without draft animals."[16]

The mir had a quite different relation to the rich peasants who also were sometimes delinquent. Sometimes they withheld their payments on purpose in fear that the community would take upon itself the delinquent taxes of poorer members, and divide the cost among the other members, making them pay their share. These rich delinquents advocated only the strongest methods against the delinquent poor. How did the council treat the delinquent rich? Examples of such cases were not remembered in Viriatino. But it is remembered that during the poor harvest of 1891–92, rich peasants as well as the poor tried to get help in food and seeds and other necessities, the repayment of which was collectively insured by the community.

"Here is the real, although not attractive, picture of contemporary attitudes in the community to the payment of taxes on the basis of collective responsibility," wrote the author of the notation cited above. "The number of people who were getting poorer because of community responsibility and other reasons increased with every year and, within communities of collective ownership, formed a real proletariat—people who nominally had rights to a piece of land, but because of poverty (and disintegration of their homesteads) could not make use of it. They gave away their land and their labor for very little to local or outside kulaks who offered to pay their taxes and other necessities, but on such terms that the debtor was bound

[16] Rittikh, p. 261.

to slavery for a long time. Perhaps it is this fact and not because of a sentimental attachment to the community, as some seem to think, that, strange as it seems, the rich peasants seldom left the community. Why should they not wish to live in communities where they were lords over their co-villagers and where they could obtain land for a small price."[17]

One might think that the above citation was written by someone who belonged to a revolutionary group, as he so well understood the class structure of the village. In reality, it was written by an agricultural official who later advanced to the position of an executive in the government office in one of the southern provinces. Whatever reasons he may have had for characterizing the village in the above way, his evaluation is basically correct.

The peasants' demand for "equalization" according to the number of people in the household was connected in the past with primitive, popular ideas about the equality of all members of the community, their equal right to land. Under the conditions of communal usage of land in the second half of the nineteenth century and the beginning of the twentieth century, when community-owned land obscured class relations, this "equalizing" became distorted and changed into its very opposite. Taking advantage of "equalization," the rich had the opportunity to be considered on a par with the poor, to receive welfare help "for the needy" from the grain foundation of the agricultural committee. And when the government distributed aid for food, the rich, supported by the general opinion of the community, received "their part" according to the number of people in their families, equally with the poor who, for example, had lost everything in fire or were without horses.

Russian peasant communities with common land existed up to the Great October Revolution. The appearance of

[17] *Ibid.*

the community at that time can be gauged from the agricultural census of July 1917. In the Morshansk district during the summer of 1917, there continued to exist not only small peasant lands but also very large estates. The average area of farm land was 321 desiatins. To private owners, not peasants, belonged 53,000, and to the peasants belonged 268,000.

In 1917 peasant ownership existed in two forms: (1) lands belonging to the community and (2) isolated farmsteads. The basic form, however, was communal ownership; out of 60,016 farms, the isolated farms numbered only 294.

From an economic point of view, the isolated farms were not at all like the "strong" farms which the Stolypin Reform was hoping to create; only 25 percent (75 farms) consisted of ten desiatins of farming land, the rest, 75 percent (219 farms) consisted of less than two desiatins each. Out of 219 dwarf farms, 196 did not have horses, and 97 had no farm animals. It is obvious that under the name "chutor" (isolated farm), proletarian households with cottage industry counted in this category of the census, even though the income they derived from farming was of secondary importance to their non-agricultural earnings.

The peasant farms that preserved their ties with the community numbered 59,722. Thus the lands of the community remained the bases of peasant farming, with the major part of the land in the district at the community's disposal.

The table on page 49 gives a comparison of these processes, as they took place in peasant homesteads in the district from 1881 until July 1917, in other words, during the time of the greatest development of capitalism in Russia.

From 1881 to 1917 the peasant population of Morshansk district grew by 62 percent; on the other hand, because the number of peasant households grew by 92 percent, the average number of inhabitants per household

PEASANT HOMESTEADS OF MORSHANSK DISTRICT

	Year 1881	Year 1917	Percentage of Increase
Peasant Population of the District	214,719	347,591	62%
Number of Peasant Homesteads	31,316	60,016	92%
Land in Pastures, Meadows, and Others in Desiatins	260,811	267,745	3%
Number of Homesteads Not Used for Farming	4,080	15,064	67%
Number of Homesteads Without Farm Animals	3,225	12,636	29%
Number of Homesteads Without Horses	6,524	24,350	74%

diminished from 6.8 to 5.7. In spite of the growth of population and the number of farms, the area of farmed land grew hardly at all (3 percent), therefore, for each homestead in 1881 there were 8.3 desiatins (22.4 acres) but in 1917 only 4.4 (11.8 acres). It is true that during these years the number of people in each household diminished; but even so, for one man in absolute numbers less land was allotted in 1917 than in 1881, 0.77 desiatin (2.08 acres) instead of 1.2 (3.2 acres).

The community's economic situation also became worse. The number of untilled farms, those which were not sown or rented out in full, increased by more than 300 percent. There was the same proportionate increase in the number of households that did not include farm animals (almost 400 percent) and horses (more than 300 percent). It is possible that the figures for 1917 are not characteristic so far as the possession of horses is concerned; that was the fourth year of World War I and horses were mobilized almost yearly, but this comparison has a meaning only in relation to the year 1881 and serves only as an index of poverty because the rich peasants bought new horses after the mobilization, but it was impossible for the poor.

The war also had an adverse effect on the peasant homesteads because it deprived them of working hands. In the same Morshansk district, according to the census of 1917, the army took 38,580 men from peasant households; more than six thousand men were detained in Donbass to work in the mines to ensure coal to the army. As a result of this, 24,138 homesteads found themselves without adult male workers. Even with horses, a family without workers was unable to till the land; this was probably the beginning of the renting-out of farms, or the hiring of help to till the land.

The especially difficult conditions in which the peasants found themselves was described by P. P. Neverov, one of Viriatino's old-timers. His father's farm was middle-sized; they had two horses, and land amounting to 4.5 desiatins which they rented out, while they lived from their own allotment. In 1914, after mobilization, not even one man was left in the family. Neverov was then fourteen years old. The family consisted of fifteen persons, but they were all women and children, and the teenage boy had to perform the work of grown men—to plow, to mow, to collect and to take out dung, and to feed the animals. In the fields, with the exception of mowing, the women would help. During the time free from work in the field, he worked at transporting wood from the forest to Sosnovka. And so it went until 1916 when one of the brothers came home.

During this difficult period, the women had to perform work that was traditionally the province of men. The women began to plow, to harrow, to harness and unharness horses; they collected dung, worked with rakes at haystacks, and generally did jobs that had not previously been considered their duty. For the most part these duties fell upon wives of soldiers. Their life became harder with every year as the war went on. When there was no horse, part of the allotment was rented out in order to get the means to work the rest of the land. The kulaks took advantage of soldiers' wives at every turn, exploiting them in the worst ways, bread on loan in return for work, day labor paid in products, and all the other methods they developed through generations, with which they could legally, "according to 'custom,'" rob a man and deprive him of the fruit of his labor.

The mir did not save the Russian peasantry from capitalism. Without much difficulty capitalism developed within its fold; by creating the village bourgeoisie, the mir transformed, at the same time, a significant part of the community into proletariat or semiproletariat. This social transformation took place in Viriatino, as elsewhere. Just before the October Revolution, along with the rich and the industrialists, there were many poor people, without horses and cows, who were considered the owners of their allotment in name only, who had long ago passed it into the hands of others.

CHAPTER II

THE GROWTH OF THE VILLAGE

The village of Viriatino is surrounded on all sides by low-lands and meadows which are flooded in springtime. Along the river Pishlyaika the village forms a long street with two rows of houses on each side and a few small side streets. At one point in the center of the village the street widens to form a square where, in former times, a church stood which has now become a village club.

In the past the village had a different layout. Old-timers' reports and the character of contemporary planning indicate that it consisted of one row of houses strung along the bank of the river. Many streets in Viriatino have, even at present, only one row of houses, that in some places stretch for considerable distances. This kind of layout was obviously dictated by the topographical conditions of the area. At first the houses were built in one row on the highest parts of the land. By the end of the 1870s, it was necessary to build more streets, and a second row of houses was completed by shortening the width of the strip of land next to the road and clearing the streets of storage places and granaries. Judging from statistics of the province and the reminiscences of its old citizens, Viriatino must have started as a very small settlement.

In the 1840s, according to the tenth revised census, the village had 70 homesteads; in 1857 it had 156, and in 1881, as the household census shows, the number reached 252.[1] In 1953 there were 456 homesteads located in 406

---

[1] The peasant homestead, the Dvor, is governed by customary and civil law, which holds that its members have joint ownership rights and joint legal obligations (Tr.).

houses. The growth of the village was determined by the basic natural increase of population and the separation of joint families which created new family units. In the development of Viriatino, however, it is possible to outline a few stages closely related to changes in socio-economic relations within the locality.

The earliest stage in the development of the village about which we have data is the first half of the nineteenth century. In that time Viriatino was inhabited largely by serfs connected to the landlord's estates. Today the old people who heard about it from their grandfathers say that the first houses in the village were situated in the direction of Sosnovka where there is now a hay yard. With the natural increase in population, there was no more space for new households since the immediate environs consisted of forest and marshes only. The landlord therefore resettled his serfs on the other side of the river Pishlyaika. At first, people built on the most elevated places from which they cleared away the woods. Some of the names of the streets in Viriatino refer to parts of the former woods, like Polana or Oreshnik streets, which in Russian means the meadow or the nut trees, etc.

The houses on Verkhniy Proulok Street were built in one row facing south, away from the river. In back of the houses and down to the edge of the water were the meadows and the vegetable gardens which were periodically under water. In another part of town, Polana and Oreshnik streets at first had houses only on the left side of the street facing north in the direction of the river. Across the street the threshing floor and other farm buildings were built. The right side of Oreshnik Street was built up probably in the sixties or seventies according to the stories preserved in a number of local families who lived on that street. At first the houses were built in one row, but not in a straight line; everybody who constructed a house did it according to his own idea. During serfdom, however, the landlord Davidov called in a land surveyor and the peasant houses were moved and rebuilt so that they formed a continuous line. During the period of serfdom, the village grew slowly, its population augmented mostly by peasants whom the landlord bought and brought to Viriatino from neighboring villages. Some families of Viriatino have their roots in other villages, the families of Ozhogin and Matrochin, for example, whose ancestors had been moved from Atamanov Ugol to Viriatino by the landlord.

During the first years after the peasant reform, the people of Viriatino erected hardly any new buildings, and the village did not grow. A new phase in its history begins in the mid-eighties of the nineteenth century when the development of capitalism brought about a more frequent division of families and, as a result, an increase in the number of houses. The newly built-up streets were populated by households which had come into being at the division of large families. Generally, at the family division, the sons divided the parents' house and buildings among themselves, or they settled on new allotments. Up to the eighties when the village was not as crowded, sons preferred to build next to their parents' home. But later the new households had to be settled at the edge of the village where the community gave allotments for new buildings. It was possible to settle in the center of the village only when somebody was leaving and wanted to sell his land.

Systematic research done by the author in 1953 revealed the existence in Viriatino of huge clusters of related families, their distribution in the village, and the history of generational family divisions. There are many people in the village of the same name. Each family in addition carries nicknames that were given to the head of families and survived through a few generations.[2] The history of the

[2] At present, family relationships are kept up mostly between people who bear the same name. Families may bear the same name and not be considered really relatives, but the old people feel a sense of kinship and seem to remember that they were once related by blood.

family Diakov-Kirushkin is a good example of subdivision and eventual choice of residence of members of joint families.

The ancestors of the Kirushkins lived on Nizhni Proulok Street. The first division of the family took place in the seventies. The three sons who separated from the family settled near the parents' house on free lots. One of the brothers, Efim, had two sons, Yakov and Alexei. When the boys grew up and married, the family divided in 1897. Yakov received the family's brick house; Alexei went to live on the left side of Sychevka, which only had begun to be built up in those years. As a result of later divisions in these families, the Diakov-Kirushkin populated a large part of Nizhniy Proulok and Sychevka streets. The ancestors of Diakov-Longanov lived in Polana, but already in the eighties, through family divisions, they populated large parts of Pesok. Grandfather Longin, from whom the family's nickname stemmed, moved from Polana to Pesok into a wooden house after he and his brother divided in 1886. He had four sons. Ivan, the elder, separated in 1895 and built next to the family, and the rest of the brothers separated in the 1900s. Fedor settled next to the parents' house. Stepan received the house of the parents and Prokofi moved to a house at the end of the same street, Pesok. As a result of these family divisions, the Diakov-Longanov family populated the right side of Pesok Street. Another family, the Diakov-Samochin, whose ancestors came from Verchni Proulok, populated the Verkhniy Proulok and Kobelevka streets. Because of the tendency of the children to settle next to the parental house, clusters of related families were formed. Today on every street one can find a few very large families, the members of which were closely related in the past.

At the turn of the century, the village continued to grow, although not as fast as in the preceding two decades. About this time its character as an administrative-business center began to take shape. In the past, the public and business buildings were grouped around the church. The new brick church was built around 1860, in place of the old log building, on stone foundations with a tin roof and an iron fence around it. Behind the church was a cemetery where priests and local rich people were buried. Close to the church stood the chapel, a district and parochial school and the house of the priest. Not far from the church square a new communal building was constructed in 1903—a large log five-corner house which had a room for meetings, a room for the village scribe, and a room where prisoners were kept. Not far from the communal house, in a large brick building, there was a liquor store. In the same vicinity, other shops were also located. Some carried small merchandise, others white bread, sugar, round rolls, sausages, etc. The first shop was opened in 1897 and was located in a large brick house near the church. Before that date, various dry goods were sold by peddlers. The village had three pubs. Beyond the river where, at present, food-producing communal farms are located, there was the house of the merchant Malikov which was surrounded by brick outhouses. The houses of the rich and the clergy were distinguished by their dimensions. The village was always well provided with water for in the courtyard of every household there was a well. Sometimes the well was dug at the juncture of two households for the use of both. In addition, there were two small artificial lakes from which water could be drawn for household needs.

In case of fire, which broke out often in the village, three barrels of water and a fire trumpet stood ready near the church. Rotating every twenty-four hours, three homestead owners, having horses ready, kept watch. In addition to fire prevention duties, every household had to participate in taking care of the reservoirs and roads. With the exception of planting white willows, which in time grew into beautiful lanes, there was little attention paid to greenery and the beauty of the village.

The Peasant Household in the Nineteenth and Beginning of the Twentieth Centuries

More than half (58.1 percent) of the houses in Viriatino today were built before 1917. In order to make clear the changes which have taken place in the traditional architecture of home and farm buildings, a historical review of the development of new types of housing is helpful.

The ancient log dwellings of the first half of the nineteenth century did not survive in Viriatino, but it is possible to reconstruct this type from the memory of some old villagers and also from similar log dwellings which survived and are still in use in neighboring villages. The architecture of the old peasant houses was typical of Southern Russia. The dwelling house stood along the side of the street. It consisted of one large room with a separately built passage around it made of logs or wicker. In the nineteenth century the layout of the huts was entirely standardized and characteristic for all of Tambov province. The oven stood in the right opposite corner from the door with its chimney in the direction of the door. In the corner of the oven a vertical pole was inserted to which planking was affixed between the ceiling and the oven and this was used as a sleeping area. The planking extended from the oven to the front wall of the house. At the door, in the left corner, diagonally from the oven, stood the dining table and above it hung the icons. Along the side walls were stationary benches. Between the door and the front wall a bench-cupboard was located where foodstuffs were cleared away after meals.

All home furniture was made by the carpenters while the house was being built and was of a Southern Russian peasant design. No ready-made furniture was bought. On the wall, in front of the stove, a shelf containing dishes hung. Another shelf was used for laying baked loaves of bread when they were taken out of the oven. To the left of the door, a cupboard was attached to the wall where, under lock and key, money and the most valuable possessions were kept. Above the windows on the front wall was a shelf for hats, yarn for weaving, and various small objects. Each corner had its distinct name and purpose. In the "honored" corner where the icons hung, the family ate their main meal, received visitors, and celebrated holidays; the corner where front and back benches met was called the back corner and it was the sleeping area. Next was the corner in which the Russian oven was located; the fourth corner was the women's quarter, the housewife's domain.

The old people slept on planks over the oven. The younger ones slept on the planks and stationary benches along the wall, to which movable benches were added. Straw covered with coarse linen served as bedding. For a cover, a homespun striped material, heavy and coarse, or felt was used. Very large pillows that two or three people shared were characteristic of this period.

In the middle of the nineteenth century, the huts in the village had no chimneys. The inside of the hut was blackened by smoke, which escaped through the oven's double doors. The inner door was shorter than the outside door and did not go all the way to the top. When the stove was heated, the inner door was closed and the outer door opened. On the back wall there was another opening to let the smoke escape, but this could be closed by a wooden shutter. In these smoke-huts there were for the most part only two windows, one facing the street and the other the courtyard. The windows were small, divided into four parts, and did not open. Later on, the style changed and two or three windows were added facing the street and made to open from the top. Old people remember that in the beginning of the nineteenth century, bull bladders were used for windowpanes instead of glass.

The dimensions of the huts in use just before the end of

serfdom were small (15.4–36.8 square yards) but the families living in them were large. The lack of space was also aggravated by the presence of chickens, calves, lambs, and maybe a pig with piglets in the hut during the coldest months. A correspondent of the Russian Geographic Society in the mid-nineteenth century described the peasant huts of the Morshansk district in the following fashion: "Together with the peasant in his hut during the winter live from ten to fifteen lambs with their mothers, two or three pigs with piglets, two or three calves, sometimes a young colt . . . and here also the cows were milked. In the evening the air in the hut was not too bad, but in morning before the oven was lit and the door opened, it was unbearable."

The interior of the huts was dirty, the air stifling. The floors were washed and scraped only before an important holiday. The room was lighted by a burning splinter; the first kerosene lamp appeared in Viriatino in 1879. All this made for extremely unhygienic conditions and promoted the spread of disease. Since the huts were small, more affluent, large families lived in a few huts located on one homestead. In the 1870s, the family of the wholesale dealer, Makarov, was made up of twenty-seven persons. They lived in three huts, two alongside the road, and one in the courtyard. One hut was used for cooking and eating, the other two were used for sleeping. The huts of more affluent peasants were spacious and much cleaner. Makarov's family, for example, slept in wooden beds. In Viriatino cottages made up of two rooms separated by a passage were rare. Some better cottages had an extension built on to them. The addition was usually made into a kitchen, including the Russian oven and planks for sleeping and benches. The other room was heated by an iron stove.

The courtyard where the cattle were kept stood open. The old form of the courtyard construction basically remained unchanged. Covered structures for cattle, firewood, and agricultural implements had wattled walls and a roof made of loosely covered straw. During the winter, for additional protection from the frost, the wattled walls were also covered with straw. At about eight inches from the wall, sticks were planted and the whole space between the walls and sticks was filled with straw. Sometimes the wattled walls were covered with clay.

The wattled structures were 25.8 to 51.6 square yards from the house. They were rounded at the corners, continued in the direction of the house and the gate and formed a closed courtyard. In large families in which a considerable number of cattle were kept, another wattled wall was built parallel to the first one. Fences separated the area between the two walls into stables. The first row of these squares was occupied by cows and sheep, and in the second row, horses were kept. During the summer months, the cows were kept between the house and the first row of the wattled wall or between parallel walls.

Where sleeping space in the house was scarce, cubicles were built outside the house within the wattled walls for married couples to sleep in during the warm weather. This kind of sleeping arrangement had been characteristic of many South Russian provinces. Outside the house a cellar was often built and perhaps a steam bathhouse made of logs. The walls of the cellar were lined with oak planks, and potatoes, cucumbers, and cabbage were stored there. In the spring the cellar was supplied with ice for preservation of perishables. On some streets where underground waters were close to the surface, cellars were made in a mound constructed opposite the house.

The question of when bathhouses first appeared in Viriatino remains open. The old people remembered that during serfdom there were very few bathhouses in the village. People began to build them in the sixties when economic conditions were easier and the peasants could afford to buy wood. The bathhouses were made of logs in the South Russian style with the oven having no chimney for the escape of smoke. During the winter this bathhouse also doubled for the shelter of young farm animals and sheep litters.

The peasant homesteads had a hayloft and shaft made of wicker all under the four-corner roof to store hay and unthreshed rye. In the eighties, 209 households, seventy-four percent of the total, had threshing barns. The threshing barns and haylofts were often on the threshing floor located behind the courtyard or in the back of the vegetable garden. The threshing shelter had no walls. In bad weather the grain was threshed in the threshing shed and in good weather on a well-pressed dirt floor next to the shed. In the shed, agricultural implements were kept—harrows, chains, carts, spokes, barrels, etc. Sometimes the homestead had a steam bath and a log granary. The granary might stand in the courtyard or on the street opposite the windows of the house.

This kind of peasant structure in Viriatino was characteristic of the mid-nineteenth century for many of the South Russian provinces, Orlov, Kursk, Voronezh, Tambov, and the adjacent districts of Tula and Ryazan. So far it has proved impossible to establish the exact time that this type of dwelling developed in South Russia. The ethnic tradition for this locality changed little during a comparatively long period, and may have been the result of the backward conditions of serfdom.

After the Peasant Reform of 1861, the villages of Tambov province, as a result of capitalistic development and the new socioeconomic conditions, began to change the traditional type of housing. The development of the migratory movement into Donbass and the orientation toward carpentry played a decisive role in this process. At the end of the 1880s there remained only two or three smoke-huts in the village. In many Black Earth districts of South Russia that had few forests, the peasants built brick structures.

In Viriatino the lack of wood for building was not felt

as acutely as in other southern districts and therefore was not a basic cause there for the change to brick. Up to 1890, that is, up to the time when the Viriatino community bought additional land, only the freehold peasant community had forests—the size of twenty-nine and a half desiatins. After buying up the additional land, the peasants received with it also a considerable amount of forested area.

The change from wooden to brick structures was the result of a number of factors. The development of mass migration to work in Donbass, the carpenters' trade and other kinds of work in the cities, brought about changes in the budget of peasant homesteads. Money appeared among the peasants. It was used to pay for the work of the stonecutters and, at the end of the eighties, to buy lime and brick. Viriatino's purchase of additional lands where there were levels of clay aided the quick growth of brick buildings. About ten years before they bought the land, the peasants dug out the clay on the shores of the river Chelnova, but the layers there, as it was discovered, were poor and, after providing bricks for only a few structures, became exhausted. Many peasants, by joining two or three households, prepared their own furnaces, built shelters for drying bricks, and manufactured them themselves, but the majority of the population bought commercial bricks. One thousand bricks cost from five to six rubles. The average cost of brick houses in the late nineteenth century and the early twentieth century fluctuated between 120 and 250 rubles. And although the building of wooden houses was much cheaper (100 to 150 rubles), the fear of fire, the ever-present danger to the peasant homesteads of Tambov province, stimulated the building of the large number of brick homes. Viriatino was ravaged many times by fire throughout most of its area.

An important role in the transition to brick building was played by a concern for village opinion. The building of a brick house, in those years, pointed to the well-to-do position of the owner. For this reason, migratory miners were eager to put the money they earned, before everything else, into building a brick house. With their low earnings they could not begin one until after a few years of work in the mines. And yet, in relatively short time, in the 1890s and especially in succeeding decades, a large part of the village was rebuilt. On Nizhni Proulok Street, for instance, before 1890 there were only five brick houses; the remaining twenty were built in the nineties and in the first decade of the twentieth century. At the present time, in the village there are two hundred and thirty brick houses that were built during that period.

Most brick houses were built alongside the street. In the building of a house, the size and shape of the lot were taken into consideration, as well as the orientation of the house to the sunny side of the street. The houses were built in such a way that most windows faced the sunny side.

The first brick houses built during the 1880s and in the early 1890s were designed according to the traditional plan of log houses. They consisted of one living room with an additional side building of plank or wicker or brick; the oven was usually in its traditional place—in the far corner facing the entrance—although it was situated not in the back corner, but a little removed from the wall and opposite the entrance closer to the door. Brick houses with a similar oven structure are often found even now. Since a brick home is difficult to warm up with one Russian oven, dutch ovens appeared about this time. In a brick house there were berths and benches built for sleeping; only a few houses had wooden beds.

In connection with the growing economic influence of the city and the development of migratory occupations (mines, carpentry, etc.), in the 1890s and especially in the twentieth century, the village's living quarters improved considerably. The change from wooden houses to brick affected not only the outside appearance of the houses but also their inside planning and furniture.

In the 1890s there was a clear tendency to separate the two rooms, the kitchen and the living room. The separation of the living room required a considerable expenditure for rebuilding and thus was possible only for the more affluent homesteads, including those who had some of their men in migratory work. The rearrangement was in large part determined by city influences. The possession of a separate living room pointed, in the opinion of villagers, to a definitely well-to-do family. It was, for example, with this in mind that F. A. Diakov in 1903 added a large brick hall to his house built in 1897. During the autumn of the same year, when he married his sister to a co-villager, in order not to lose face before his brother-in-law and neighbors he transferred the oven from the living room into the brick hall and made a kitchen out of it. When a new brick building was put up, the structure was often divided by a wall into two rooms, kitchen and living room.

The influence of migratory work can also explain the appearance in Viriatino of another new way of planning the dwelling. Gradually, houses began to appear in which, in order to make a more rational use of living space, the oven was placed differently. The houses were built parallel to the street; the kitchen had two entrances opposite each other, one opening on the street and the other on the courtyard. The oven stood in the corner farthest from the street, facing the street entrance. This innovation, because of the two entrances, required a lot of fuel so such houses were built only by the most affluent segment of the population, and not until the twentieth century. But though this plan was slow to win widespread acceptance, it is now quite popular.

With the shift to brick building, the houses became larger. The old log houses were comparatively small. According to the statistics of 1881, in Viriatino 252 homestead owners had 254 houses, with the following dimensions: the largest number of houses (180) were built 18 by 18.7 feet; probably these were typical middle-class housing in Viriatino. The rest included four dwarf houses (15.4 square yards) and twenty-five small houses (23 square yards), which probably belonged to poor households without horses.

The average house had seven inhabitants, that is, for each person there was from 2.2 to 10.5 square yards of space. Since the number of people comprising a family varied greatly, and as the large, undivided families may have reached twenty, even thirty people, the norm of 10.5 square yards was met rather seldom.

The brick houses were large. Regrettably, we have no detailed statistics and must limit ourselves to approximate figures. One-room brick houses were built in a 21 by 36 foot area; two-room houses took about 23.4 feet. The number of square yards per person, in comparison with the log huts, was growing. For example, in the old wooden house of Diakov's grandfather in the 1880s, there was 45 square yards of living area. When in 1895 the family built a brick house of 58 square yards, the living area per person became larger. In Matrochin's brick house, which had two rooms in 1884, there were 85 square yards of living area. In that house twenty people lived, and the living space per person amounted to slightly over 3.9 square yards.

Considerable changes in furnishing were noticeable in the beginning of the twentieth century. With the introduction of two-room housing, the homes became cleaner and more spacious. The kitchens of this period were not very different from the old wooden huts, but an effort was made to give the living room a parlor look. On both sides of the living room stood dutch ovens and often wooden beds were ranged along all the walls according to the number of married couples. Grown-ups slept on mattresses filled with hay or straw; the children, as before, slept on benches and on the floor where straw was placed for them and covered with a sheet. Next to the beds hung cradles for infants, and above the beds hung rods for clothing and diapers. The women spun while sitting on benches placed next to their beds; weaving was done, in turn, on a family loom which stood in the kitchen or in the living room. In the front corner there was usually a table which, during holidays, was covered with a cloth. During the summer the family ate in the kitchen; they slept and received guests in the living room. During the winter, because of the lack of fuel, they basically lived in the living room; the kitchen was heated very little.

The penetration of city bourgeois tastes into the village was manifested in wall decorations: cheap, popular prints, brightly printed postcards, round disks made of colored paper which were usually bought in the village of Sosnovka, which had a large merchant center located near the railroad. The cultural level of the population in these years was very low. From Sosnovka, bourgeois tastes first entered into Viriatino, through the better-off part of the population. In the beginning of the twentieth century, in some more affluent households, the beds were separated by a curtain. (The first curtain appeared in Viriatino in 1905 in the family of Makarovs, because of their connections with Sosnovka.)

Many of the brick houses still standing in the village are lengthened, multiroom structures. The multipartitioning of houses is connected with the division of families who, faced with shortage of land, had to build as cheaply as they could.

During the period of brick building, when the peasants were feeling the scarcity of all sorts of land, the shortage of land for building became especially acute. Thus, at family divisions, the old building lots were sometimes subdivided among the individual families, a practice especially common among families of former state peasants whose lots were nestled among the lands of the community of former serfs, and therefore could not be enlarged. For example, when in 1887 the Burkin family divided, their lot was split into three parts; two sons received each 9/100 and the third received 12/100. Since there were already two brick houses on the homestead lot, one was given to the oldest son, and the two remaining sons received the second house and divided it between them.

When the additional land was bought, the new families, the community of former serfs, were given lots for building in Sosnovka, but peasants were reluctant to settle there, preferring to divide their old houses. This can be explained by the fact that, if one was building with brick, it was more economical to build one large house instead of two small ones, so that later it could be subdivided for two or three families. Therefore, in anticipation of a division, large families from the beginning built houses of large proportions. If an undivided family could not afford to build a large house, they put up a small one and added more rooms as the family grew and divided.

Many brick houses in the village have complicated histories that are often very difficult to reconstruct; the houses were rebuilt and their plans changed a number of times because of family division.

Four families now live in the long brick structure of the Beluev family. In the nineteenth century, there was only one family and the house occupied only a fourth of the site of the present one. The first family division occurred in 1900. A new brick room was built for the separated family; a kitchen was then added on to each room and, as a result, the house became a double one, each part consisting of a kitchen and a living room. When the family again enlarged, they divided between themselves (in each half) both kitchens, and living rooms were divided in half, and after a few divisions, a multifamily house grew up. Naturally, each time the existing house was subdivided and additional structures built on to it, the whole plan of the living rooms was changed, and the ovens were put in the most practical place, regardless of the traditional way of arranging things.

Sometimes when houses were divided the new units consisted predominantly of living rooms, but more affluent peasants added brick kitchens to their rooms. An example of this kind of remodeling can be seen in the brick house of the Matrochin family which was built in 1884. When the original brick house was built, the living quarters were divided by a wall into a kitchen and a living room. The oven then stood in its traditional place. In those years, the family consisted of twenty people. When the members of the third generation married in 1888, the Matrochin subdivided. The oldest son, Mitrofan, with whom the mother remained, received the kitchen; Aleksei and Semen took the living room. Five years later, in 1893, Aleksei and Semen separated, and Aleksei went to live in a previously constructed brick house in Oreshnik.

In 1903 Mitrofan, the oldest brother, with the money he earned in Donbass, added a brick kitchen to the side wall of the living room and behind the kitchen built a hallway of wooden planks. The oven was transferred to the kitchen and placed in the middle of the lateral wall facing the door. In front of the stove there was a window looking onto the court. In 1904 a kitchen was added to the side wall of Semen's half of the house, as well as a brick hallway and gates. The entrance to the hallway was from the street; the entrance to the kitchen was through the side wall. This change necessitated moving the Russian oven, which fitted most practically in the corner next to the door with the outlet directed to the back wall of the kitchen, which faced the courtyard. The dutch ovens in both parts of the house were placed in the middle of the wall, facing the courtyard. In this instance, traditional planning disappeared when additional kitchens were built.

As stated above, brick houses were characteristic of middle-class households. In the 1900s, as class disintegration intensified and the economic situation of the peasantry became worse, the number of poor households in Viriatino grew. Regardless of whether the poor families sent some of their men to Donbass, or whether they busied themselves with odd jobs not far from the village, they lived in very poor conditions. Their houses were small wooden huts, and the furniture was shabby.

As we were told by Puchkova, in her father's family there were seven children, two sons and five daughters. The homestead had a land allotment for only one person. They kept a horse and cow, but they had to sell the cow because of lack of fodder in the wintertime. The family lived in a poorly constructed wooden hut, 14.8 feet square, in which there was no furniture except the table and stationary benches. People slept on straw and covered themselves with spreads. Because the hut was so badly made, they had to purchase new wood for repairs with the money that had been planned for the dowries of the daughters (which they had raised only with great difficulty).

Puchkova became a widow at a young age with five little children to support. The oldest son emigrated to Donbass when he was seventeen and did not return. The second son worked as a shepherd from the time he was twelve years old. The family lived in a smoke hut until 1914; the household kept no cattle and had no outbuildings. Puchkova leased the land allotment, which was enough for three people, to neighbors for farming, receiving straw and hay in return.

The houses of rich peasants were outstanding in size, the planning of living quarters, and the furnishings. Sayapin, a timber merchant, had a large two-story house; the ground floor was brick and was used for storage but the upper part was wooden. Sayapin also had houses in Morshansk and Otiasy. Another timber merchant, Sleptzov, who also owned a large land allotment, had a house that consisted of two large rooms, divided by a hallway. Part of the living room was used as sleeping quarters. Food was cooked in the kitchen where farmhands slept. Behind the house there were outbuildings, cellars, sheds, and pigsties, constructed in a rectangular plan for storage of food and implements. All the homestead buildings were brick. A large brick house, built in 1908, which belonged to

Zhdanov, has been preserved until the present day. The upper floor consisted of a living room and a kitchen; down below there were storage rooms. A miller had a wooden house, consisting of a few rooms.

The brick houses were built by specialist stonecutters who came from the surrounding villages of Kosmachevka, Ot'yas Yard, Krasnaya Sloboda. The walls of the first such houses were built three bricks thick, but these were few, and toward the end of the nineteenth century, many houses were built with walls two and a half bricks thick. Between the bricks, a space was left which was usually filled with a broken brick and limestone solution. As a result of the technically deficient way in which the bricks were laid, the old houses were cold and damp and a great deal of fuel was needed to warm them up. When the outer walls were two and a half bricks thick, the main walls that subdivided the house into rooms were two bricks thick. Most of the houses built in the twentieth century had walls two bricks thick. The brick houses usually had deeper foundations.

The ceiling panels in the early brick houses were inserted into slots in the wall. At the beginning of the twentieth century, carpenters of the village who had also worked on city buildings introduced into Viriatino a new style of ceiling with thick beams running across. This looked more attractive than the traditional style but was twice as expensive.

Most of the brick houses had thatched roofs; bundles of straw were laid across the supporting beams and kept in place by thin sticks. At the turn of the century a popular new, better method of building thatched coverings was introduced. This kind of roof required a lot of straw, and one house usually used about twelve carts. It was, however, very practical because it could stand up without repair for thirty years. Unfortunately only specialists made this kind of covering and they usually came to Viriatino from the village of Lamka.

At the end of the nineteenth century, tin roofs appeared in Viriatino. Initially tin was used mostly in the houses of the well-to-do. But in the first ten years of the twentieth century, tin became popular with poorer people as well because, in view of its fire-preventing properties, the district office sold it to the peasants on credit in order to encourage its use. The construction of this kind of roof was very primitive; the plates of tin rested directly on the brick walls and were reinforced by planks of wood, a method that put too much unbalanced pressure on the brick walls, so that they often collapsed.

Windows in the brick houses of this period were made with an oval arch, but the old wooden structures were completely devoid of decoration. When the people started to build with brick, they tended to give more thought to the appearance of the house. Many old brick houses were decorated with geometrical patterns invented by the stone-cutters. The façades were ornamented with polished brick set in such shapes as triangles, rhombuses, and rectangles. The windows were also decorated with patterns that resembled two draping curtains, and cornices were likewise embellished with decorated brickwork. Different colors were used to highlight the designs. In spite of these decorations, however, the brick houses built at the turn of the century had very little aesthetic character in their architecture.

There were not many changes in the style of outbuildings during this period. The rich peasants began to build brick storage sheds with iron doors. Less affluent households had another kind of storage shed, usually built on the street facing the house, and made out of beaten clay. The fences which had originally enclosed the homesteads of large families were torn down when the families divided and rebuilt around each individual family unit.

In Viriatino, brick houses were built until the First World War. During the war, in connection with the general economic collapse, the brick industry, and with it brick building, ceased in the village.

Thus, in Viriatino, during the years of the intensive development of capitalism, great changes in the building of houses took place, affecting the outer form of dwellings, construction methods, the layout of the interior, and even the furniture. The changes touched not only the well-to-do peasants, the village bourgeoisie, but also the average middle-class peasants.

The dwellings that have survived from prerevolutionary times, in which many families of the collectives now live, once belonged to the middle-class peasantry. The majority of the houses consisted of one unit, but a separate kitchen and living room were characteristic of better-off homesteads. The tendency to isolate the parlor from the daily living space, the changes in interior design, and the buying of furniture mirrored the influence of the cities and industrial and commercial centers. In particular, the neighboring commercial village of Sosnovka exerted a direct influence on the living standards and housing of the well-to-do levels of Viriatino peasantry. But equally important was Viriatino's link to the industrial centers through the migratory worker. The growing cultural awareness of the migratory coal miners resulted in a greater demand for home improvements.

CHAPTER III

PEASANT DRESS

Up to the 1890s peasant clothing in Viriatino was made mostly of homespun material because the possibility of buying manufactured cloth was very limited. Only in a few instances, in the preparation of some sorts of cloth, for example, or in the manufacture of particular kinds of clothing and footwear, did the peasant use craftsmen in the neighboring villages, dyers, feltmakers, shoemakers, and tailors. The responsibility of making clothing was a heavy burden upon the women of the family. Most time-consuming was the spinning and weaving of materials made out of flax, hemp, and wool. In the autumn, winter, and early spring, all the women were busy with this work. Little girls worked preparing thread for weaving by the time they were seven or eight. When they reached twelve they were considered proficient spinners and at the age of fifteen they were already occupied in the bleaching of linen. As weaving required a greater mastery of technique and more stamina, only women between the ages of twenty and forty were involved in that work. Spinning began right after the clearing of the fields in September and any free time—especially on winter evenings—was given over to spinning. Hand spindles and spinning wheels operated by foot were used to prepare thread. In every house there was at least one spinning wheel and sometimes two or three. When spinning time began, this equipment would be brought out from storage and placed close to the window. Weaving usually began early in the spring and continued until Lent. Material was woven in a simple cross weave.

The people of Viriatino knew a more elaborate weaving technique, but it was no longer in use by the 1870s. The canvas technique was used sometimes for embroidering women's blouses that had been bought in Sosnovka.

Hemp and, to a lesser extent, flax were used to make coarse materials. After the material was woven it was bleached. Bleaching began in May and continued to September and October. This was usually done in a meadow near the river. The women would set up a large caldron there, with a plug at the bottom, which could hold twenty pails of water. They laid in the caldron thirty or forty pieces of material which had previously been soaked, covered the pile with an old piece of material, and spread wood ash on top of it. Then boiling water was poured into the caldron. The water was boiled in large iron pots on a campfire or in a primitive brick oven. When the water in the caldron grew cold, the plug was pulled out and the water collected in a wooden bucket. The ash water then would be reheated and poured again into the caldron.

To bleach the linen successfully required refilling the iron pot twenty to twenty-five times. After it was removed from the caldron, the linen was rinsed and then beaten with large rolling pins. During the next few days, it was spread out on the meadow. With this the process of bleaching ended. After the linen was rinsed, dried, and pressed out on a wooden roller, its preparation was complete.

Besides coarse linen, the peasant household manufactured pure woolen and partially woolen material. Thin woolen material was used for women's skirts and thick wool for outer clothing. The technique for making woolen material and coarse linen was the same. Finished thick woolen material was then sent to a fulling mill for conversion into felt.

One important facet of the home production of clothing was the preparation of "onuch," long pieces of linen that were wrapped around the feet and worn in place of socks. Sheep's wool was used to make stockings and socks.

The women preferred wool sheared in the spring for the knitting as it was softer and easier to spin. Felt for the boots was made from the autumn shearing, and sheepskins were used as linings for winter clothing.

Material made of hemp and wool was dyed black, blue, red, and orange. Black was the only color dyed in the home, and this was done by pouring a specially prepared hot liquid over the material. But more often the peasants would give their material to special dyers in Sosnovka. The favorite color scheme in Viriatino, as well as in many other Russian villages, was blue, often combined with white and red. It is for this reason that dyers were often called "bluers." Viriatino also used a small number of printed designs.

All the sewing, except that of outer garments, was the duty of the women. They sewed by hand with hemp thread. Sometimes padding was fastened to a table and it was used as a pin cushion to facilitate the working of the material. A tailor was brought into the home to sew overcoats from thick woolen cloth or sheepskins. He was paid a wage and food. Tailors from the neighboring Shatzkiy district were considered superior craftsmen. Felt shoes were likewise made by craftsmen from other districts, and they also worked for money and food at the home of the people who employed them. Sometimes they lived for a time in the home of an employer, or they rented a place in the village where they lived and worked.

It was the men's duty to manufacture the bast slippers called lapti,[1] which were made from the bark of young

---

[1] *Lapti*—Slippers, ancient Russian footwear made of bast (bark of a young linden tree) by a shoemaker, or homemade. They were considered a symbol of poverty. A rhymed anecdote is recorded by Roman Jakobson in "Commentary on Russian Fairy Tales" in *Russian Fairy Tales* (Pantheon: New York, 1945), p. 649:

> Peter the First braided lapti
> And put a curse on them;
> "To braid lapti," he said,

linden trees. They wove the narrow strips of bark on a last with the help of a hook. There was no bast in Viriatino, and they had to buy it at the fair in Sosnovka or illegally take it from the forest reserve.

The style and cut of different articles of clothing, especially those that were homemade, were determined by the width of the material and the traditional taste. In terms of ethnographic categories, the clothing of the peasants of Viriatino belonged to the Southern Great Russian type, the characteristics of which were manifested in women's clothing of the mid-nineteenth century. Men's clothing had less of a local character than women's, although it was subject to some regional modifications.

In the second half of the nineteenth century, the man's outfit consisted of the Russian peasant tunic shirt (low standing collar and side buttoning), pants, and a felt hat. The shirt was made of homespun linen. Sometimes, under the outer shirt he would wear an undershirt of the same style but without the standing collar and with an opening at the neck. Pants were made of linen bleached or dyed blue, usually in a striped pattern, and consisted of straight legs connected by two triangular pieces of cloth cut very amply. Elderly men held up their pants by means of a drawstring, but young men had theirs finished with a waistband fastened by a tin or copper buckle. Shirts were worn outside the pants. Waists were gathered with a leather belt or a cord. Hats, made of wool felt, were tall and conical in shape with a narrow brim. During the winter, hats made of sheepskin with earmuffs attached were worn.

Women wore a long shirt, skirt or sarafan (a loose dress flared from the bodice, attached to the shoulders by thin straps with a gored skirt), an apron and kerchief. Viriatino

---

> "is to eat once a day,
> but to mend worn lapti,
> is never to eat at all."
> And he cast away the awl.

The use of lapti is limited since in winter and autumn they are too light to walk in snow and rain. They wear out quickly (Tr.).

peasant dress in particular consisted of a skirt, a kerchief headdress, a sleeveless vest gathered at the back and sides, and slippers with rounded toes (Moscow type). A long linen shirt which had an upper and a lower part, often of different materials, and was gathered by a cord, was worn by girls until the age of fifteen or sixteen or, in other words, until they were considered eligible for marriage. From that time on, during holidays they wore homemade woolen skirts or, in wealthier families, sarafans. An informant remembers that until the age of fifteen or sixteen she was dressed only in a shirt even when she went out to bleach the linen. Only after she was sixteen was she given a skirt to wear.

Married women wore skirts over their shirts. The skirts were, of course, homemade and of wool woven in large plaid designs. The basic colors were usually dark blue, or black, and plaids were of white and red, or just white. The skirt was made of four panels connected by inserts of white or blue linen in the seams at the front.

By the 1890s skirts were sometimes made without the inserts, and such skirts are still seen in Viriatino today in a style widely known throughout Southern Russia. At the hem and waistline ornamental red bands were sewn on. The holiday or Sunday-best skirts were more elaborate. They had braid at the hemline, and were sometimes made from better-quality sheep's wool, a kind of material that was thinner, more even, and had a sheen, though it was still practical. In the affluent families, skirts were made with inserts of blue with store-bought material. The everyday skirt was shorter and simpler. While working, the women would tuck in the hemline of their skirts at their waists. In Viriatino the old people remember that formerly women wore homemade woolen skirts of a type characteristic of the costume of freehold peasant tradition. In the 1860s and 70s, they were worn only sporadically.

Under this skirt was worn usually another woolen skirt in a plaid or a two-colored material with a red background and a blue cross weave. Women wore aprons over the outer skirt. Some older women wore a type that had sleeves, but most aprons began at the waist and were trimmed at the hemline with a band of material. In the middle of the nineteenth century the sarafan for girls of marriageable age in well-to-do families began to become stylish in Viriatino, as in many other villages of South Russia. The sarafan was worn with pride and some of our informants in this study, now eighty-year-old women, did not forget to mention that they had owned sarafans. They were made from store-bought material, polished cotton, plain cotton, or silk. At first they were cut so that the panels flared at the bottom, but now that kind of sarafan is a very dim memory. In the 1870s the only type popular in Viriatino, as elsewhere in Russia, was one made of straight panels with straps at the shoulders. Such a sarafan was quite expensive to make because it required ten arshins of store-bought material.

The sarafan was worn over the long shirt. To make themselves look more impressive the women often used to wear three or four skirts made of a homespun woolen material underneath. Over the sarafan they would wear an apron which covered the whole front of the dress from top to bottom. The belt of the apron was tied in back under the arms between the shoulder blades. At the waistline, under the apron, another belt of silk or braided paper was worn. Women did not wear underwear. Under the sarafan and skirt, as noted above, they wore only the long shirt, sometimes two if it was cold. They slept in the same things they wore during the day, that is, in the shirt and inner skirt, and sometimes in the outer woolen skirt as well. No one living in the home was supposed to see a married woman, especially an older married woman, without her outer skirt and head kerchief.

Complicated kerchiefs were part of women's attire, a characteristic in Southern Great Russia.[2] The Viriatino

[2] Great Russia is a name traditionally given to the central provinces of European Russia as distinct from Malorussia (Ukraine) or Belorussia (White Russia) (Tr.).

peasants long ago rejected this type of complicated head-dress and were content with the simple kerchief. The old people remember that women used to go to church in silk kerchiefs to which a "backpiece," a beaded piece of cloth embroidered with gold thread was attached at the nape of the neck. A particular type of headdress topped with peaks like two horns was worn in neighboring villages but not in Viriatino. It was said in one village that the priest objected to these horned headdresses and suggested the village women follow the good example of the women of Viriatino in not adopting such elaborate devices. Kerchiefs for everyday use were homemade, but those for holidays were made of polished cotton, wool, or silk in loud colors.

The girls usually wore one long braid. They could go out without any head covering but they preferred to wear some kind of kerchief. For ornaments they used glass-bead necklaces with icon pendants. For earrings they wore pieces of wire on which they threaded glass beads or copper rings. Only the rich women had silver or gold earrings.

The outer garment worn during the warmer part of the year was a vest, the Ukranian type of natural gray or dyed black that was made of thick homespun woolen cloth. These vests had fitted waists, were pleated or gathered, were usually without a collar, and fastened at the throat and waist. Old women made vests out of store-bought broadcloth.

The long-sleeved kaftan which served as men's and women's autumn and spring wear had a similar cut. A light, short kaftan was called "the cool one." The peasants wore old "cool ones" for everyday use, while the new ones were reserved for holidays. The short ones reached approximately to the knees. The longer and heavier kaftans were called "zipuns." Zipuns were made of thick homespun woolen cloth, and in their cut they resembled the short kaftan. The zipun was an outer garment used for everyday and holiday wear, and it was worn when working, going to market or to church. During the wintertime a fur coat made out of sheepskin was used and this was covered with fabric.

Besides the basic outer garment, a supplementary garment was worn outside during the frost, on stormy or rainy days, and when the peasants had to travel. This overcoat was made of homespun heavy wool. It was very long, reached down to the heels and had long sleeves that covered the wrist, and a large collar with a scarf that could be used as a head covering. The making of a "tulup" —the overcoat—was an expensive undertaking. It required many sheep's skins and, therefore, was far from being available to every family. Even middle-class peasants did not own them.

The basic type of footwear for men and women was slippers made out of Linden fiber. The fibers were woven diagonally so that the toes were rounded. This type of slipper is known from the ethnographic literature as the Moscow or Vyatich type. On holidays slippers with an extra layer of more evenly woven rows were worn. During winter, corded soles were attached to the slippers and straw was tied on the top. The foot was wrapped in long pieces of woolen or half-woolen cloth before the shoe was put on. Most men used strips of leather and women woolen ties to fasten the slippers to the foot, although poorer people used cord. The leather boots for men and women which looked like galoshes were fastened to the foot with strips, like the slippers, but this kind of boot was very little known in the village. As one Viriatino informant said: "Our grandfathers went around in homemade slippers. They would buy one pair of boots to last for twenty years but would be dressed in slippers during winter and summer. When grandfather married in 1860, there were in the village only three pairs of leather boots." Not everybody owned even a pair of felt boots.

The development of a money economy in the village brought a change in the whole material culture of the peasant and with it a change in his clothing. Alterations in

clothing took place very slowly and began to be felt in
Viriatino only about the mid-1890s, but a special development took place in men's costumes during the first decade
of the twentieth century. The changes affected first of all
the material from which the garments were made. In this
period, as before, homespun garments existed, for the
business of spinning and weaving did not stop in Viriatino
until the October Revolution. Weaving was done even in
those families whose entire income was from non-
agricultural seasonal work. The number of articles of clothing made out of homespun material gradually diminished,
however; the linen shirt and old-style pants were now worn
as underwear, or for work, and remained fashionable
only among old people and poor families who used the
shirt and pants made out of store-bought materials only
five times a year during the great holidays. Shirts made
of store-bought cotton or of a plaid material which the
peasants themselves wove out of hemp were widely used
as an everyday garment for men. For the most part, clothing gradually began to be made of fabrics bought in stores,
such as plain and printed cotton and, to a lesser degree,
silk, sateen, and cashmere.

Shirts were made out of white or printed cotton or
sateen, with the side closing as before. They were sometimes embroidered. A less popular type of shirt was made
with a bodice and full-gathered sleeves with cuffs; these also
had a side closing and a short collar, and were embroidered
with colored thread in a cross-stitch design. Very popular
among the peasants in Viriatino were shirts in fiery colors
—shocking pink, red, green, or rose. Over the shirt was
worn a woolen vest with a sateen or silk and satin back,
or a jacket made of wool, which sometimes was worn just
over the shoulders. Pants were made out of cotton or woolen
material and the style was the usual city cut. Some people
wore pants cut a little fuller than usual and tucked into
boots. On their heads they wore caps. This, in the main,
was the Sunday-best costume of the Viriatino young peo-

ple. It became stylish around the turn of the century, and was used for holidays, engagements, weddings, and all grand occasions. As the use of store-bought materials and the new styles that came into vogue demanded more careful cutting and sewing, some articles of clothing had to be sent out to tailors or dressmakers who were professional people and owned sewing machines.

New influences seeped into Viriatino along different routes. The innovators who introduced the new styles were seasonal workers who worked in cities and industrial centers. But informants remember that in the 1880s–90s, when workers went off to the Donbass for seasonal mining, they left dressed in thick, crudely worked, linen shirts, with coats and pants of the same thick, crude material. They did not even take a change of clothes with them; seven months later they would return to the village in the same outfit, by then dirty and torn. The people used to call this outfit "miners' attire," and it was worn until it was actually falling off their bodies. Instead of the usual slippers, however, they wore leather work boots in the mines. At the turn of the century, and especially after the Revolution of 1905, the migrants went to work in everyday clothing taking the miners' attire with them as a working outfit. Besides this, they took one change of underwear and an extra outer shirt. Steam baths made their appearance in the mines at this time. From Donbass the miners brought back to the village not only the money they earned but also the clothing they bought. Every young miner tried to buy himself at least one new outfit.

Diakov remembered that from his earnings he used to set aside fifteen rubles for his own use, food and clothing. Of course, not all the miners could spend as much on clothing, and the quality and amount of clothing varied greatly. Another informant, Nagorova, remembered that when her husband was about to be married, he owned only one rose-colored sateen shirt which he had bought in Donbass. On the other hand, Diakov, who came from a more affluent family, remembered that in 1908 he returned from Don-bass with a wardrobe of pants made of thick wool, a belt, and a shirt with a diagonal side closing (a special miner's style). Besides these he also owned four sateen and two plain shirts, five or six pairs of pants, one pair of plain boots and one pair of patent leather, and galoshes. When seasonal miners worked in the fields in Viriatino they did not wear the traditional peasant footwear but kept their boots on in spite of the protests of their parents. The miners' holiday attire resembled that of shop clerks, arti-sans, and other lower middle-class people in the city with whom the Viriatino workers came into contact and who served them as models. In comparison with other seasonal workers, the miners from Donbass had an especially fes-tive holiday costume. They sported fiery-colored sateen shirts, pleated pants, and patent leather shoes. Only the miners in the village had shirts with a diagonal chest clos-ing and two rows of buttons. Shirts of this type were not made in Viriatino but were imported from the miners' settlement, as were other types of men's holiday clothing.

Another source of city influence was the nearby village of Sosnovka, which had a considerable petite bourgeoisie consisting of tradespeople, entrepreneurs, and others whose way of life was like that of city people. While preserving some features of the traditional form of peasant dress, these circles of the village bourgeoisie strove to demon-strate at the same time, by their dress and bearing, that they were not of the common people.

The influence of Sosnovka on the kulak and more affluent families in Viriatino, who adopted the new styles and customs, was especially noticeable. Their clothing was distinguished by good-quality material, the use of more subdued colors in comparison with those of the miners, and slight alterations in traditional styles. Thus, while a miner wore a short coat lined with cotton fleece in place of an overcoat, village bourgeoisie wore lined fur coats or overcoats of heavy wool called "poddevka." The poddevka resembled the zipun in that it was gathered at the waist, the back was given shape by two seams, and it was drawn at the throat and waist. For example, old Sleptsov, a kulak, dressed in a sateen shirt, vest, a poddevka, and boots or, during the wintertime, felt boots with galoshes and a good fur-lined overcoat. Even for traveling he used a good overcoat. But the poor wore only a zipun and bast slippers, both winter and summer.

The same changes could be observed in women's clothing, though these occurred at a slower pace. As a rule, the women did not leave the village, but occasionally they accompanied their husbands to the mines and worked there as cooks. New influences came mostly via Sosnovka. The sarafan became the basic costume of peasant women but at the same time the "poneva" (the woolen skirt) was still in use. During the holidays, instead of the traditional old women's "kichka" (a special form worn on the head over which a kerchief was tied) it became usual to wear a small piece of lace or brightly colored silk on top of the head, with the hair braided high on the head into one braid and not covered. This headdress was not only decorative; it also had a symbolic meaning. It was placed on the bride's head, for example, at the wedding to symbolize the change in her status from girl to married woman. The everyday headwear for married and unmarried girls remained the kerchief.

Before World War I a citylike style, a jacket and skirt, became popular among the women of Viriatino. This was a holiday outfit and very few people wore it, mostly young women of more affluent families and especially of those families who sent out seasonal workers. Most Viriatino women could not break away from the sarafan, but in order to follow the new style they wore a jacket over it. Sometimes this costume was supplemented by a silk scarf, usually black, and a kerchief for the head or shoulders. One can see such attire in the family portraits of 1910–17.

As for footwear, shoes with elastic inserts or buttons

or lace were fashionable in the cities and in workers' settlements. Homemade woolen stockings were replaced in the summer by white cotton store-bought stockings. One informant claimed that "in former times we had half-boots which we wore to church. When we returned from church, we would dust them off and store them back in the chest. In the evening we went to the street parties in 'lapti,' our bast slippers. Our parents kept their shoes for twenty-five years." As a rule, people went to work in bast slippers. As these slippers were also worn for bleaching linen while water was still standing in the meadows, it is no wonder such sicknesses as rheumatism were widespread. Felt shoes were expensive. Although some people owned them, they were saved for church while in other families leather shoes were used even for work. Members of the kulak family Sleptsov did not even know how to weave bast slippers.

In the autumn, spring, and winter women wore short, fur-lined coats just like the men. Sometimes they bought coats and jackets from cities and industrial centers, but they very seldom wore them. Tradition here was still very strong, and women who left for Donbass would leave their short, fur coats in Viriatino to have proper overcoats when they came back home.

The attire of a Viriatino peasant, as was generally the case with all Russian peasantry, reflected his socio-economic position. An especially sharp distinction in clothing appeared toward the end of the nineteenth century in connection with the growing class differentiation in the village. Earlier, the predominant use of homespun materials for most clothing concealed the difference between the well-to-do and the poor peasants, but the use of store-bought material brought the distinction into focus. Store-bought material was used by all economic groups in the village but, of course, the amount and quality was determined by the amount of money available. In the 1870s and 80s everyday clothing differed from holiday garb only in that the latter was decorated, but at the end of the nineteenth and in the first decade of the twentieth century the difference became one of quality. At that time a Viriatino peasant could not afford to buy all his clothing and therefore only material for holiday outfits was bought. Clothing also came to differ in style. During the holidays, the women wore sarafans, short decorated skirts, shoes, and gay kerchiefs ("skolka"), and the men wore sateen or silk and satin shirts, woolen pants, and boots. For work they still wore everyday clothing. Of course holiday outfits became worn out and ordinary looking in time, but they were treated with great care because they were expensive and not very durable. Women took special care of their holiday clothes and what the men brought from the mines lasted them twenty years. Because of this some women accumulated twenty to thirty sarafans in their hope chests. Holiday clothes were worn for work only during haying, when, according to old tradition, women would wear sarafans, batiste shirts, and gay kerchiefs for their heads, while men wore white shirts, good pants, and boots or shoes.

Besides holiday and everyday costumes, the Viriatino peasants also had ceremonial costumes for special rituals connected with the important events in their lives. But while they kept this ritual clothing for a very long time, it seems that it did not play as important a role as it did in other regions. The attire for funerals, mourning, and burials was especially distinctive. However, even here, except for soft shoes and shrouds, nothing special was made for the dead person. There was much more emphasis on preserving the old forms. For instance, in the first decade of the twentieth century the older women were buried in poneva, long shirts, and kichka, in other words, in their traditional costume. Parts of the ancient costume, the poneva, for instance, were also considered ritual garments. One informant remembered that she wore a poneva only when she attended a funeral because on such occasions it was considered becoming to a married woman. The mourning shirt, an ancient tradition in Russian peasant clothing, was usually made of a plain white cloth. Wedding costumes preserved fewer of the traditional features. Usually the best holiday attire was saved for the wedding. Brides appeared for the ceremonies in sarafans and skirts with blouses, and men came in shirts with side closings.

The distribution of clothing and footwear within a family was uneven; children and teenagers had fewer things. Youngsters usually received hand-me-downs or clothes made over from adult attire. Little dresses were made for infants out of their mothers' and fathers' shirts. As soon as the child began to walk he was given a long linen shirt. Boys up to the age of ten or twelve wore nothing else, but in the 1880s this was true only until they were six or seven. Girls wore their long shirts up to the age of fifteen or sixteen. Warm outer clothing and footwear were scarce. Two or three youngsters shared one fur coat in many families. One of the old members of a collective farm reminiscing about life in her family who were middle-class peasants recalled "for three girls there was one made-over fur coat; each girl had a heavy short coat and also sarafans. The youngest one wore the same dress and the same bast slippers every day during summer and winter. During the winter, however, she would wear extra wrappings around her wool stockings."

At the turn of the century, as a result of increased earnings, peasants started to buy store-bought clothing, especially for their children. Most often, this phenomenon could be observed in the families of migrant workers who would bring home gifts of children's shoes, printed cotton, sateen, and other materials. In the family of the carpenter Nagorni, for instance, there were always little dresses, stockings, and shoes for the children. The old people, who did not approve of such spending, considered buying shoes for little children a waste of money.

The whole family was responsible for supplying a young man with clothing. But as migratory work in Viriatino became the rule, young men on the verge of getting married used their own money to buy clothes. With girls the arrangement was more complicated. When a girl was about to be married, she made herself enough clothing to last almost all the rest of her life; it was one of the basic parts of her dowry. The number of articles she owned and their quality were determined by her economic status, and the kind of sarafans which were made in the 1890s were considered a measure of the bride's wealth. Besides her dowry, the bride had to make some clothing for her groom. According to the acceptable norms this included a few shirts, underclothing, a belt, a vest, and sometimes even a fur coat. In return, she would receive from him a kerchief, shoes, a sarafan, earrings and rings, and sometimes even a fur coat. Those who were more affluent would have their fur coats lined with black sheep's fleece; those who were poorer used anything they could get because, as they reasoned, once it was covered with fur it would not show.

Generally speaking, the peasant clothing in Viriatino changed very slowly. The change from the old fashions to the new only began to be noticed by the end of the nineteenth century, and more specifically during the prerevolutionary period of the twentieth century. But even then the use of factory goods did not completely replace the use of homemade materials and bast slippers. The whole structure of the village, the century-old tastes and habits which seemed in harmony with a state of "seminaturalness" supported the preservation of the traditional styles of peasant attire.

CHAPTER IV

FAMILY STRUCTURE AND FAMILY LIFE

The Peasant Family After Serfdom

In order to understand the processes and basic changes that took place in the structure and general way of life of the peasant family during the years of Soviet rule it is necessary to review in detail the Russian peasant family of the past. In this respect Viriatino provides a most interesting example, as its traditional extended patriarchal family structure survived until the Great October Social Revolution and was felt even later during Soviet rule.

The reasons for the prolonged existence of the joint family stemmed from the peculiarities of the economy of a village located in the middle of the Black Earth Belt. Capitalism developed more slowly in this region than in, for example, the steppes of Southern Russia, and the remnants of serfdom were manifested in all aspects of life. The fact that their farmland consisted of several tiny holdings in scattered areas forced the Viriatino peasants to preserve—even at the time of the greatest development of migratory occupations—a form of agriculture requiring a large number of workers. For this reason they relied on the joint family as the best means of assuring that all available labor remained on the homesteads.

It is also necessary to consider the importance of any additional earnings to the economic base of the peasant family. Families which had a surplus of farmhands in relation to the size of the farm could, to a very great extent, count on the earnings of the extra members of their family from migratory labor to strengthen their own home-steads. As ethnographic investigation revealed, the tradition of large joint families was preserved most of all among the well-to-do peasants. There was hardly any economic reason for maintaining the large joint family among those families not owning draft animals who lived in tiny huts in the 1880s in an area of from twelve to seventeen square meters. Because of the lack of horses, most of their allotted land had to be leased out. These families also participated in the migration to the mines. It was probably the only way they could support themselves. The mines were not merely an additional source of income for them, but their main-stay. These families never reached the dimensions of the joint families that had ample land.

At the same time, the increase of earnings from work in the mines set into motion a deeper involvement with a money economy, and this exerted a tremendous influence on the economic and social structure of the family. This explains the great changes which took place in the family structure in the second half of the nineteenth century and especially in the late eighties. The changes can clearly be distinguished when later developments are compared with the peasant family structure of the period of 1860–70, when many features of pre-reform structure were visible.

Our information about the state of the peasant family on the eve of the end of serfdom is very scanty and reveals no clear understanding of its size and structure. On the basis of family stories, the older local people believe that the families in those times were predominantly large, about twenty-five to thirty people. Sometimes the families of four or five brothers lived together. However, insofar as we can piece information together from their reminiscences, there already existed a tendency for the families of older brothers to separate.

Some light on the size of the family in pre-reform times is shed by the documents recording the sale of the landlord Davidov's estate to the peasant families of Viriatino. Most of those families who purchased land in 1808–31 had twelve to fifteen members. Since the land was usually bought by poorer families, one could assume that the size of well-to-do families was larger. The size of some families can be substantiated from memories of the types of houses which they built. In many poorer households, separate summer huts were built for married couples, while complexes of two or three houses that preserved a common household economy were characteristic of well-to-do families. The slow growth of the village up until the last quarter of the nineteenth century is striking. Only in the eighties did the village start to grow intensively in all directions.

During the first two decades after the Peasant Reform, the internal structure of the peasant family showed no visible change in spite of the changes that took place in the economic structure. But great changes in all aspects of life, particularly in family relations, took place in Viriatino between 1880–90 with the further development of capitalistic activities. Divisions of families became more frequent. Both partial and complete division of the joint family began taking place at an accelerated pace, and the size of families significantly diminished. According to the census of 1881, there was an average of seven people per room of living space. This does not mean, of course, that joint families disappeared altogether; apparently the two forms, the joint family and the small, immediate family, existed together for some time. According to old people in Viriatino, the middle class homesteads were run, as before, by two or three married brothers living together.

At the turn of the century, with the formation of a working class in mining areas and the growth of a working-class political movement throughout Russia, the individual image and way of life of the migratory peasant changed. His mingling with workers involved in politics also had an influence on the general cultural level. The demand for consumer goods increased. Peasants wanted to be dressed in the style of the city, to better their own existence, rather than send all their earnings home, and generally to improve their working conditions. The growth of these desires, without any doubt, represented a heightened self-awareness which manifested itself in the younger generation and could not help but leave its influence on the patriarchal structure. At the turn of the century, relations within the joint family were on edge. There was an impetus for young couples to associate more with each other. This same tendency showed itself in the practice of miners' putting aside some of their earnings for personal needs and those of their immediate family, which, according to informants, was one of the main reasons for family conflicts and divisions. But family life on the whole was changing slowly and still preserved its patriarchal form. Even though they could support their families from their miners' pay, the limited scope of the communal peasant's world-view forced migrants to cling to their small piece of land. The drive to preserve ties with the land was partially explained by the negative attitude of the middle-class peasants toward the migrants who cut their ties with the village and moved to workers' settlements.

Straining to support and save declining farms, the peasants clung to the old family structure in which the traditional relationships and the rights and duties of each member were strictly regimented. The representative of the oldest generation, the grandfather or, after his death, the grandmother, was considered the head of the family. In cases where a grandmother was head of the family, the direction of the farm was the responsibility of the oldest son. When both members of the oldest generation were dead or senile, the position of family head fell to the next oldest. The head of the family was the overseer of the whole family structure. His function was to direct the field work and the division of labor among the men of the family. Specifically, he established a rotation of migration to the mines among sons and grandsons, and had charge of the family property and capital. All the earnings of family members from work outside the homestead were put into a common purse and spent for the needs of the joint household. Into the family purse also went what the women earned selling eggs or moss, berries or mushrooms they gathered, and bleaching linen, for instance, although as the informant Diakov said, "with what they earned, you could not buy kerosene or a pair of boots."

A division of labor along sex lines was characteristic in times past. The wife of the head of the family was in charge of household duties; in the case of her death, the house fell to her oldest daughter-in-law. Women were responsible for all housework, the preparation of food, cleaning, washing, the care of children, tending the cattle, and drawing water. Men helped in the care of livestock. They cleaned the barn, removed manure, changed straw bedding, and took care of the horses. Women fed the cows, calves, pigs, sheep, and fowl. The sale of eggs was one of the principal sources of women's income.

During the autumn and winter, women spent all their time free from household duties spinning and weaving for their family. This work was preceded by the heavy labor of preparing hemp. Little girls also took part in the spinning and weaving. Girls of nine and ten were taught to spin and at fifteen or sixteen to weave. Women over forty, for the most part, no longer wove because such work was considered above their strength if done extensively. Women sewed family garments, with the exception of the winter overcoats which they had made by a tailor, and knitted wool stockings, shawls, and gloves. The weaving of bast slippers was considered men's work and boys from early years were taught how to do it.

Field work was strictly divided between men and women. As noted above, men's duties consisted of plowing, sowing, reaping, gathering, bundling, and transporting. Women stacked hay, turning it over to dry, and at harvest they bound the sheaves. They also helped with chain threshing.

All work in gardens except for the initial plowing was done by women and children. It was a man's job to bring in fuel and feed the livestock.

In the division of duties among married women living in the same household, it was necessary to consider the needs of the household as a whole, and also those of the individual families. In the sharing of basic housekeeping work, a strict routine was established for the mother-in-law and her daughters-in-law. Each woman had a day when she acted as cook and overall housekeeper, assisted by the teenage girls and unmarried women. Because of the isolated position of a daughter-in-law in the joint family of her husband, she could generally rely only on her own children to help when her day came. On the other hand, the mother-in-law was assisted in all her chores inside and outside the house by her own daughters.

While the bulk of housework was the responsibility of married women, girls of marriageable age had many chores, especially spinning. In the first year of her marriage, a young daughter-in-law served as a helper for the mother-in-law at the oven, as they were not allowed to prepare food. Not until the second year was she allowed to have a turn at the stove, to cook together with the other daughters-in-law for the whole family. The women rotated among themselves the weekly job of baking bread, and took turns in preparing the steam bath if the family owned such a thing. During the time left free from housework, women wove and spun, sewed, darned, and knitted. Some labor was done collectively, as for instance, the washing of floors and the family laundry. Underwear was homespun and very coarse and was not washed with soap but with the same arduous process used in bleaching linen, requiring the participation of all the women of the family. When daughters-in-law did their own family laundry, those who had fewer children divided the grandparents' washing.

In the house everybody had his own allotted space for work. Girls and women spun sitting on benches at the window, or in a circle around the fireplace when it got dark. When they were working with hemp, the dust was so thick that it hung like a curtain in the air. When the women began their weaving during Lent, one or perhaps two looms were brought into the room.

The family also had a definite order of daily activities. They got up early and went to bed late. In families where there were carters they rose between 2 and 3 A.M., and everybody else got up at the same time; because of the close living quarters it could not be otherwise. While the woman who was to cook that day lit the stove, the other women disassembled the beds, put away the bedding and the benches on which people slept, straightened up the room, swept the floor, and washed the table. There were three meals a day. The family ate breakfast together and then everyone went about his own work. If someone had to leave the house before dinner, which was at noon, he would pack some food to take with him. At suppertime the family sat around the fireplace and ate whatever was left from dinner; food was seldom prepared for supper. Places at the table were assigned in a definite arrangement. The head of the family sat at the head of the table and next to him was placed his eldest son. Men sat on one side of the table on benches and women on individual stools on the other side. In the last decades of the nineteenth century this traditional arrangement was reshuffled with married couples sitting together. Usually at the corner of the table sat the woman whose chore it was to serve food that day. When there were many children in the family they were fed separately. All ate from a common bowl. Table manners were determined by considerations of rank, but the rules of etiquette were less strict and tense in comparison with those which governed common meals during serfdom. As the old people remember, at the time of serfdom it was customary for the head of the family to hold a switch in one hand throughout the meal ready to swat those who laughed too loud or talked too much.

Rye bread was the staple of the Russian peasants' diet. A batch of bread was baked once a week in the Russian oven, sometimes on cabbage leaves. Pancakes and blintzes were made from a combination of rye and buckwheat flour, rye kvas,[1] and from rye flour alone. Until the 1880s, wheat flour was seldom used because it had to be bought at the market. Later on it became an everyday commodity for well-to-do families, but poorer people saved it for big holidays.

The basic hot dish, served almost daily, was cabbage soup. Depending on the family's economic situation, it was made with or without meat and enriched with milk, sour cream, or lard. At the turn of the century, probably because of the influence of the migratory workers, cabbage soup began to be called "borscht." The ingredients did not change, however, and it was cooked without beets as before. Another very common soup was made from wheat flour and cooked with potatoes or lard. When cooked with potatoes, it was first boiled for a while and then the liquid was removed and enriched with butter, lard, etc. The remaining potato pulp, "kasha," was eaten with milk or oil. Between the 1880s and 90s, millet kasha appeared on the table almost as frequently as cabbage soup. Other kashas were made from buckwheat, but not as often since it was more expensive and not everyone grew it.

Kvas played an important part in the diet not only as a beverage. During the winter as a first course it was prepared with sauerkraut and horseradish. It was sometimes cooked with peas, particularly during feasts, and during the summer the poor would add bread crumbs and chopped scallions, while the more affluent added cucumbers, onions, and eggs. On festive days such as weddings, kvas was served with meat and horseradish.

Toward the end of the eighties, potatoes took the place

[1] *Kvas*—A fermented beverage prepared from dried black bread (Tr.).

of kasha. They were cooked with their skins on and served with pickles, sauerkraut, or sometimes simply mashed with oil on the top. The peasants did not fry potatoes. Some of the old people interviewed remarked that it would have been difficult to fry for a family of ten to fifteen people.

Dishes called "salamata" and "kalina" were very common because they enabled the peasants to economize on bread. They made a loose dough of rye flour, baked it, and ate it with or without milk. The inhabitants of the village, as an eighty-eight-year-old woman related, called this dish "Viriatino salamata." The affluent of the village, however, very seldom ate it, serving it only when they were tired of kasha. During Lent when food became very dull, people even ate guelder-rose berries, which were collected after the first frost because their bitter taste had disappeared by then. These were the fare of the poorer peasants; in well-to-do families it was considered a disgrace to eat them.

As everyone prepared food in the same way, the only differences in the diet among the different classes of the peasantry were in the quality and nutritional value of the ingredients used. In the well-to-do family—for example one that consisted of twenty-five people and owned a few horses, cows, and pigs, and more than a score of sheep—a lot of milk was used and meat was eaten twice a day, with the exception of fast days. In the poor families potatoes in their skins were generally eaten along with kvas, sour milk, steamed kalina, and a kasha for supper. There was not enough bread for everybody and even kasha was not always available.

In order to give more importance to themselves, the older women would strictly supervise the traditional preparation of foods by their daughters-in-law. All attempts at innovation were met with scorn and were refused. Even though by the turn of the century there had already appeared in the village many new foodstuffs which would better the everyday fare, yet up to the time of the social revolution the diet generally remained unchanged and primitive.

Traditional Family Relations

The patriarchal structure of the family determined its traditional relationships and created its overall moral atmosphere. The order of things, developed through centuries, was based on the unquestionable authority of the oldest member of the family.

Any manifestation of independence or revolt against custom was not tolerated. Fear of one's elders and the scorn of one's neighbor prevented nearly all innovation. An old-timer named Starodubov explained much of the village's conservatism. The migratory workers, he pointed out, had better food when they worked in the mines than they were offered at home. In the village, for example, the potatoes were cooked in their peels and never fried, even though fat was available. The men ate the family fare with no new dishes. Any criticism from a migrant worker was met with something like "you just came here and you want to bring new rules."

Families generally lived together on good terms. Most fathers treated their daughters-in-law equally well, for if they showed any favoritism it immediately created a rift among the women. Quite often, however, married couples did not get along peacefully because marriages were formed by the parents who had little consideration for the young people's wishes. Sometimes husbands beat their wives savagely. How peaceful family relationships were depended mostly on the tactfulness of the head of the family, on the character of the mother-in-law, and on the relations between the young married people.

The main source of misunderstandings and quarrels was the disparity of earning power among the men. Those who went to the coal mines had a chance to contribute money to the family purse, while those who remained at home could not do so, and this situation sometimes provoked the dissatisfaction of the parents and disharmony among the daughters-in-law. It must be noted, however, that bickerings among the young people were carefully concealed from the parents. "We daughters-in-law did not let on that we were quarreling in the presence of our parents," said one woman reminiscing about her life in a large, joint family. Parents who had the right to withhold a share due the offender in case of joint family separation were not so much respected as they were feared. But the character of the peasant family changed gradually. By the 1900s the manifestations of fear and submission among the younger generation so characteristic of peasant families under serfdom had largely disappeared and were much simpler and more relaxed.

It is interesting to examine the way in which families separated; it was supported by a strong tradition. According to the laws of 1906 and 1913, all matters concerning family separation were under the jurisdiction of district courts, but elderly villagers remember that difficult cases were appealed before a village committee. Its decision took into consideration the reason for separation and the value of the family's possessions. It should be noted that although the law of 1886 requiring the consent of the oldest member of the family to the division of property was later annulled, the village committee continued in any controversy to take all statements and claims into consideration first. When family conflicts were not resolved at home it was not uncommon, however, to bribe some members of the committee.

Preparation for the separation was made ahead of time, so that each member received some of the family property. By the common efforts of the family, new houses were built but as a rule were left uninhabited up to the time of the separation. Usually a family decided to divide when it had accumulated sufficient property, including living quarters, outbuildings, and livestock. At the separation all the family possessions were assessed and divided according to the number of smaller family units, each getting an equal share. After the death of a father, property was divided among sons by lots, drawn in the presence of one or two appointed neighbors. If separation took place during a father's lifetime, he decided what portion each of his sons would receive and which one would remain behind to share what he kept.

Special attention should be given to the position of the daughter-in-law. The daughter-in-law's complete dependency on the family is illustrated by a proverb well known in Viriatino: "Work—whenever it is forced upon you; eat —whenever it is given to you." Her condition was further aggravated by her husband's dependency on his family.

On the other hand, in Viriatino, as everywhere else in Russia, what property and possessions she had were considered separate from those of the rest of the family. In the first place, her property included a dowry, which not only provided her with the necessary clothes, but also with sheep, whose wool and offspring could be sold. Any other property and money she inherited were considered her own, to take care of her needs and those of her children, for according to tradition not one kopek of the family budget under the charge of the head of the family was to be spent on a daughter-in-law. She was entitled, however, to food, an overcoat, and shoes, and she was dealt a ration from the family supply of wool and hemp. Necessities such as clothes for herself and her children, bedding, even such small items as soap, had to be bought with her own money. In most families the bulk of the daughter's dowry came from "woman's earning." Only expenses for the wedding ceremony and reception were paid from the family purse.[2]

---

[2] The same basic order was also prevalent among the kulak families. This is why the relationship between the daughter-in-law and the parents of her husband very often assumed an especially hostile character.

This arrangement was logical as long as the peasant household retained its rural character, but with the growth of a money economy and a taste for more goods, the woman's obligations under such a system became a heavy burden which forced her to seek the most profitable work she could find. The traditional odd jobs for women in Viriatino, such as collecting moss on the swamps for calking tree stumps in the neighboring villages or gathering berries to sell, provided a negligible income and were no longer satisfying. Linen bleaching which was more profitable became, therefore, a common home industry, but it was very difficult and unhealthy work and as a result of it many women suffered from rheumatism and tuberculosis.

The laws concerning what a widowed daughter-in-law could inherit and her position in the family after the death of her husband deserves special attention. When the widow was left with children, her husband's share of the family property was held for her and she usually continued to live with her in-laws. If the family separated, she received a share on an equal basis with her brother-in-law. If, however, at the time of separation the widow was childless, her position was more uncertain. She had two choices, either to return to her family, or, given the opportunity, to remarry. On leaving her late husband's family, she was allowed to take her personal possessions and his clothing. When her relations with her father-in-law were good and he treated her well he might give her a sheep as a dowry for her second marriage.

If the woman complained of unfair treatment to the county's chief magistrate, her petition almost always went unheard. As a rule, such matters were passed on for decision to the village assembly which would invariably uphold the father-in-law. Diakov described a characteristic situation. His eldest sister was widowed after twelve years of marriage. As long as her little boy was alive she continued to live with the family, but when he too died, her father-in-law threw her out of the house. She appealed to the head of the village assembly but was informed that "she was entitled to nothing." She then approached the county chief magistrate, who sent the case to the village assembly. She was told to "look for a husband. You have nothing coming to you, and no one to stand up for you."

If a widow had no sons, only unmarried daughters, she was still entitled to a share in the household. However in such cases she was much more dependent upon the good will of her father-in-law. Cases of tyranny and arbitrary rule were frequent, especially in kulak families. The relations between daughter-in-law and the parents of the husband were often especially sharp. Diakova, aged seventy-five when the study was made, related that when her husband was killed in the Russo-Japanese War she was left with a little girl. Her father-in-law ordered her out of the house as soon as he received the news of his son's death. She appealed to the head of the village assembly, who recommended that she leave the house, stay in a rented room, and bring her case against the father-in-law to court. When the case came up, the county court referred it to the village assembly, and there, as always happened, it was dismissed. It was only when the case came up a second time in the county court that she received an allotment of land for one person, a horse, and a hayloft. Usually the widow's household was the poorest in the village, as a rule without a horse and a cow, and she and her children were forced to hire themselves out all their life.

Cases of inheritance received by orphaned children were frequent and characteristic of the customary law of the period. On remarrying, a widow lost her right to her late husband's property (the house, outbuildings, livestock). All this was sold and the proceeds of the sale were distributed among the orphans up to the age of legal maturity. The village assembly selected a relative or even a stranger with experience as guardian; money inherited in this way became the personal property of an orphaned girl, and after her marriage, she could spend it according to her own judgment.

All these characteristics of a patriarchal family structure were preserved longest in wealthier families. Where life was oriented toward increasing the family wealth, especially in kulak families, the rules of conduct were severe. For example in the family of the kulak Kabanov, the women were made to work even on holidays. "We were blinded by constant spinning and weaving," said Kabanov's wife. In poorer families, forever in need, the traditional order weakened sooner. In these families the women were much less closed in; girls and young married women worked between chores in their own households as day laborers for the kulaks or landowners, doing such jobs as weeding, and so developed an independent outlook that was reflected in their strong position within the family.

By the turn of the century young married women enjoyed relative freedom. Even when their husbands were away during the winter working in the mines they were not forbidden to socialize at block parties and to take part in holiday entertaining. When the mother-in-law went to the fair she took along the daughter-in-law, and there the two of them would often collect orders for bleaching linen. In other words, to some extent they set up an independent household operation.

It is a pity we have no data concerning the strength or the extent and manifestations of the more distant ties of kinship in Viriatino. Elderly local townsmen claim that in former times such ties were broader and stronger; even cousins twice removed were invited to weddings, for example. Of course a lot depended on the number of relatives; the fewer relatives the stronger were the ties that bound them. But regard for second cousins was considered obligatory.

Relatives, particularly close ones, tended to practice mutual help, mostly in terms of labor, and especially in cases of emergency. After a fire, relatives would help to rebuild the house; when a horse died they would bring their own to help in the field work, and would lend each other grain, bread, etc. However, when long-term aid was called for, a business arrangement was made with relatives as it was with strangers.

Diakov's sister married into a family that was headed by her husband's stepfather. The stepfather had children of his own and the stepson was treated in the family almost like a farmhand. Diakov's parents suggested the young couple move to their house and live there until they could put away enough money to build a home of their own. There were forty pounds of grain per month per person. Straw was taken from the sister-in-law's field and used by the family for the livestock; milk for everybody came from the parents' cow. The son-in-law had an allotment of land for two people, but since he had no horse the field was worked with the family equipment. This work was estimated at thirty-five to forty rubles, and from this sum was deducted the amount that was estimated for the work done in the fields by the son-in-law and his wife. During the winter the son-in-law went to work in the mines and the income was saved for the building of the house. Expenses for clothing, shoes, and taxes were paid from the young couple's own earnings.

Extra help needed with farm work was ordinarily provided by the nearest neighbors, but neighborly feeling on the whole was fairly weak; the neighbors did not participate in family celebrations, for example, and only relatives attended funerals.

Family Customs

The character of the marital relationship had been basically determined by the patriarchal structure of the peasant family. It was customary in Russian villages for girls to be married at seventeen or eighteen to young men of eighteen or nineteen. Any considerable age difference was permissible only in the case of widows, who were likely to marry widowers with children. Usually a bride was selected from the same village or from one nearby. Those who were married in the 1880s and 90s maintain that marriages had usually been arranged by the parents in accordance with the parents' choice and the feelings of the young people involved were not taken into consideration. As was to be expected, a great deal of personal unhappiness and even tragedy resulted from these arrangements. One older woman living on the collective farm told of her betrothal to a man with whom she was deeply in love. She used to go out with him and walk in the street, having met him on "the stoop of the house" (the customary place for local courting). They agreed that after he next returned from the mines he would send the matchmaker to ask for her. But during the miner's absence another bachelor proposed. The father preferred the second suitor and decided to give him his daughter because he was a good worker.

"I cried that I didn't want to marry," the woman related. "My betrothed sent me letters from the mine but I was illiterate and could not answer them. I cried for him —rivers of tears—but regardless, Father had his way." Similar examples typical of that time could be given. Older people remember instances of young couples meeting for the first time at the altar.

In negotiating marriages primary consideration was given to the needs of the household and the abilities and skills of the persons involved. The young people were often measured by the attributes of their parents—"the apple doesn't fall far from the tree." But by the turn of the century marriages were beginning to be arranged more and more in accordance with mutual personal inclination. The personal desires and choice of young men became manifest as they achieved some measure of independence. Characteristic in this respect is G. P. Diakov, a former seasonal mineworker, who testified, "I got married—did not ask my father. I acted as my own matchmaker [1908]. When I got home from the mine, I said to Father: 'Now go, as it is customary, to a "drinking party." ' Father was pleased. A year earlier he had wanted to marry me off, but I had asserted my independence. My brothers and sisters married according to their own wishes, not under the yoke of our father." Other peasants in the collective affirmed the same.

Characteristically during the same period, the family customs of the kulaks were significantly stricter. The families lived in greater confinement; for fear that marriageable daughters might develop undesirable attachments, they were, for example, reluctant to allow them to go to the "street" during the holidays. This is the underlying reason for the high degree of intermarriage among kulak families; the local Kabanovs, Sleptsovs, Ludanovs, Makarovs, Starodubovs, were all involved in a close interfamilial bond which undoubtedly increased the social and economic importance of the wealthiest kulaks in the village.

The wedding rituals of Viriatino during the last quarter of the nineteenth century, as far as it is possible to judge from the reminiscences of the old people, retained many characteristic features of the traditional South Russian rites, but even so they had changed considerably and had become somewhat disorganized. Much of what had been meaningful in detail and custom was lost and forgotten. When parents decided to marry off their son and the prospective bride was selected, some close relative of the girl, most often the eldest brother and his wife or a sister with her husband would go to her parents in order to ascertain their willingness to the match. When the answer was in the affirmative the bride's parents would say, "Let them come to make a match and to agree what should be bought for the bride for *posad* (ceremonial seating of the bride during the wedding).

A few days later at the home of the bride a "little drink-

ing party" would be arranged. The bridegroom's parents
and close relatives would come and bring some wine and
vodka and appetizers. Only the closest relations of the
bride were present; the girl herself did not come out to
greet the guests. An agreement would be reached concerning the sum of money which the bridegroom was required
to contribute (partly for the clothes that the bride would
make for him). For a proper trousseau the bride needed
a sarafan, blouse, shoes, a silk kerchief for the "sitting"
ceremony, and, as a rule, a fur-lined coat. It should be
noted that the bride's dowry did not figure importantly
during the discussions, as was the case among the North
Russians. The date for the wedding and the number of
guests of both families who were to attend were then decided upon. During the drinking party, guests and hosts
sang and danced. According to the older people of the
village, merrymaking on these occasions sometimes lasted
for several days.

The betrothal period usually was quite short. Directly
after the small drinking party, relatives of the bride and
groom went to the market in Sosnovka, where they made
the necessary purchases (mainly materials for the "sitting"
garments). Then the groom's family entertained the bride's
relatives who had taken part in the shopping in the village
tavern. The bride's girl friends gathered daily at her house
until the wedding day to help prepare the dowry. As far
back as the 1900s a custom called "cutting" existed, according to which the groom treated the girls who had cut
and sewn the wedding gowns. Subsequently, however, according to E. A. Diakov, this custom became only "the
glory" (so preserved as a traditional survival) since the
dowries not only of well-to-do but of middle-class families
were made by professional seamstresses.

After the betrothal the suitor usually did not see the
bride again until the "drinking party" which took place
at her house about two weeks before the wedding. Relatives of the bride and groom were invited; in cases where

families were too large, invitations were limited to first cousins. When the day came, wine was bought by the bucket and an opulent feast was prepared on three or four tables, depending on the number of guests. All of this was, of course, ruinous for families of limited means. The parents of the bride, godparents, and eldest relatives sat at the first table. The bride and groom were seated at the second, along with her female friends and his companions. Remaining relatives and children were relegated to the third and fourth tables.

The dinner began with the prayer "that everything would go well and that the young people would live in harmony with one another." The groom's family toasted the bride's relatives; the father of the groom offered vodka, and the mother offered refreshments. Afterward the bride's relatives toasted the other relatives, and the whole day was spent in singing and dancing.

The day before the wedding two or three of the bride's closest friends would stay overnight at her home to help her arrange the hope chest. In the evening, also, the girls sewed the "strange shirt" (a small shirt, pants, belt, and socks, a precise facsimile of the male outfit in miniature) which is used during the sale of the bride's bedding. At the same time, a broom was decorated with paper ribbons. The symbolism of this is completely forgotten by now. While the bedding was being transported, according to some of the old villagers, the broom was fastened to the collar part of the horse's harness; according to others, one of the groom's relatives, probably the best man, wore an embroidered towel over his shoulder attached to his waist, and all during the trip would continuously make sweeping motions with the broom. That same evening, a girl friend would braid the bride's hair and tie it with a ribbon which the bride would give on her wedding day to her best girl friend. The old people cannot recall whether this custom was accompanied by particular incantations, another sign that in the last decades of the nineteenth century the customs of the traditional eve spent by the bride with girl friends had already begun to vanish. The term "Devish-nik" (maidens' evening) is still familiar to the older people, however.

On the prenuptial evening there was also a celebration at the house of the groom for his friends as well as the friends and relatives of the bride. The groom served refreshments and strolled about with his harmonica while the guests sang and danced. In Viriatino in the 1890s a wedding lasted at least three days, in earlier times as long as five or six.

On the morning of the wedding day the bride and her girl friends went to the steam baths. After the bath, if she was an orphan, she visited her mother's grave and wept as she talked to her.

The bride, unassisted, dressed for the wedding. Her girl friend only unbraided her hair as both wept freely. The old women say that they heard from their own grandmothers (who would have been married in the 1840s and 50s) that at that time it was the custom for the bride to wail and lament, sometimes accompanied by women who specialized in incantations. After she was dressed, her parents and godparents blessed her with the icon and seated her and the girl friend at the table. Meanwhile at his house the groom was involved in preparations for his departure to call upon his bride. He too dressed himself, and his father gave him some money to put in his boot in order that it might multiply. Before his departure, the parents blessed him with the icon of Christ the Redeemer. The groom left the house with his best man (*druzhko*), the matchmaker, and the other principals in the wedding ceremony and proceeded from the bride's house to their future home. The first person they met was offered two glasses of vodka.

After the groom arrived at the bride's cottage, the best man purchased, in fun, the seat next to the bride from her younger brother. The best man, whip in hand, got to his feet, filled a glass with wine, and put twenty kopeks on the table. The lad, after some bargaining with the older man, drank the wine, reached for the money and attempted to run away with it, whereupon the buyer sought to strike him. After this scene the groom seated himself next to the bride.

It was customary for the bride and groom not to eat before the wedding ceremony. When the time arrived for the couple to leave for church, the priest, if he were present, or the best man, escorted them out. A kerchief tied to the middle finger of each right hand was worn by both bride and groom. Thus by holding each by the kerchief, their escort led them from the room.

In accordance with ancient tradition, weddings usually took place on the feast of St. Michael's, November 8, and on the first Sunday after Easter. Twenty or thirty couples would wait to be married on these days. The first to be married were those who could afford to pay for the wedding ceremony; the poorer couples had to wait in the church, sometimes far into the night.

After the wedding, still in the church, the female matchmaker and the best girl friend braided the bride's hair in two plaits and covered her head with a *kichka* (headdress). If the plaits were uneven in length it was considered to be an omen of early widowhood. At the end of the century fashion changed and the bride's hair was piled up under a cap of silk and lace, usually worn low on the forehead. As she left the church, someone would throw a kerchief at her which covered her whole head and forehead.

The wedding procession headed for the cottage of the bride's family where the couple was met at the gate by the parents with salt and bread. Once inside the couple was seated at the head of the table and congratulated on the official celebration of their nuptials. Then they were invited to the next table for refreshments. The best man, the matchmaker, and the groom's relations were seated at the same table. The parents of the groom were not present. Refreshments were served on three or four tables, the traditional holiday dishes of Viriatino: cabbage soup, dry meat, fish, cold soup, *blinchiki* (pancakes), fritters, and of course vodka. There were no ritual dishes especially for Viriatino weddings. The wedding guests would begin to sing, and would, ultimately, dance.

When the time came for the new wife to leave for her home, friends and relatives went through the motions of selling her bedding to the best man and matchmaker. This was the time for the girl friend to produce the "strange shirt." For every mistake in the making and sewing of the "shirt" the price offered for the bedding by the buyers went down. The money received from this "sale" went to the girls, who in turn used it to "gild" the couple. After the bargain was concluded the best man and matchmaker, followed by the bridal procession, carried the bedding to the couple's home, singing and dancing. At the head of the crowd was one of the husband's relatives, who would present the bride with a mother hen along with a wish that it should multiply.

On arriving at their new home the couple were met at the gate by the groom's parents who presented them once again with the symbolic bread and salt. The couple was again placed at the table of honor to receive more congratulations, after which the best man led them to the next table for what is called "a never-ending chat." Until about the middle of the 1880s a custom existed whereby the wedded couple were seated separately behind a curtain. Toward the end of the celebration they were led out for the "gilding," which was done as follows. The old people from the first table moved to the table shared by the newlyweds, who then stood at the table's edge. The groom's parents would be the first to "gild" the couple. The son offered a glass of vodka to his father and the bride to his mother; as the parents drank the couple bowed low before them, and the elder ones placed money in one emptied glass. The same ritual was repeated with his god-parents, with her parents, with her godparents, and finally with all the other couples present. It was all accompanied by jests, "The wine is not good!" "It's bitter!" and many more of the same. The gilding lasted for at least two hours, after which the company sat down to supper. Then, the matchmaker and best man escorted the couple to bed (this custom had disappeared in Viriatino about the first decade of the twentieth century). In their bedroom the young wife would pull off her husband's boot and take out the money.

The next day the best man and matchmaker received the couple, offering them pancakes and other delicacies. Again guests would gather, and everybody went to the home of the bride's parents for another party. The group later continued on to the newlyweds' own house and gilding was resumed.

Celebrations continued through the third day in the same fashion. Toward evening of the last day the bride was "uncovered." Until the middle of the 1880s she sat for three days behind the "curtain" and was led to the guests always covered with the silk kerchief. In later times when the kerchief was no longer worn for so long, the ceremony of "uncovering" was done differently. The kerchief was placed over the bride's head and the young couple lowered their heads while the guests smashed clay pots. The mother-in-law would take the kerchief from the bride's head, put it on herself, harmonicas would appear, and she would dance to their accompaniment.

After the unveiling the bride was allowed to dance and partake in the festivities. Old people tell us that on the last day the bride was given formal tests of her knowledge and skill, such as the preparing of hemp. During the testing she would pick up the wet hemp and facetiously beat the guests over their heads with it. They would also give her the broom that had been decorated for the wedding and throw money under her feet while she was made to sweep the floor.

This covering of the bride's head with a kerchief, the groom's offer of two glasses of vodka to the first person he met on his initial departure, the parents' greeting the newlyweds with bread and salt, and putting money in the groom's boots are all elements of magic which have been retained in the ceremonies. One of the very oldest customs was the presentation to the couple of a mother hen which was passed from hand to hand by members of the procession as they danced.

Special wedding songs connected with various stages of the rites are now almost completely forgotten. In later days ordinary folk songs and couplets were sung. The ritual chants seem to have disappeared quite early, largely because of the relatively weak tradition of music in Viriatino. (In other areas of Southern Great Russia there is a rich tradition of wedding music and poetry.) The shift from specific wedding songs to more general popular songs occurred simultaneously with the disintegration of the ritual.

In a comparison of wedding customs at various periods, a succession of changes can be observed. The rites were shortened and simplified; the time for celebrations was also shortened. Whereas in the 1880s it was customary to celebrate weddings over a period of from four to six days, by the turn of the century this had shrunk to three. The time for preparation of the wedding feasts was also considerably shortened. In the 1880s the matchmaking alone was celebrated for several days.

In a number of cases various stages of the traditional rites began to be omitted; instead of both a small and a large drinking party there would be only one small one. Some people would have the big drinking party together with the wedding in order to reduce the expenses. The initiative in these changes was taken by the young people, especially those who worked in the mines. G. P. Diakov, detailing the circumstances of his own wedding in 1908, said: "We had only a small drinking party. I did not consent to a big one, it was not necessary. Those who were better off wanted big drinking parties, but for myself I considered it unnecessary." This testimony is very characteristic of the revolutionary period of 1905–7, when old customs were dying out because they were incompatible with the new ideas of young couples entering upon marriage. For instance a custom once widely practiced which continued only a few years into the twentieth century was that the best man and matchmaker would put the newlyweds to bed on the wedding night and wake them the next morning. The roles of the participants in wedding rituals also changed. The groom began to assume a more active role, going with his parents to the prospective bride's home when they asked for her hand. Before the turn of the century this would have been unthinkable.

The wedding of Egor Diakov is very typical of the new order of things. Returning from the mine in the spring of 1911, he found himself unable to find a bride who suited him, since the more desirable girls had been married during the previous autumnal wedding season. One of his female relatives recommended to him a girl from the neighboring village of Griaznoe. Diakov, accompanied by his elder sister, went to meet the girl and was taken by her appearance and manner. Thereafter he assumed an even more active role of courtship, accompanying his parents to the small drinking party where they sat down with the bride. The couple animatedly discussed the forthcoming wedding and Egor visited the girl often before the nuptials. This clashed sharply with custom and convention and serves to indicate the growing independence of young men who more and more often overrode the form and significance of the old marriage traditions. But the traditional attitude toward marriage as an economic and practical arrangement still endured and pragmatic motives continued to exert their influence on the selection of a bride.

The religious beliefs which had a great influence on the structure of the peasant family complemented the patriarchal system. The rotation of work, the ways in which free time was spent, and the diet were determined by the dates of the Church calendar which paralleled the ancient agrarian rituals everywhere in peasant Russia. The folk calendar, which is of great importance in the life of the peasant, will be discussed in the next chapter. Here we are concerned with the character of activities in the home during the holidays.

About three days before a holiday a great house cleaning would begin. The women washed ceilings, walls, floors, and whitewashed the stove. On the eve of the holiday, all members of the family traditionally took steam baths. The holiday fare was prepared; some of the items were bought ahead of time at the bazaar. In Viriatino there was a characteristic absence of specific ritual food. The only exceptions were the baking of pancakes during the Maslenitza,[3] as well as on the day when the dead were remembered, and on the ninth of March in celebration of the Forty Martyrs, the preparation of Easter bread with white cheese and the dyeing of eggs for Easter and Holy Trinity. The same dishes were prepared for any of the family or Church holidays, either cabbage with meat, or simply plain cooked beef, mutton, or, less frequently, poultry, fish, blintzes, or potato pancakes. During the holidays at Christmas and Easter which were preceded by

---

[3] *Maslenitza*—A week preceding Lent. In the traditional folk calendar, it is a period of magical rites and observances connected with the resurrection of life in the spring. It is the gayest season of the year. The proper names are Maslenitza (Butter Week) or Syrnaia Niedela (Cheese Week). The traditional *blini,* pancakes or raised rye flour, are served with butter and/or sour cream. In olden times a ritual significance was attached to eating *blini,* and the first pancake was given to a beggar in memory of the dead.

In Soviet Russia the religious meaning of Maslenitza is gradually dying out, but the tradition of carnival masquerading, amusements, and especially the preparation of *blini* are still popular (Tr.).

long periods of fast, the family ate early in the morning immediately after coming home from church. At Christmas time it was customary to eat early. The holiday meal began with vodka, which the head of the family offered to everyone. After dinner the older people would lie down to rest and the younger ones would go visiting relatives of the wife's family. The young also went to the street parties, which usually took place on especially important holidays during the day and in the evening up to eleven or twelve o'clock. On the eves of holidays and on Sundays, no one worked. Annual holidays were celebrated for not less than two days, while celebrations began two weeks before Christmas and not less than one week before Easter. Holidays therefore played an important role in family life.

The keeping of fasts was especially important. Not only important fasts were kept, but also those on weekdays, including Wednesdays and Fridays. More than two hundred fast days were observed during a year. Fasting, which meant fewer meals, restricted even more a diet that was already limited. On fast days the family ate wheat porridge with kvas, potatoes with salt, and peas with kvas. Fast-keeping was also required of the children. Small children did not get even a spoonful of milk on important fast days, or on the Wednesdays and Fridays of abstinence. Especially difficult was the observance of St. Peter's and Assumption fast days which occurred during the busiest part of the farming season, and it was no accident that after the October Revolution these were the first elements of peasant tradition to be done away with.

Religious beliefs left their marks on other aspects of family life, especially those most important events in the life of man, birth and death. A whole complex of rites was connected with the birth of a child. Many children were born to families in Viriatino—abortion was a sin. A peasant was pleased when a boy was born for when the reapportionment of land was brought about he would receive another share. In the long run, though, parents' feelings made the best of a situation, and no distinction was really made in terms of preference for children of either sex.

Women gave birth in the room where steam baths were taken, on a table upon which straw was spread beneath a piece of cloth. If the event happened to occur in the house the woman was placed on the floor on a piece of rag. A woman about to give birth was removed from the house not only out of consideration for those who shared the crowded living conditions, but also because from ancient times there had existed the belief that it was necessary to protect the woman, and especially her infant, from the gaze of strangers. Only much later, at the turn of the century, did women begin giving birth in the house in a more hygienic environment, in a bed covered with coarse linen. She was assisted by the midwife. The relationship of the expectant mother and her family to the midwife had its roots in the ancient customs connected with her function. Before the mother was carried back into the house three or four days after the birth, a ritual "hand-washing" took place. The mother poured water on the hands of the midwife and, in the same water, washed her own hands. Afterward the midwife was presented with a gift of linen. She also was given a place of honor in the rituals that took place the day following the birth.

Baptism took place in the church. The midwife brought the infant to the church, and the godmother carried it home. Dinner was prepared when they arrived home from church. Many holiday dishes were served, blintzes, studen,[4] meat, and, of course, the vodka with which the dinner started. It was customary for relatives to bring gifts of food The godmother and godfather were seated at the most honored place at the table. Next to the godfather sat the father of the new mother; next to him, the father of her husband. Next to the godmother sat the new mother; next to her, the

---

[4] Jellied beef and pork stew (Tr.).

midwife. Some informants remembered that both the mid-wife and the mother-in-law served at the table. Merrymak-ing continued for two or three hours, and the infant was brought in toward the end of the dinner. The midwife placed two plates on the table and the relatives contributed to both plates, one for the midwife and the other for the infant—this was called "the gift for the tooth." After two or three days the woman would again take up her daily household chores. As one informant put it: "After giving birth, one didn't stay in bed long. Three days after the birth one would return to the stove, lift heavy pots, and feed the piglets."

The baby slept in a cradle slung by ropes from a hook on the ceiling and lined with straw covered with coarse linen. A tiny pillow was placed under the infant's head. At the turn of the century the old-fashioned cradles made of bast had started to disappear and, by 1910, were no longer sold in the bazaar. Cradles made out of wooden planks with bottoms woven of cord came into use instead. The sides of the cradle curved inward so that the mother would be more comfortable feeding the infant. In well-to-do families different kinds of cradles were used; they were made of four pieces of wood connected to form a frame, and the linen was stretched over this. This kind of cradle was brought to Viriatino from Sosnovka, where it first appeared in the years 1870–80. Its popularity spread partly as a result of the intermarriage of people from the two villages, especially among the upper economic classes of Viriatino.

The infant was breast-fed until it was a year or a year-and-a-half old. Afterward it was taught to eat at the family table. In the beginning it was given an additional feeding of porridge and milk, but after it started to teethe, it would eat borscht, porridge, and potatoes with the family. Bread and porridge were used as pacifiers; the mother would put chewed bread, sweetened with sugar, or some wheat porridge into a rag and give it to the infant.

Because of unhygienic living conditions, the mortality rate of children was very high. Any infectious disease like scarlet fever, diphtheria, or dysentery grew to epidemic proportions. An especially large number of children died in infancy due in large measure to the fact that, as a rule, sick infants were taken to local medicine men and women who explained any childhood disease by the "evil eye." A baby was brought to the medicine woman and she sprinkled him three times with some unknown liquid. An infant could be cured of crying too much, it was believed, if he was taken at the break of dawn to a chicken coop and the following incantation repeated three times: "Dawn, dawn, you beautiful maiden! As you calm yourself, as you become silent, so too, you, God's servant (the name of the baby) calm yourself."

The conditions under which children were brought up were difficult. In the busiest season of the summer, the baby was taken in its cradle to the field or left at home in the care of an old grandmother or a young girl; sometimes it was left alone. As one woman related, "When you came home the baby, who had been crying for a long time, was all wet, with flies swarming around his pacifier." In families where there were many children, the care of infants was given to one of the women who had the most even temperament, who was considered the most likely to act fairly and not make a distinction between her own and somebody else's child. The children would be afraid of her but, at the same time, have respect for her.

Children were brought up strictly, and complete obedience was demanded of them. As one villager put it, "Once a thing was said—that was it!" Though parents showed concern for their children's welfare, no especial closeness or affection was felt between parents and children or brothers and sisters. Diakov, remembering his youth, related that though his mother took watchful care of him, he never shared his most intimate thoughts and experiences with her or, for that matter, with his brothers; it was not the custom. There was, however, a greater bond between mothers and daughters, and this closeness was preserved even after a girl's marriage. The young bride always remained a stranger, to a certain extent, to the family of her husband. In the difficult moments of her life, she would always go to her own parents, especially her mother, for advice and help.

Youngsters from earliest childhood were accustomed to the work of the peasant. Little girls were taught how to spin. From the age of seven or eight, the boys began to work along with their fathers, going out to the fields with them, fetching water and wood. By the age of eight or nine, a boy was sent out to tend the cattle, and by his thirteenth year he would help his father in all his chores. There was no carefree childhood for the youngsters.

The education of the children was of no special concern to the parents. Boys went to school but were not forced to study. "If you wanted to, you could study; if you didn't want to, you didn't have to," said one informant. At the turn of the century it was considered necessary for boys to complete at least two grades at either the village or the parochial school, but no attention was paid to the education of girls. "Girls aren't going to be inducted into the army, and they can spin and weave without any education" was the general opinion of the villagers.

Among the most stable family traditions were those rituals connected with the burying of the dead. Burials were conducted according to church precepts, but many archaic features were attached to them. Old women washed the dead of both sexes. The elderly were buried in homespun materials, but by the end of the nineteenth century young ones were customarily buried in clothing made of store-bought material. Old women were buried in skirts. These customs persisted into the first years of Soviet rule. Clothing "for death" was prepared by individuals for themselves during their own lifetime. If a girl or a young man died, paper flowers were laid on the head and chest.

The dead person, covered with coarse homespun linen, was placed on a bench in the honored corner of the room with his head under the icon. If the dead person was an old man his whole body was covered with linen; if a young man, he was covered with a cotton sheet.

All night long elderly people and nuns read prayers. The dead person remained in the house more than twenty-four hours. If he was going to be buried after mass, he was brought to church in the morning. If no mass was to be said, he was taken to the cemetery toward evening. Two hours before the dead person was taken from his home he was placed in a coffin lined with homespun linen. The coffin was made and the grave dug by the relatives. When the dead person was removed from his home, a priest was necessarily present. After a short requiem mass, the coffin was carried on towels; outside the gates it was put on a bench and the priest would recite a short litany. Relatives and neighbors, those who were not going to the cemetery, then paid their last respects to the departed. Usually only the closest relatives went to the cemetery. Women would wail and carry on. The open coffin was normally carried by hand, but if it was too heavy, it was put on a cart. On the way to church or the cemetery the procession would stop a few times and the priest would recite the litany. At the grave he performed the funeral services. Relatives bid goodbye to the departed, the lid was put on the coffin, and it was lowered into the grave; everybody present sprinkled a little dirt over its top. The grave site was marked by a cross. After all this a requiem mass was celebrated.

When the relatives returned home they held a memorial service. First the priest was offered food. Later, after he departed, everyone would sit down at the table. Sometimes there were enough people to fill two or three tables, and then those who were closest to the dead person sat at the first. They started with wine, then usually cabbage soup was served, meat, blintzes, and potato pancakes, noodles, and, finally, a millet kasha with milk. During the days of abstinence, the kasha was made with oil instead of milk. Prayers were said when everybody had eaten. Everyone sang the prayer "In Memoriam" and then went home.

On the following ninth, twelfth, and fortieth days the death was recommemorated. First the relatives would read prayers; afterward a supper was served and the family sat up the whole night. On the fortieth day they revisited the cemetery. A date six months after the death was observed, as was the first anniversary, after which the traditional period of mourning came to an end.

The dead were remembered on special religious holidays. On the eve of a holiday each family sent one of its members, either an elderly woman or a young girl, with a note and an especially prepared cake to church for the general services of the day. The next morning a wake was held. Blini were baked and the elderly woman or the young girl took them to the church. After the celebration of a requiem mass, everyone present at the church would go to the cemetery, where, on each grave, relatives would spread a towel and put the blini on it. The priest would walk around saying prayers. Blini and sums of money were given to the church official; part of the former was crumbled over the grave, and before they left the cemetery the relatives would offer each other the rest. At home each member of the family would eat a piece brought back from the cemetery, representing a communion with the dead. Some of the details of this "communion" resembled traditions surviving from ancient cults of ancestor worship. Of special interest in this respect is the custom of holding a wake on the Saturday before Maslenitza. In the morning on that day every housewife would put one of the first baked blini on a towel or dish before the icon, setting it aside for "the parents," and when the family started to eat the blini, they would remember all parents. This mixing of Christian elements with those even more ancient demonstrated the unusual permanence of traditions relating to an understanding of death and life after death.

As we can see from the above descriptions, there were

very firm family traditions in the life of the people of Viriatino up until the October Revolution. Yet in spite of the fact that this traditional and religious outlook was responsible for the very slow evolution of the family, by the start of the twentieth century some families had begun to differ considerably in their cultural level from the rest of the people. These were not the kulak families who, although they differed in their economic and cultural standards from the mass of peasantry, were also more conservative and backward. The new features of family structure sprang up in direct proportion to the progressive influence of city and industrial centers; and this means that the most progressive element of the village was found among the families of migrant workers. One could especially single out the Nagorni brothers who, according to the opinion of other inhabitants of Viriatino, had the most cultural influence on their co-villagers. They were carpenters; their father's and grandfathers' generation had had the same occupation, and every year they would visit large cities like Moscow or Rostov on the Don. From this Nagorni family later came the first representatives of the Viriatino "intelligentsia." One of the brothers was a man who wrote a great deal, read the works of Tolstoy, Nekrasov, and others, and subscribed to a newspaper. He always socialized with the co-villagers. They visited with him, and very often discussed political subjects, quite an innovation for Viriatino since even ordinary house-visiting was not the custom. The Nagorni family lived on their income from carpentry. Their allotment of land, enough for one person, was leased out and they used their horse only for carting wood and feed for the livestock. No spinning was done by their family; the young people dressed in city-like clothes. Life at home in the Nagorni family had a city-like character which was expressed in the furniture, the food, and the clothing. The living room had quite an urban atmosphere. The table was always covered with a tablecloth. Next to the table stood an easy chair in which the head of the house liked to sit and read. Besides stationary benches there were also chairs and, in the corner, a closet. There were curtains at the windows, and the walls were hung with inlaid wood paintings, as was customary among the rich families of the village. There were also oil paintings in glass frames. Even their diet was in marked contrast to that of their neighbors. The city influence manifested itself in their choice of beverage—tea. Meat was not only boiled, as was customary in Viriatino; it was sometimes fried or stewed. Another innovation for the village was the kind of pirogi they baked, which were made of rice, eggs, and raisins. The food for the little children was prepared separately. Even during the days of abstinence when the whole family was keeping the fast the children received dishes made with milk. While this represented a certain deviation from the proper observance of religious traditions, that did not disturb the women of the family. The family of the second Nagorni brother was of about the same cultural level.

The life style of the migratory miners also differed considerably from that of the other villagers. One example of this is the family of Zhdanov, who started going off to the mines when he was about fourteen years old. He liked to read and when he returned to the village he brought many books with him. He also owned some volumes of political literature, one of which was the *Works of Lenin*. To the great annoyance of his wife, all his free time was spent reading. He was an atheist. When his son was born in 1918, he named him Lev in honor of Tolstoy. His personal outlook, however, had very little influence on the rest of his family.

But while such people existed in the village before the First World War, it should be noted that the most fundamental changes in family structure, the formation of a new domestic way of life, and the raising of the cultural level of the families in Viriatino took place after the victory of the October Revolution.

CHAPTER V

VILLAGE LIFE, CUSTOMS, AND MANNERS

The Backwardness of Village Life

Before the Revolution, social life in all Russian villages was characterized by backwardness. The peasant's horizon was very narrow, and what took place outside his homestead, his village, and his own family was of little interest to him. He had only a dim understanding of the events that took place elsewhere in Russia and in the outside world. During the nineteenth century the Viriatino peasants did not receive newspapers, and it was only in the twentieth century that the wealthier peasants began to subscribe to them. Important regulations were sent in from the district committee to be read at the meetings of the village communal house. Bits of news seeped in from the migratory workers, and the village really got its news by word of mouth.

All family and social norms of conduct, all interpersonal relations in the village, in the family, and among the young people were affected by the religious superstitions and the regimentation that derives from a patriarchal tradition. The breach of generally accepted norms was severely condemned by public opinion. This resulted in limited social exchange, while the time-honored traditions of family rituals, holidays, and leave-taking of army recruits and migrant workers were stressed. Until the 1890s there were no cultural institutions of any sort in the village; and later, when they did appear, they did not play an important role. The population was almost completely illiterate, and fist fighting was a popular village diversion.

Through the centuries the world of the Russian peasant, his life and customs, were most strongly influenced by the control that the Church exerted. The priest was essential to every important event in the peasant's life. He was present at the birth of a child, at weddings, funerals, at the departure of the migratory worker or the enlisted man for army service, at the celebrations of yearly festivals, and many other events. To a certain extent, even agricultural work was connected with the Church calendar. During Church holidays, all work stopped in the field and in the house. In years when Lent and Easter coincided with the beginning of sowing, the peasants of Viriatino usually postponed work in the fields for a few days, although every lost day in the spring could have a bad effect on the quality of the harvest. On Sundays and holidays, the women never spun or wove. It was considered a sin to disobey the rules of the Church and the breaking of these rules provoked condemnation of the individual by the whole village community. The priest looked after the parishioners' adherence to the Church's regulations with a vigilant eye. The parishioners had to fast, go to confession, come to church services, especially during the holidays. Four times a year—on St. Michael's Day, on Christmas, Epiphany, and during Easter—the priest was paid for making the rounds of all the houses and performing services. During Easter a cart followed him and the villagers' offerings of food were put into the cart. If a peasant did not go to church and withheld the customary payments, the priest reprimanded him, or sometimes even refused to perform an appropriate rite. The memory of a certain event still lingers in the village, and even now the story is told. A peasant by the name of Losev did not pay the priest his dues for five years. Consequently, when Losev's son was about to be married, the priest refused to perform the marriage ceremony. The elder Losev had to bake enough loaves of bread to fill a cart and present it to the priest. The priest then fed his farm animals for a whole week with the bread, and the marriage was performed.

Another example of the priest's power was the fact that debtors were married in neighboring villages in order to avoid a confrontation with their own priest. But that was possible only in cases where the bride came from a neighboring village. In addition to his religious duties, the priest acted as an informer to the police; he scanned the political loyalty of the populace and especially kept an eye on the miners and teachers.

Superstition was at the root of the peasant's religion. It stemmed from illiteracy and poverty. Almost all the peasants believed in God, but their faith was expressed in the performance of religious rituals whose content they did not really understand. The peasants, especially the women, understood the sermons very poorly and often did not know how to recite the prayers. Questions of religion were much better understood by those peasants who graduated from parochial schools, some of whom functioned as church officials while others sang in the church chorus. The undivided family presented a fertile ground for the preservation of religious traditions. These traditions were so strong that though those peasants who worked in the mines often became alienated from religion while they were away, on their return home they went back to church and kept the fasts.

Changes in the world view and daily life of the people of Viriatino were noticeable after 1895, and even more so after the turn of the century. This was a period that saw the most intensive penetration of capitalistic interests into the village as well as the development of mass migratory work, especially in the Donbass. While migration from the village disrupted the closed circuit of village life it also widened the outlook of the people. Lenin noted the progressive influence of this migration when he mentioned the change from a sedentary, subjugated, ingrown existence. In the place of those peasants who trusted the priests and feared officialdom, there grew a new generation who visited industrial centers and cities and learned something from the bitter experience of the hired laborer's nomadic life. The hard work in the mines and the close contact with fellow workers who were labor organizers contributed to the progressive mood of the peasant who was absorbing proletarian class ideology and developing a revolutionary temper. Without a doubt, these migratory workers influenced the disintegration of the patriarchal family.

After the revolution of 1905–7, a more anticlerical, antireligious mood prevailed among the peasant miners. There was much truth in the villagers' opinion that the miners were godless. Even now the old people understand that their alienation from village life was the result of their work in the Donbass. According to Diakov who worked in the mines for nine years, "when we emerged from the mines we were as black as the devil, and who would think of God?" Because of their contact with the organized workers some of the miners came back to the village confirmed atheists. On the eve of the revolution of 1906–7, some free thinkers were already refusing to receive the priests. The more progressive of the migratory workers began to understand the mercenary interests of the priests. "When a poor man died, the priest did not sing the mass in the proper manner. The priests only cared to finish it as quickly as possible, because they were paid very little," said Diakov. The amoral conduct of some of the priests and their role as police informers further undermined the authority of the Church in the eyes of the peasant.

Peasant Calendar Holidays

The yearly cycle of the seasons with their rituals and customs occupied an important place in the life of the people of Viriatino. The peasant agricultural cycle which fused Christian Church observances with ancient pagan beliefs was the basis not only of the religious ritual, but also in great part of the economic, social, and family life of the village. The peasant's calendar determined the beginning and end of home and field work, the form and schedule of holidays, and family celebrations like weddings or betrothals. Each season had its special tempo. After threshing time, the nights grew longer, and in the evenings young girls began to gather in each other's homes to spin, knit stockings, and weave. On Sundays people went to church both morning and afternoon. Not much was done during the day. The young people prepared for block parties and in one or two homes, perhaps, some social drinking was in progress. So it went from the fifteenth of September to the eighth of November. For eight weeks there were evening gatherings, drinking, parties in the street, and church services. On some days, the fourteenth of November for example, fasting was observed. After that the girls would take up their spinning again and the men would work at odd jobs such as delivering fuel. Men hired to deliver fuel worked until the sixth of December, the Day of St. Nicholas. By that time, women were soaking flax and had begun to weave the cloth that men and women wrapped around their feet when they wore straw slippers. From the Day of St. Nicholas to Christmas there were no holidays, but these were quite free from labor, and women did not work at their spinning again until after the New Year.

During Shrovetide the most important days were Friday, Saturday, and Sunday when block parties and fist fighting competitions were the order of the day. After this came the "Great Fast." During "Clear Monday" women and girls who spun would push their spinning tools down a hill of snow, a ritual that was meant to purify them of their sins. Work would resume again at Easter time. During this period the spinning was finished and weaving began.

These were the highlights of the autumn-winter season, and they emphasize the close relationship of the Church ritual calendar with the whole economic and social life of the peasant. Yearly festivals were widely celebrated in Viriatino when, like the Christmas holidays, they blended in with the agrarian calendar. Some of the Church holidays, on the other hand, were hardly noticed when they conflicted with work in the fields.

Many holidays were celebrated only in family circles and followed a definite, well-established tradition. Holidays which fit in with farm work were treated as social events. The custom of observing these calendar rituals was South Russian in origin, and different in a number of ways from practice in North Russia. In Viriatino the first important holiday after the fall farming was St. Michael's Day, November 8. On that day people came from neighboring villages; many weddings were held in which at least half the population took part. The sixth of December was St. Nicholas' Day; from then until Christmas a period of abstinence was observed, during which there was no socializing or block parties. On Christmas Day the people were supposed to go to church. After the morning mass there was a breakfast consisting of meat, pancakes, and eggs. The Christmas holidays lasted for two weeks and were full of rituals and diversions. The children sang carols and praised Christ, visited homes and wished the hosts and hostesses good cheer. The street was filled with people and fist fighting competitions were arranged.

The New Year customs were ancient ones; adults and children wore costumes and masks and made the rounds of homes singing carols and wishing the people whom they visited good fortune and cheer. Probably because of its playful character this custom has continued until the present. New Year's caroling was known in all the provinces of Russia; the Middle Black Belt and Tambov area had their regional versions of the songs. The carolers who made the rounds of the village in groups of five or six were usually teenagers, bachelors, and sometimes young widows and soldiers' wives. Betrothed girls did not partake in these entertainments. Most often, too, the carolers belonged to poor families; the more affluent peasants did not allow their children to go caroling because they considered it a kind of alms collection.

In the nineteenth century carolers frequently dressed as lords and ladies or as gypsies. By the turn of the century the costumes sometimes represented peasants. Those who masqueraded had their faces made up with the aid of charcoal, flour, and different dyes. Some were also dressed in the usual peasant outfits with their bright colors. Conventions governed the style of costume. Ladies, for instance, had the same colorful skirts as the gypsies, but added frills at the hem and tied kerchiefs to their heads in such a way to resemble hats. The men had beards made of sheep's wool or unraveled cord.

Caroling began after the mass and went until dark. When the masqueraders entered a house they sang songs, and danced to the music of a harmonica or balalaika. Some of their songs carried the threat that if they received nothing for their efforts, the next child to be born in the family would be a girl instead of a boy. Songs with wishes for a good harvest or with religious and Christian themes were not included in the Viriatino repertoire. Besides the traditional songs, the women and girls recited short verses about love. They were not very different rhythmically from the limericks, *chastushki,* which made their appearance in the village in the twentieth century.

Generally the peasants allowed the carolers to come into their homes; it was entertainment for the whole family and to refuse them entry was to run the risk of being reputed a miser or of otherwise engendering ill will.[1] If the owner of the house refused to admit them, he would be laughed at and they would wish him a bad harvest and all kinds of misfortune. The carolers were given gifts of pancakes,

[1] Chicherov, B. I., Russkie Koladki i ikh tipy. In Sovetskaia etnografiya, 1948, no. 2, pp. 108–9.

meat, grains, and small coins. They either divided the gifts among themselves or put the collection into a common fund for a party. The grain was usually sold and with the money they would buy vodka, nuts, candies, and other delicacies.

From Christmas until New Year's the girls indulged in telling each other's fortune. At the bazaars in neighboring villages they bought horoscopes which, because of the low cultural level of the population, were very popular, especially between 1890 and 1900.[2] Besides the cards and books sold in the villages by merchants there were also the traditional fortunetelling devices, tearing out stems of grain, foreseeing the future in the behavior of a chicken, measuring a courtyard with a wooden shovel, melting wax, throwing a boot out of the house and observing the direction in which it fell, etc. The girls gathered in groups to tell fortunes, but the men did not participate. A chicken was brought into the room, and grains were set out on the floor along with a looking glass, a saucer filled with a little water, and a piece of charcoal. If the chicken approached the looking glass first, the girl's future betrothed would be an elegant man; if it touched the charcoal, he would be a coal miner; if it drank the water, he would be a drunkard. On the threshold they placed a wooden vessel used for kneading dough; a girl would walk backward and try to sit down on it. If she succeeded, this was a sign that she would be married within the year. Girls would take out some stems at random from a bundle of grain, and if a full grain came out, it meant the holder would marry into a rich household. They would throw their shoes and boots in front of the gate to determine in which direction their future home would be located. Before Christmas they would melt wax and after it cooled observe the resulting shapes very carefully. If they were in the form of rings, it was a sign that the girls would be married, if they resembled a

[2] Solokov, U. M., Russkii Folklor, Moscow, 1941, p. 189.

coffin, that they would die, etc. Some girls went into the steam baths at the New Year and looked into a mirror. This divination was considered very frightening and not many had the courage to try it as one was supposed to see the face of one's future husband in the mirror.

In some of the villages of the Tambov province during the New Year the men also read omens in order to learn about the future harvest. In his article "Beliefs of the People of the Tambov Province" Bondarenko brings together some interesting material, and he notes that in the Kirsanovsk district in order to guess the yield of future harvest the oldest member of the family would leave a few grains of rye overnight in the snow. If there was a little covering of ice on the grains in the morning, the bread would be plentiful the following year.[3]

Men did not generally take part in the girls' fortune-telling passion, although sometimes the young men would join in, but that would be done in fun; on such occasions they would try to frighten the girls. For that reason, those who took the divinations seriously did not join in large groups but preferred to get together in twos and threes. Married women did not take part in these activities though they did speak about their "experiences" to the young people.

After the evening church services on Christmas Eve, teenagers would chalk small crosses on the doors of houses on different homesteads, on gates, and on farm equipment to chase away the "bad spirits." After mass on Christmas they would go to the river for a ritual called the "blessing of the water" where they collected some "holy water" which they brought home to wash themselves and to sprinkle on the livestock. This water was then kept for a whole year and if someone became ill he would be washed in it. The ritual feeding of the livestock was also a remnant

[3] Bondarenko, B., Pover'ia Krestian Tambovskoi gubernii in Zhivaya Starina, 1890, vol. 1, p. 119.

of agrarian magic transformed into a Christian custom. On the morning of Christmas Day the head of the house would take a pail filled with unthreshed grain and bread crumbs to the courtyard, sprinkle it with "holy water," and give it to the animals to eat. Some of the peasants would walk around the courtyard three times, holding a hatchet in their hands "for the well-being of the animals." This ancient custom began to disappear long before the Revolution.

After dinner at Christmas time the people took to the street to talk and have fun together. Fist fighting competitions were arranged. On the third day after Christmas all entertainment was curtailed, however, and up to the time of Shrovetide housework occupied the evenings.

The people remembered their dead relatives on the eve of Shrovetide, called "memorial Saturday." The Shrovetide holidays began on a Monday, and again there were fist fighting competitions. Young people and adult men and women went sledding down frozen hills and cut steps at certain places to facilitate the ascent.

This recreation on the street lasted for three days, from early morning until late in the evening. On the next morning, called "purifying Monday," the girls and married women who usually did the spinning went sledding down the hills to "cleanse themselves of their sins." On Palm Sunday the peasants who had duties at the church would go into the forest and bring back some branches of evergreens which they distributed after the services. People flogged each other with the branches and said, "the palm smites, beats to tears, and now one for good health." Or they would say, "The palm smites in order to live a hundred years and not be sick." The branches brought from the church were placed behind the icon where they were left until the livestock went out to pasture for the first time.

Eggs were colored during Holy Week, and especially on Saturday. On the eve of Easter the people went to church to kiss the shroud of Christ. Attendance was required at both the morning and the afternoon services. After the morning mass the priests and their parishioners exchanged greetings and religious salutations, and each parishioner gave the priest an egg. During the first day of Easter, and up to the end of the fast, the people—mostly women, children, and old men—went to the cemetery to "christo-sovatsia"[4] with the dead. They took with them pancakes and eggs and rolled some of the eggs on the graves. The priests, the men who sang the psalms, and the deacon would walk around the village from Monday through Thursday receiving donations. People would gather in the streets for recreation only after these rounds were completed. During Easter the young people went around singing in groups; some also played ball. Weddings were held one week after Easter. Peasants, especially the young ones, loved to watch wedding ceremonies. On St. George's Day, April 23, they went to the fair in the neighboring village of Sosnovka where they could ride on the carousel. This was also the day when the livestock was taken out to pasture for the first time. Every head of the household took his animals out and prodded them with a "palm," saved from Palm Sunday. The priest blessed the herds and the shepherds. During the Voznesenie, Ascension Day, the peasants went with banners into the fields. They went swimming from this day on.

The houses and the farm buildings were decorated with greens for the holiday of Pentecost—the fiftieth day after Easter. Birch trees grew along the street near the houses, and a yellow dye was made from their leaves for coloring eggs. Everyone on the farm received one egg, and little children on the street played egg-rolling games. Holiday crowds gathered on the outskirts of the village. Young

---

[4] Traditional ritual greeting "Christ has risen" accompanied by three kisses. In this case it is symbolic sharing with the dead relatives the Easter eggs (Tr.).

people working in the meadows sang songs and played games. Wreaths were made from the branches of a young birch tree. If the wreath a girl had made was wilted, she would remain in the house of her parents. If it was still fresh it was a sign that she would be married. On the following Monday an ancient ritual took place, at which time they doused themselves with water. Grown men and women took part in this activity. On this day they also prepared brooms for the whole year.

In Viriatino there were other customs directly related to farming which had as their goal the safeguarding of the future harvest. At Easter the head of the household put a palm in a pail filled with oats that had not yet been planted. If Easter was late and the oats were already sown they filled a pail with millet and stuck a pussy-willow branch into it. The pail stood on a table and next to it a loaf of bread and a small heap of salt were placed. A small bundle of straw was put under the table. When the priest came to the house he blessed the pail with the grains. Wafers (*prosfory*) were baked before the spring sowing by a villager and were sent to different homes in the village. Then on the first day of sowing the peasants would go out into the fields and take the wafers with them. One of the children had to eat them in a furrow.

Parties and Games

Types of relaxation and their timing were regulated again largely by the Church calendar. Block parties during the 1870s and 80s were held only on important religious holidays, but in the last decade of the century they were held on Sundays as well. Despite protests from the priests, these gatherings usually took place on a meadow near the church. The participants were young married couples, single men and women, and adolescents. Groups of young people gathered from different corners of the

village, sometimes more than a hundred strong. Traditionally the girls stayed in their own groups, but in more recent
years the sexes mingled. Arriving at the festivities the
young people arranged themselves in groups of fifteen to
twenty, sang songs, and danced. Groups formed according
to neighborhood with different blocks remaining separate.
A young man could court only a girl from his own neighborhood, and, if this rule were broken, he was often
beaten by the other boys. Such outbreaks occurred even
in the beginning of this century.

Homemade pipe instruments accompanied the dancers
until the 1890s; the balalaika and the harmonica came
into use much later. Circle dances and choral singing were
organized. Some of the old songs had disappeared by the
turn of the century, while other traditional tunes continued
to be sung at such gatherings. The most popular dance
was "Rassypucha." In the winter time the young people
danced in fur coats and boots, or in straw slippers. A traditional ball game was played at Easter. During the summer when the young people gathered in meadows to sing
songs, dance, and play games, most parties took place on
the holiday of Troitza. Until harvest times, there were no
others.

These block parties were almost the only form of entertainment and social contact for the young people until
the October Revolution. At these events they would get
to know one another, and afterward the young men accompanied the girls to their homes, being careful not to
be seen by passers-by. Most of the old miners who married
women of their own choice met their wives at these block
parties or in the evening get-togethers which were also
popular.

The evening get-togethers took place in autumn and
winter. Older women remember that in the time of their
youth (1870–80) such social events did not exist. Originally, girls gathered only for spinning. For example in the
last two weeks of December, after the end of field work,

ten to twelve girls from the neighborhood would get together in the evenings to spin and knit together, each
bringing her own work from home. A mother allowed her
daughter to visit with her girl friends on the condition that
she would complete a certain amount of predetermined
work that evening. If she did not, the mother would not
allow her to go next time. Most often the home in which
the girls gathered belonged to a widow who had a daughter. As they did their work, they chatted and listened to
fairy tales told by elderly women who would drop by. The
favorite fairy tales concerned Prince Ivan and the Gray
Wolf, the Firebird, and the Bova Prince, Nikita Kozhe-
miak. Sometimes they would put the work aside briefly to
dance and sing. Toward the end of the evening, boys who
had not left the village in search of seasonal work,
bachelors looking for wives, would drop by. Usually the
young men were not invited into the house but from time
to time girls came outside to see them. Sometimes a young
man would manage to slip into the house and sit with the
working girls, making jokes, and treating them to candy
and cookies. The conduct of the young people had to be
strictly proper. While a young man could walk a girl he
liked home, he could never enter her house.

At the turn of the century the relations between young
people became more relaxed and gatherings were arranged more for entertainment than work. In the early
1900s there were usually two or three houses in the village,
most often those in which women lived by themselves, that
became popular meeting places for the young people. The
young men would arrange for a party with the women
in advance. Every man would pay from ten to fifteen
kopeks for himself and for the girl he was courting. The
boys brought wood for fuel and kerosene for the lamps.
Some money was spent for nuts and candies, and other
food, like apples, was brought from home. During the holidays sweets and baked goods were served. As these gatherings were a way of matchmaking, parents, with the ex-

ception of the rich, were glad to see their children participating. The girls did little work at such events, and spinning wool was carried to the party as a pretext.

The man who knew how to play a harmonica was an indispensable guest. All evening long the young people danced, sang, and played games. A popular choral dance-game, "Gaily We Talk," was arranged as follows. A circle was formed, and a leader walked slowly around the inside, eyeing the girls, while the chorus sang:

In cheerful conversation,
The young man makes merry.
He looks around for a girl
Close to his heart.
He moves closer, takes the girl by her hand.
"Be kind to me, please, chase away my boredom.
I will dance with you once, and kiss you many times."

At the end of the song the leader would select one girl, sit down with her on a bench in the middle of the circle, and kiss her. The next round started with the girl as leader.

Second in popularity was the game called "Collecting." All participants sat in the center of the room. In unison the others asked, "Tell us, Collector, about whom are you dreaming?" "About a pigeon," he would answer. "Which pigeon?" they asked. The leader named a girl who came forward and sat down next to him. He kissed her. Most of the games were similar in that they all ended with the girls being kissed. During the holidays, at public gatherings and parties at home, games called "Sticks" and "Hide-and-Go-Seek" were also played. In the twentieth century a game called "Telephone" was probably brought home by the migratory workers. Card playing and coin flipping, "Heads or Tails," were played by the young men. The most popular dances were the traditional Russian ones; the waltz and the Krakowiak made their appearance after the October Revolution. Songs from the city were also sung in addition to the popular peasant songs. Peasant songs and dances themselves became influenced by those of the city and these changes were widely adopted. After 1905 there were also the revolutionary songs for the workers. Above all, the *chastushki* verses ("limericks") became a great favorite of the youth.

The people of Viriatino were very moved by the departure of recruits for the Army or of workers leaving for the mines. Everybody took a part in the send-offs. The migratory workers left the village in groups of thirty to forty usually at the beginning of October, when work in the fields was finished. The groups of workers would hire a horse cart to carry their baggage to the station since it was forty kilometers from the village, and they themselves would travel all the way on foot. A mass was celebrated for them in the church the day before their departure. Their families would come to pray for a safe journey, and the whole village would turn out to say farewell at their departure. The women wept. The men would return home before Easter, however, since they were needed for the spring planting. On their return they ordered a thanksgiving mass to be celebrated and, feeling free and gay, they would drink for three or four days, especially the young men. They also took the opportunity to show off the new city clothing that they had purchased in the stores at the mines; they walked the streets playing harmonicas and balalaikas, singing songs, and generally trying to impress the villagers.

The farewell celebration for the army recruits took a somewhat different form. It was a tradition that for a whole month before joining the army the recruits had an extravagant time. They gathered in each other's houses for drinks, walked the streets with balalaikas, and generally fooled around. The village assembly usually designated a small sum of money for their entertainment. Sometimes the recruits pulled pranks and would herd cattle into winter crop fields and then demand a ransom which in turn was spent for drinks. Women never took part in this but they did cook food for the future soldiers.

On the day of departure the family of a recruit would arrange a farewell dinner for him to which the closest relatives were invited. They would come with gifts of money ranging from twenty kopeks to three rubles. The parents gave their blessing to the son for his "services to the Tsar." The recruits took with them a small bag containing some underwear and clothing, some food (like salt pork, bread, and millet), and they dressed themselves for the trip in the most worn-out clothing available. They reported to the induction center at Morshansk with their families, wives, and children, if they had any, and the families stayed there for two or three days until the men left town. A homecoming recruit was also greeted with celebration and drinking.

The passion for fist fighting competitions can be explained by the low cultural level of the people of Viriatino in prerevolutionary times. Such exhibitions were usually arranged in most villages of the Tambov and Voronezh provinces during holidays like Christmas, Epiphany, and Shrove Tuesday. After the turn of the century fist fighting competitions were held only on Shrove Tuesday. This rather wild form of entertainment persisted in the folk tradition. The competitions usually took place after dinner, about four or five o'clock in the afternoon. Two teams, each representing half the village, faced each other on the meadow near the church. They fought in their street clothes. It was strictly against the rules to use anything but fists; whoever broke that rule was eliminated from competition and possibly even punished by the others. Not only adult men but adolescents also took part. Youngsters started the fight; adults would join in later. Each fighter selected a partner equal to him in age and size; old men, for example, would fight one another. Some needed a few drinks to bolster their courage.

The whole village turned out to watch. Spectators stuffed their pockets or wrapped up in handkerchiefs quantities of sunflower seeds which they nibbled during the fight. The women did not remain indifferent spectators but encouraged and urged on the players. They also gave them first aid when it was necessary, and some wives tried to cool the zeal of their husbands if they already had bloody noses and torn clothing. It sometimes happened that these games ended with accidents in which men were permanently disabled or even killed.

The kulaks of the village usually did not participate in these competitions as they were afraid some poor villagers might take the opportunity to get even for having been exploited by them. They were still very much absorbed by the fighting, however, and even though they did not take part themselves, they were eager spectators, urging the contestants on and offering them drinks. Sometimes kulaks went so far as to provide poorer peasants with some additional warm clothing so that they could be on the team.

Priests were the only people who objected to the games, but nobody listened to them. Migratory workers also held such competitions at the mines, and players often arranged themselves into teams divided along national or local lines; for example, the Russian workers fought the Tartars, and the Tambov peasants fought the Voronezh peasants.

Holidays and important events in family life were celebrated with plentiful drinking everywhere in Tsarist Russia. Depressed by their hard way of life, the peasants looked for an escape. During the holidays most of the men drank and the women joined in at family celebrations. By the 1890s there were three saloons in the village. On occasion men squandered their land allotments and ruined their families financially because of their addiction to drink. In this way Lisov's father while drunk gave away his land for ten years' use to another peasant, and his sons were forced from late childhood to hire themselves out. The Viriatino peasants tried to refrain from drinking at the mines, being afraid of losing their hard earnings, but sometimes a miner would return home empty-handed.

The Sanitary Conditions of the Village

During the first two decades of the twentieth century, the standard of living in Viriatino did not satisfy the most elementary requirements of hygiene. For this reason, the number of diseases present in the population was very high. Because of the hard physical labor expected from them, peasant women suffered not only from "female maladies," but from rheumatism and tuberculosis as well. The bleaching of linen was especially hazardous to many women's health. The miners also developed tuberculosis, and sometimes whole families would be wiped out by the disease. Because of heavy work the peasants developed hernia, heart failure, and kidney ailments. Low standards of cleanliness caused bad skin conditions, pimples, sores, and itching. Childhood diseases like diphtheria, scarlet fever, and measles, chicken pox, typhoid, and dysentery reached epidemic proportions. Pulmonary diseases, grippe, and malaria were the consequences of the cold climate and some peasants suffered from scurvy.

The disease that hit the people hardest was syphilis, brought to Tambov province in the middle of the nineteenth century by traveling wholesalers. It was especially prevalent on the route along which cattle were brought to market, where it was spread at fairs and inns. Later, it was brought back to the village by the migratory workers, miners, and carpenters. In the 1870s and 80s a considerable number of peasants, adults and children, were afflicted with the disease. In 1876, according to a report from the sanitary authorities in the district to which Viriatino belonged, 41 percent of those afflicted were children. Dr. Nikolski's report stated that "poverty and what goes with poverty, the absence of sanitary conveniences,

crowded living conditions, people of all ages and both sexes
sleeping in the same beds, the practice of communal steam
baths where almost the whole village used the same switch,
everyone eating from one bowl, smoking one pipe, sharing cigarettes, took its heaviest toll on the children, the
most innocent of victims." Among children the disease
was generally mistaken for scrofula, and parents would
usually consult the "wise men" for a cure.

The Morshansk district authorities were forced to take
administrative measures to combat syphilis. Women whose
husbands worked outside the village were obliged to notify
the district doctor immediately on their return and arrange
for a medical examination. In the village itself, the authorities, including the police, were supposed to see to it that
the regulations were observed, and to inform the district
doctor immediately of suspected cases. Special clinics were
opened in many villages; they functioned most during the
summer when the migratory workers were home. In 1875
a special section of Sosnovka hospital was devoted to the
treatment of venereal diseases. But in spite of all these
precautions, the number of people afflicted with syphilis
increased every year. A large number of cases occurred
in the 1890s. In the Sosnovka district in 1911 there were
twice as many cases reported as in 1876. No exact data
were kept on the number of cases occurring in Viriatino,
but it is known that syphilis was widespread there.

To cure all kinds of illnesses the peasants relied on home
remedies, and visits to the "medicine men or women."
Very often women would travel to another village to
be treated by the medicine man there if he was believed
better than the one in her own village. Many folk remedies
had real merit. When somebody caught a cold, he would
take a steam bath. Stomach ailments were treated with a
distillation of plants made with water. Rheumatism was
cured by applying hot sand or by setting the sore limb on
a pan under which pieces of smoldering wood were placed.
Sometimes rubbing alcohol or compresses were used. But

most home remedies were, of course, very irrational. In this category above all was holy water. Together with the "medicine man," two male peasants who had served as nurses during the Russo-Japanese War gave medical advice as did one of the priests who had no idea about medicine at all and who, by confusing the application of different medicines, brought more harm than good to the village.

Viriatino had no hospital or medical clinic. Until the 1860s the peasants used to go to the neighboring village of Kulevatovo where a wealthy landowner had established a small medical station. In the 1870s a hospital was opened in Sosnovka, a wooden structure that had a receiving room, a pharmacy, and two wards, one for men and one for women, each with fourteen beds. No space was allotted for the delivery of babies. Sick people with infectious diseases were placed in a separate, specially constructed barracks. At the beginning of the twentieth century a new stone building was built which included an operating room but had only an eight-bed ward. As a result, by 1911 the ratio of the population in the surrounding area to the number of hospital beds was twice what it had been in 1870.

The hospital served neighboring villages in a radius of from twenty-five to thirty kilometers. It had two medical stations in separate villages. The hospital staff included a doctor, two "feldshers" (semiprofessional medical practitioners nearly equivalent to a real doctor), a nurse, a cook, a laundress, and a watchman. Subsequently the number of feldshers was increased to four, but up until the Revolution there was only one doctor. This small staff could not serve the population of such a large area, and sometimes peasants who came to the hospital or the stations had to wait two days before seeing the doctor or the feldsher. The hospital could handle from one hundred to two hundred patients daily but people visited the doctor only if their cases were difficult or hopeless. The hospital was very far from most villages, and the peasants were unwilling to take their horses away from farm work for such a long journey. At the same time they had very little faith in the effectiveness of medicine. Doctors were strictly forbidden to make any attempt to discuss matters of health with the peasants. However if measures had to be taken to prevent the spread of disease this was always done under the pressure from the administration, and this always frightened the peasants, who were mistrustful of all official edicts and tried to escape them by any means at their command. As a result they had to be forced to be vaccinated against smallpox. The head of the village assembly was obliged to gather together parents and their children to be vaccinated by a specially designated feldsher sent to the village and yet many children did not appear at the appointed time. In 1896 it was recorded that in the medical district served by the Sosnov hospital only a third of 3107 children were vaccinated. This same state of affairs existed well into the following years.

Even more rarely would women visit a trained midwife. In most cases they would ask for help in delivery from certain old women in the village who practiced a form of midwifery.

A proper understanding of medicine and sanitary and hygienic requirements spread extremely slowly among the peasants. More often than others the migratory workers sought medical help, but the women preferred to visit the medicine man, especially when their children were sick. The old medicine man's remedies remained popular even up to the first years of the Socialist Revolution.

CHAPTER VI

LITERACY AND THE INFLUENCE OF RETURNING WORKERS ON VILLAGE CULTURE

As is well known, up to the time of the Revolution the level of literacy among the peasants was very low. The Tsar's regime was not interested in advancing education among the people. According to Lenin the "Ministry of Enlightenment" was, in fact, the "Ministry of Darkness." At the beginning of 1917, seventy percent of all the people of Russia were illiterate. The literacy level among women was especially low. Before the Revolution, because of the rigid class structure, the schools could not serve to introduce culture or any practical knowledge into the village. The system of primary education was not sufficient enough to exert any kind of lasting influence on the cultural level of the peasant, or to enlighten the darker side of village existence, and the conditions of the peasant's way of life were not, of course, conducive to the retention and development of the little knowledge he received in school.

The village of Viriatino was no exception since many children never went to school. In 1917, on the eve of the Revolution, only two children of a village carpenter were able to receive a high school education, and in 1918 a member of this same carpenter's family became the first inhabitant of the village to graduate from a university, with a degree in forestry. In fact, up to the 1870s there was no school at all in Viriatino. Some of the peasant children were taught to read and write by the priest and the deacon. All of these were, however, boys who belonged to affluent families. In 1872 the Morshansk district opened an elementary school in the village with three grades. In 1875 it had eighty-three pupils, of whom only three were girls. In the 1880s the number of pupils diminished. As a result, by 1881 there were in this village of 1835 inhabitants, 922 adults of whom only forty-six were literate. Not one of these was a woman. Thirty-three boys were enrolled in the school at this time and no girls attended.[1]

The school building that was built in the 1880s did not satisfy the most basic educational or even sanitary requirements, and could not house all those who wanted to learn. It was nineteen and a half square feet and very badly constructed; there was not enough furniture and not enough teaching equipment. The school was dirty; one teacher wrote in a report in 1885 that "because of the negligence of the caretaker the school was often cold, practically never swept, and very seldom washed." The basic cost of running the school was paid for by the district and the village itself. According to official data, the district paid four rubles, forty-nine kopeks yearly for each child in attendance, while the village and private citizens shared a contribution of four rubles, sixty-nine kopeks. The central government supplied only twenty-four kopeks. Because of the negative attitude toward education, the village community barely provided for the basic needs of the elementary school. As a rule most of the village leaders ranged from semiliterate to illiterate and were little interested in improving either its physical conditions or the lot of the teachers, and this attitude had an equally negative influence on the village schools.[2]

In 1889 a two-grade parochial school opened in Viriatino, but it never had more than thirteen students. The instructors in the parochial school were even worse than those in the government school. Until 1903 there were no

[1] Sbornik statisticheskich svendenii po Tambovskoi gubernii, vol. 3, Tambov, 1882, pp. 50, 86.
[2] Gosudarstvenniy Arkhiv Tambovskoi Oblasti, 1895.

steady teachers and the priest and his assistant taught without either a plan or a curriculum, very often leaving the children unattended to perform their other duties. The peasants preferred to send their children, especially the boys, to the government school and only if there were no vacancies there would they send them to the parochial school. As a result the majority of the pupils in the latter were girls.

At the turn of the century, the number of children receiving an education increased somewhat so that by 1896 there were seventy pupils enrolled in the government school. By 1906 there were one hundred and twenty and by 1916, there were one hundred and fifty, of whom nearly half were girls. But the overall percentage of illiteracy among the peasants remained very high. Not all who started school finished their education. The average for a district school was that out of thirteen who began, one graduated. In 1875 five boys and two girls graduated from the school in Viriatino; in 1909 eight boys and one girl, in 1916 three boys and three girls. Parents took their children out of school as soon as they were barely able to read and write. One informant, Kabanov, who was born in 1892 to a poor family, remembers that his father would not let him finish school. One spring he simply said, "Take the books back to school. We're going to plow." The economic realities of life in a joint family also contributed to the negative attitude toward the education of children. Another informant said that his uncle who lived in the same household forced him to drop out of school two months before final exams because plowing was about to begin. His father was working at the time in the coal mines and the son had to replace him in the fields. According to an old woman in the village, it was difficult for her children to study because her father-in-law was against it. "The girls are not going to be soldiers," he said, "and because you have only one son, the army will not take him away." This opinion was upheld by the priests. Another informant, Diakov, aged seventy-six, said that when she had learned to read the priests told her, "Now that you can read the prayers well enough, you don't have to study anymore. Now let another child have the chance to learn. You are not going to become a scribe."

Many peasants did not send their children to school because they lacked the proper clothing and shoes. For this reason the children of one family would often take turns going to school; one year one child would go, and the next year another. It is interesting to note that even by 1906 when the attitude toward the education of girls had begun to change, there were still three times as many boys in the school. Kulak families held especially negative views about educating girls. Almost all the children of Sayapin, a lumber merchant, and Popov, a mill owner, remained illiterate.

Instruction in the village school was rigidly organized, and no deviation from the program was allowed. According to Lenin, "There was no relation between the people's labor and the instruction they received in a capitalistic society. This was a deadly, scholastic, governmental kind of teaching muddied with priests' influence, which everywhere, even in a democratic republic, would keep out fresh, healthy ideas." The government and the ruling classes were not interested in widening the peasant's horizon by providing him with practical knowledge. The manual of methods and procedures handed down by the district office in 1897 recommended outright that the teachers "not be carried away with a desire to share with the children all the knowledge they had about a given subject." But a few teachers did somehow manage to spark interest in those pupils who had a desire to learn and they taught things outside the prescribed curriculum. Some people in Viriatino even now remember with gratitude one teacher who taught them the elements of astronomy and geography. Another, a woman who taught at the parochial school, led excursions on her own initiative into fields and meadows for nature studies. The people also remember with great respect a teacher who continually stood up in the assembly to urge the peasants to send their children to school and even organized a library. Such zealous persons were few, however. Many more were thickheaded, barely educated, and reactionary. Such teachers remained aloof from the peasants, looked down on them, and did not take part in the social life of the village. The largest percentage of teachers came from two social classes, the priesthood and the lower-class city-dwellers. Very few came from the peasant class, and it was very difficult for those who did to obtain a position. The daughter of a feldsher of peasant stock who graduated from the teachers' seminary spent over a year without finding work although there were vacant positions in the district.

Before the 1890s, books were a rarity in the village, although sometimes religious books or fairy tales were bought at a fair or bazaar in Sosnovka. Only in 1896 did the district open a small library in the school that was designed to serve adults. The money set aside for its upkeep was not large, but the sum was increased in 1902 and again in 1912. In the latter year the library held a collection of one hundred and fifty-three books, of which sixty were on art, twenty-one on religious and moral subjects, and seventy-two on popular science. The popular science group contained thirteen volumes on history and eleven on geography.

When asked about the reading taste of the villagers, teachers used to say that the greatest interest was shown in stories about peasant life and fairy tales. From classical literature, they read the fables of Krylov, Pushkin's *The Captain's Daughter,* Gogol's *Taras Bulba* and *The Inspector General,* the stories of Turgenev, Mamin-Sibiriak, and Grigorovich. Very seldom were the brochures about village farming read. Books with a religious or moral tone did not have much of a public. These reading habits were characteristic of the young peasants who were the main users of the school library. Literate adults more often read the *Lives of the Saints* or the Bible. An old peasant woman reminiscing about the 1880s when she was a child remembered that during the holidays she would read books about Saints Aleksei and Nikolai Ugodnik aloud for the family. In the 1880s and 90s, editions of fairy tales about the "Little Humpbacked Horse," the Bova Prince, and Eruslan Lazarevich were printed in large quantities by enterprising publishers.

By the beginning of the twentieth century, the number of peasants who read books had increased greatly. Some people had collected small libraries and others would borrow books from them. Young people got the reading habit in the Donbass. Older citizens of Viriatino recalled that after the Revolution of 1905–7 small libraries were gradually compiled in some of the mining camps by the miners who bought books at the bazaars. Sometimes during the rest hours miners would read aloud from these volumes, and a few booklovers even brought them back to their villages. Adventure stories were widely distributed in the village at the turn of the century. They were usually books by T. M. Reid, Jules Verne, and cheap detective stories.

In the years 1908–10 young people often spent their evenings in each other's homes reading books aloud and sometimes discussing them far into the morning. One man who was an initiator of these reading circles would read books in advance and recommend the most interesting ones to his friends. Girls attended these gatherings, but it is reported that they did not pay much attention to the reading.

At the turn of the century, the first newspapers made their appearance in Viriatino. Some affluent peasants, the storekeeper, and the priest subscribed to several of conservative leanings. In a teahouse at the Sosnovka bazaar the peasants could reach such newspapers as the ultraconservative Moscow *Page,* a tabloid, and the *Stock Market News* without buying them. Reading these kinds of newspapers did not improve their political understanding, nor did the "Evening Reading Groups" organized by the district. Set up at the end of the 1890s, these gatherings at which teachers, doctors, or priests gave talks were supposed to have an enlightening effect on the peasants, but the general political character of the meetings was plainly reactionary. The peasants gladly came to them, however, and on some evenings when lantern slides were shown, the attendance reached 120 to 150 people. The books they were offered at these gatherings were of a religious and moral nature, patriotic books, books about the lives of the saints, about icons doing miracles, about the holy places, and about the three hundred years of the Romanov Dynasty. Readings with literature or geography as a theme were very seldom attempted. Lectures on methods of village farming which would have interested the peasants were also ignored. The person responsible for the readings was not the teacher but the priest, who had to answer to the district for their effectiveness. The readings produced a seemingly literate people but, in effect, they were a means of distracting the peasants from more important social issues.

The Growth of a Revolutionary Consciousness

The first Russian Revolution of 1905–7 exerted a great influence on the peasantry. Former miners in the village told how revolutionary propaganda spread in the mines where they worked during the spring of 1905, and how they read illegal literature in their barracks under the covers. Forbidden pamphlets and leaflets were brought back to the village by the miners who gave them to their co-villagers to read. After "Bloody Sunday" in Petersburg, political interests gained headway in all industrial centers of Russia. The political strikes and confrontations did much to awaken the peasantry and draw their sympathies closer to the Revolution. The Revolutionary workers sent out from the cities to their own villages enlightened the villagers about what was taking place in the cities. According to Lenin, "In the Russian village a new type of peasant was ripening, a politically aware young peasant. He communicated with strikers. He read the newspapers. He spoke to the peasants about events in the cities and explained to his village comrades the significance of the political demands, calling on them to rise against the nobility, the priests, and officials."[3]

In Viriatino a group of revolutionarily inspired peasants appeared, all of whom had been miners.

Especially vivid in the minds of the older generation were memories of Ion Andrevitch Diakov who circulated political books among the peasants. Ion was an orphan who at an early age migrated to the mines where at short intervals he worked until after the October Revolution. Ion was a good orator. The Viriatino migrants remember his fiery speeches in the mines during 1916. After the establishment of Soviet rule, Diakov was voted as the first chairman of the Kulevatovo county executive committee.

A particular center of cultural influence for the people of Viriatino was the family of Nagornov which, by village standards, had a rather high income. Nagornov kept in touch with peasants who had revolutionary leanings and supplied those he was able to reach with political literature.

It is difficult to pinpoint the exact nature of the political literature that passed from hand to hand in the village. What the peasants remember best are popular pamphlets like "The Reasons Why Russia Is Poor" and "To Sow and Reap Understanding." In the mining camps the migratory peasants became acquainted with the Social Democrat leaflets and brought them back to their native villages. In December 1905 in the village of Sosnovka, a peasant from Viriatino was arrested in a saloon for reading such literature aloud to other workers. The pamphlet from

[3] Lenin, V., *Works,* v. 23, p. 235.

which he was reading was entitled "An Announcement from the Deputies of Soviet Workers of Uzovsk District." The man arrested said he had received it from a delegate of the deputies of Soviet workers before leaving the mines. It was known that in Uzovsk the Social Revolutionary Party was carrying on important work among the laborers.

In the spring of 1905 there were peasant uprisings in the Tambov, Kirsanovsk, Morshansk, Lipetzk, and Lebediansk districts. Peasants stormed landowners' estates, setting fire to the granaries and issuing demands for lowering the rent on leased lands, raising wages for hired farm labor, and removing some district officials. In many instances the landlords' fields were destroyed by cattle that were turned loose in them. One hundred and thirty estates in the province were destroyed. In the villages nearest Viriatino there was also some peasant unrest. In one village the peasants beat up a village headman; in another they cut down seven hundred trees and brought the trunks home. The same peasants also cut down a few thousand trees in a forest reserve.

The peasant uprisings were spontaneous; they had no leaders and for this reason were quickly put down by the police and guards. The center of the revolutionary peasant movement closest to Viriatino was Sosnovka, where there were many poor peasants. To judge from the documents of the period, the Morshansk district official was very disturbed by the developing revolutionary spirit among the peasants and many times asked the provincial authorities for their assistance. During November 1905 he informed the governor of Tambov that peasants from villages close by were meeting with people from Sosnovka, making plans to storm the landowner's estate and to stage a pogrom in Sosnovka itself. A reinforcement of guards arrived, arrests were made, and some of the peasants were exiled. During the summer of 1906 there was a new tide of peasant uprising, more widespread than before. According to police reports the peasants not only intended to storm the landlord's estates but were going to put up an armed resistance against the police if they attacked the crowd. Again reinforcements were called in and numerous arrests were made. The uprising was stopped. During the peasant uprising, leaders would arouse the crowd against hired farmhands who worked the landlords' estates, and, when they temporarily captured an estate, they would replace those workers with peasants from local villages. All this must have been directed by the leaders of the Social Revolutionary Party. This subversive movement caused a conflict between the peasants and the workers, and doomed the uprising to failure.

Although the peasants of Viriatino did not take a direct part in the unrest, one can see from documents in the archives that there were Social Revolutionary Party agitators in the village who came from the cities and who apparently had old ties with the local people like the Nagornov and Diakov families and others.

How can the passive role played by the people of Viriatino in the Peasant Movement be explained? Local activists now account for this phenomenon by pointing out that in the years 1905–7 there were no longer any large estates near the village. The landowner Davidov already had sold much of his land to neighboring villages, including Viriatino. Some of it he sold to industrialists like Sayapin, and what remained in his possession was bid for by the village of Kulevatovo, which was located next to the estate. Thus the Social Revolutionary Party's appeals did not bring much response from the Viriatino poor, who were by then more working class than peasant and who recognized their blood ties with the miners from Donbass. Under no condition, however, could one call them passive toward the Revolution of 1905–7, because the migratory miners did play a direct part in the revolutionary conflicts. Some of them were arrested and subjected to reprisals. One of the participants stated that in Donbass there was a large revolutionary underground, that meetings were called by the Social Democrats, leaflets distributed, and so on. Miners from Viriatino took part in this underground movement.

By the end of 1906 the strength of the peasant movement had been sapped and the revolution was checked. But it left a lasting impression on the consciousness of the peasants, and a new kind of revolutionary mood found expression just before 1917.

During World War I the economic level of peasant life was sharply lowered, a direct result of the general economic breakdown. There was not enough food or consumer goods and villages were hungry. Because of the lack of manpower, farm output dropped. In Viriatino most of the men were called into the Army and the rest were mobilized to work in the mines of Donbass. The burden of farm labor was laid on the shoulders of women, old men, adolescents, and children. The situation was especially critical in the families where only women and children were left behind. The small monetary allowance from the government did not help. Many families could not work their land allotment by themselves and were severely exploited by the kulaks. The needy peasants' dissatisfaction with the situation created by the kulaks was growing. With bribery kulaks liberated their sons from army duty, and they also received special consideration when horses were commandeered from other peasants. People in Viriatino remember that at the time the community had in its possession a few pieces of farm machinery, reapers, cutters, and so on, which had been given them by the government especially to aid families whose sons had been sent to the front. But, in effect, these machines were taken over and exploited by the wealthier peasants of the village and became a source of income for them. Soldiers at the front learned about the miserable conditions at home from the letters of relatives, and they became profoundly bitter. The overall depression produced by the war and the gradual breakdown of the national economy was felt no less in Viriatino than in other villages throughout the country. The flood of paper money which the Tsar's government was forced to print to cover wartime expenses did not correspond to the volume of trade, and because of this inflation was unavoidable. Quite suddenly in 1915 the prices of goods rose and the value of the ruble dropped daily. Speculation with goods took place on a large scale. People hoarded goods with the expectation that, as prices rose further, they could be sold under the counter for a profit. The chief object of speculation was grain. People profited from speculation not only in the cities, but also in the villages. That part of the population which could not produce its own grain and had to buy it suffered most. In Viriatino there were a number of families that were forced every spring, and sometimes during the winter as well, to buy bread on the black market from the local kulaks in order to survive till the next harvest. During the war the number of such families increased because the former middle class of the village became impoverished. The price increase of bread was a real catastrophe for these people.

Because of this situation the money brought back to the village by the migratory miners for saving had to be spent instead. The miners who were forced to work in the mines had regular, steady earnings. Because the wages during wartime were higher they could send money home. Though from the amount of money which the miners were able to send home one might think that the villagers could live quite well, actually they were paupers. The paper money quickly lost its value, and it was pointless to save it. Moreover, they needed it all for daily requirements. Before the war, the miner's wages were usually saved to build a house, to buy a horse or cow, or to purchase clothing, shoes, and other household needs. Only the very poor had spent the money to buy bread for the family. Now it was an everyday occurrence.

The constant malnutrition and overwork that was the

lot of women and children brought about widespread disease and raised the mortality rate. Vacant huts with doors and windows boarded up began to appear. At the same time news reached the village of the defeat of the Russian Army at the front and the huge number of casualties.

Early in the war, because the village was weighed down with grief and despair, the church collected a rich harvest, although it could not keep up with the number of funerals needed. But this heightened religious sentiment proved itself short-lived for the war went on and God did not rush in to shorten it. People died as before and the belief in miracles waned, now replaced by hatred for those who involved them in this bloody conflagration.

In the mines where the people of Viriatino worked, revolutionary leanings grew in strength with each month as the economic situation of the country deteriorated and the fiasco at the front became obvious. Every so often there were strikes in the mines which took on an increasingly political character. Underground literature was distributed in the miners' barracks which explained to the masses the meaning of the imperialists' war and exposed the rottenness of the Tsarist regime. The central government dirtied itself not only through immorality, but through bribery, stealing funds from the treasury, and direct treason. The names of the Tsarina, Rasputin, Sukhomlnov, and Miasoedov, which were so hated at the front, were just as hated among the workers. People began to talk more and more often, and more openly about the necessity of doing away with the monarchy and getting out of the war.

During the war, although the miners could not leave their jobs and were unable to return home during the summer, they did not break their ties with the village, and their political mood communicated itself to Viriatino. They opened the peasants' eyes and planted a faith in them that life was going to change and that those who came back from the front and from the mines would be able to curtail the abuses practiced by the kulaks and save the people from poverty. Never before had the cries for abolishing the monarchy and giving the land back to the peasants been so strong as they were at the start of 1917. The greatest rallying point was Lenin's call to turn the imperialists' war into a civil war. The nation was on the edge of the great events that began with the February Revolution of 1917.

PART II

THE SOVIET VILLAGE

CHAPTER VII

ECONOMIC LIFE OF THE
CONTEMPORARY VILLAGE

Peasant Domestic Economy Prior to Collectivization

The revolution of February 1917 found most of the male population of Viriatino either at the front or at the Donbass coal fields. The people remaining in the village were primarily women, children, and old men. Public affairs among both groups of peasants were still under the control of the wealthy. A small group of Narodniks, comprised primarily of peasants and teachers, took no part in these affairs and did not consider opposition to the village bourgeoisie one of its goals. Thus, there had been essentially no change in the social structure of Viriatino. But in the fall of 1917 when the soldiers and miners gradually began returning home, the course of events in the village began to take a different direction. The brewing discontent of the masses needed only political guidance to come to the fore. After the February Revolution the political parties that had been developing underground became openly active.

Following the February Revolution, the migrant miners participated in strikes at the mines and were witnesses to struggles between political parties. One of the miners described the situation: "You go out into the street in the morning and there are flags and speakers everywhere. Under a black flag are the anarchists—'All governments are a violation of nature.' They are good speakers and they sound convincing enough. You listen to the Social

Revolutionaries—they too are against the tsar. But they want a provisional government. We listen to them all and then we think about it." The Bolsheviks also listened . . . It was difficult, however, for a migrant miner to join a specific party; his class consciousness as a proletarian had not yet been formed and he felt tied to the peasantry. Not all the miners who later aligned themselves with the Bolsheviks and joined the Communist Party believed in its cause when they returned home in 1912. Nevertheless, they appeared at meetings, where they actively harassed the wealthy landowners, one of whom was forced to go into hiding and was never again seen in Viriatino.

When the soldiers and miners began the job of restoring their neglected farms they had their first practical lessons in politics; the profiteers had managed to turn the war into a source of tremendous profit, while the families and farms of the soldiers were in irredeemable debt to their wealthy neighbors and the village kulaks. The class struggle was becoming so clear that it was not difficult for the village proletariat to understand its essence. There were spontaneous gatherings at the village meetinghouse. Using an outdoor table as a rostrum the men delivered speeches, and many heated debates arose, especially about land and peace. Newspapers were read aloud at these meetings.

When the villagers learned of the October Revolution and of the formation of a Soviet government, a Viriatino soviet of peasants, soldiers, workers, and deputies was organized. This group declared itself the governing body of the village. There were no Bolsheviks in the village soviet—in fact, not one deputy had declared himself as affiliated with any political party. This, however, did not mean the soviet lacked a political image. The members included men who had been at the front and miners who were already influenced by the ideology of the Communist Party.

In the county of Kulevatovsk a land committee was organized. The landowners' property rights were abolished, and all their holdings registered. On March 29, 1918, an emergency meeting of the county land committees and soviets of Morshansk districts together with representatives of the rural communities resolved to distribute the land among the peasantry by establishing an allotment quota of 2.7 acres per person in three separate fields (a crop rotation precaution). In carrying out this resolution each district had to take into account the population of the villages and redistribute the total acreage in accordance with the established quotas. The residents of Viriatino needed an additional 321.3 acres to fulfill their quota, and these were apportioned to them in April 1918. With the receipt of their full quota, they renounced any claims to the use of the remaining undistributed lands of the former landowner, Davidov.

When it came to apportioning the plots of land, the clash of interests became evident. The wealthier peasants insisted on receiving the lands they had previously been farming. The village soviet decided to carry out a complete redistribution of the land and accomplished this the same way that the prerevolutionary community had done it; land was divided into two categories—the lands formerly allotted and the lands belonging to the landowners. Land was chosen from each category according to its productiveness and distance from the village and was divided into parcels which were turned over to the peasants by means of a lottery based upon the size of their families. With this redistribution, the fields turned out to be divided into long and quite narrow strips, and both the open field system and compulsory crop rotation were reborn. The three-field system again became the only possible system of agriculture because the tradition of communal farming among the peasants was so strong. This fact was not surprising to the Bolsheviks. Addressing the delegates of the committee on poverty in Moscow, November 1918, Lenin said:

> We didn't want to force strange ideas about the uselessness of equal division of land upon the peasantry.

We felt that it was better if the peasants saw this themselves, through their own experience. Only then could we ask them how we could overcome the ruin and preponderance of the kulaks that take place during land division. Division was good only at the beginning. It was necessary to show that the land was being taken from the bourgeoisie for the peasantry. But this is not enough. The only answer is communal work of the land.[1]

Conflicts arising among the peasants in regard to the allotment of lands were settled by the village soviets, but some of the disputes were carried to higher authorities for decision. In Viriatino one such conflict concerned an entrepreneur named A. F. Goloveshkin, who had rented land from a landowner and then leased it in lots at increased prices to the peasants. The village soviet had refused to allot Goloveshkin any land and he appealed this decision to the Kulevatovsk county land committee. Unable to reach agreement with the Viriatino village soviet on the claims of Goloveshkin, the county soviet sent his complaint to the district soviet in Morshansk with a plea to "clarify" to Viriatino the necessity of apportioning some land to Goloveshkin. As his name appears in the household register for that autumn, the district committee apparently ordered the village to apportion the entrepreneur his quota.

The above correspondence indicates that the land policies of the Kulevatovsk county soviet and the Morshansk district soviet were contrary to those of the Soviet government. Saboteurs and other vermin, in the committees of these (and many other) soviets, were taking all possible steps to distort and mutilate soviet laws. In the fall of 1918, after the counterrevolutionary uprising of the kulaks in Morshansk, the executive committee of Tambov province dissolved a number of local organizations for harboring a nest of anti-soviet, Social Revolu-

[1] Lenin, V., v. 28, p. 156.

tionary and Menshevik party elements. Among those dissolved was the executive committee of the Morshansk soviet.

In order to strengthen the dictatorship of the proletariat in the villages and to create a counterbalance to the conciliators and anti-soviet elements in the village soviets, the Communist Party organized the poor people. In the Morshansk district of Tamborsk province, Poverty Committees began forming on June 18, 1918. Two were in Viriatino: one assigned to Perkinsk county and the other to Kulevatovsk. No information was found in the archives as to the activities of the Perkinsk committee. The Kulevatovsk committee, which apparently later represented the entire village, had one hundred members by the middle of August 1918, about sixty or seventy poor peasant households. In its membership lists there were marks to indicate that all the members were "communist-bolsheviks." It is doubtful that this was so, but undoubtedly the committee was under the influence and political control of the bolsheviks. Their chairman was V. M. Kabanov—a miner who had worked for fifteen years at the Donbass coal fields.

According to the records of this committee, in August 1918 there were 375 peasant households in the village. Capitalistic leasing of the land was forbidden, and the use of hired labor in peasant farms was made difficult. The poor peasants received land allotments on which they could work without having to sell their labor to the kulaks. The Poverty Committee saw to it that the profiteers did not regain their former economic strength or influence the soviet administration.

But although the allotment of land helped the peasant slightly, his standard of living began to rise only very slowly. It was difficult for the poor peasant families to recover from the ravages of the First World War. They were without cattle, and the war's toll of human lives had thinned their number. They received land from the Soviet government but they had no horses or plows with which to work it. There was no way to obtain cows or sheep. In Viriatino, sixty-three families (16.8 percent of the total number of households) had no horses and seventy-three (19.4 percent of the total) no cows. Once the civil war began the Soviet government could not give out loans for the purchase of working cattle; in consequence, the lands of the very poor peasants were left almost completely unsown. They planted only the absolute minimum necessary to keep from starving.

A considerable number of the very poor peasants nevertheless did manage to get a few horses and cattle, and their farms fell into the category of "one-horse" farms. These made up more than half of all the farms in Viriatino (218, or 58.1 percent) and certainly middle-class peasants who had lost some of their horses during the war formed part of this group. In 1918 this middle-class peasant element was economically unstable and a good deal larger than in prerevolutionary times. There were only eight farms that had no cattle whatsoever.

There were eighty-six (22.9 percent) peasant households with two horses in Viriatino. These were well-to-do households that had managed to maintain their economic independence despite the ravages of the years 1916–18. After the revolution some of the very rich households who had exploited their poor neighbors pretended that they belonged to this rank of the merely well-to-do. As later events demonstrated, these capitalist elements in the village were only temporarily quiet and possibly had made themselves appear no richer than middle class because they were seeking to avoid conflict with the committees of the poor peasants. They had sold some of their cattle and persuaded their neighbors to do the same. From this practice originated the slogans "Cut up your cattle" and "Don't increase your crops." More active than the village bourgeoisie (who were much too visible) these outwardly middle-class families later became the main power behind the kulak uprising. Finally, the presence of a numerically small group of eight families (2.2 percent) owning three or four horses and two or three cows showed that not all the farms of the village bourgeoisie had been liquidated.

The history of the kulak uprising which took place in the autumn of 1918 in the Morshansk district has not yet been fully studied, so it is hard to tell to what degree the activities of the Emergency Foods Committee temporarily set up in that district influenced its origins. There is some basis for conjecture that the district supply commissar (of food) brought about a great turmoil and caused a great many panicky rumors among the peasants with his miscalculated orders. Some of the poor subordinates to the supply commissar, in following his directions (in the inventory of grains and other products), did not always do what was best at the given moment for the revolution. The activities of the Viriatino Poverty Committee, however, showed at the outset that it had a correct understanding of the political line of the Communist Party. It registered the grain of the new harvest, permitted no cutbacks in the sowing, and helped those without horses to work their fields.

The fall of 1918 saw the migrant miners off to the Donbass as usual, but the civil war had already reached the area where the mines were located (now known as Voroshilovogradskaya oblast). Some of the men from Viriatino joined the ranks of the Red Guards and together with the other Soviet forces started to break through the rebel Cossack villages. Germans occupied the Donbass. The mines were still and all work stopped. Other migrant miners returned to Viriatino and strengthened the proletarian backbone which upheld the Poverty Committee and, by implication, the soviet regime. It was only because of the size and strength of its proletarian nucleus that Viriatino never became a center of kulak and Social Revolutionary rebellions and did not shelter roving bands of rebels during the years of civil war.

In the second half of 1919, the Social Revolution Party

considered that politically the moment had come to stab the Red Army in the back. The Red Army repulsed this attack of Denikin on the southern front.[2] The Social Revolutionaries then spurred a kulak uprising in the Tambov province. They organized the kulaks and army deserters into a large unit directly responsible to a central headquarters at the head of which was a man named Antonov. The Social Revolutionaries planned to destroy communications between the breadbasket of the South, the East, and Moscow, and thereby to prevent the proletarian centers from getting food supplies. In 1920 the center of uprising was the Kircanovsk district. But anti-Soviet bands under Antonov were moving from village to village in the neighboring districts, and they also came to Morshansk. The Red Army would disperse parts of the band in one place, but they would only reassemble in another and would suddenly attack units of the Red Army, killing members of the Poverty Committee and village Communists as well. They imposed themselves on the people for food. Military strategies taken by the Soviet commandants in the Tambov province could not effectively suppress the uprisings because the kulaks and a large number of the middle-class peasants who were taken in by Social Revolutionary-kulak demagogy hid the bandits and replenished their ranks. The poor peasants and the proletarian farm laborers and migratory workers gave strong support to the Soviet Regime in those places where uprisings were instigated. They took the brunt of the bloody terror of the Antonov bands which stole horses and food from them and threatened to kill all who opposed. Only a few people, perhaps as few as ten, went over to the side of Antonov's bands, but it was done secretly because the village as a whole was much against the uprising. Rifts occurred in some middle-class families

[2] *Denikin* was one of the counterrevolutionary military leaders on the southern front during the Civil War which followed the October Revolution (Tr.).

when members of the same family found themselves politically opposed.

Viriatino was terrorized in 1920 by a small group of local hooligans who beat up and even robbed their co-villagers. At the head of this band was a nineteen-year-old named Zhiriakov who had left his family after the death of his father. During one of these attacks Zhiriakov was arrested by the police. But a band of Antonov's men rescued him as he was being taken to Sosnovka, and Zhiriakov thereupon joined them and organized a full-scale raid on Viriatino. Swooping down on the village, his henchmen robbed the poor villagers. Zhiriakov himself stormed into the house of Losev, a person who had previously denounced him as a thief and bandit, and cut off the man's arms in a beastly rage. In a nearby village the band razed the community center and burned its library, mainly with the intent of destroying any political literature. As a desperation measure the civil-district government was temporarily replaced by a military government which gained full control. In Kulevatovsk county the first order became that of arresting and bringing to headquarters all those people who were involved in any way with the bandits, army deserters, black market racketeers, and gossipers who spread rumors and provoked panic.

In the spring of 1921 the Tenth Communist Congress took place in Moscow and it was there that Lenin presented his proposal of natural taxation. It was decided by the Congress to revoke the surplus appropriation system in favor of food taxation.[3] The news made a great impression on the peasants. Because of these measures there was a definite drawing back in Tambov by the middle-class peasants from

[3] *Lenin's natural taxation* refers to the payment of taxes by the peasant in the form of agricultural products. During the first few years after the Revolution peasants were required to turn over to the State all foods grown on their farm except the minimum to keep their families from starvation. The money the peasants received for their products had, at the time, little buying power (Tr.).

Antonov's bands. Losing the support of the peasants, the bands also lost all political future. The peasants ceased to provide them with food or horses, and the number of these units very soon diminished as the peasants started leaving for their homes. Antonov's days were numbered. The Red Army defeated the rest of Antonov's men in a few decisive battles in the summer of 1921, driving them back into the forest and swamps. On July 5, 1921, the commandant of the Tambov province reported that his forces had defeated the bandits and had thus created a mood favorable to the soviet government among the peasants who had been infuriated by the terror which the bandits brought to Viriatino and had begun to form village resistance units for self-defense. These local army groups (composed of local population and demobilized Red Army units) were under the personal military responsibility of a Soviet commandant, and only in areas where it was certain that the villagers were pro-Soviet.

At the same time that the fight against Antonov was raging the Viriatino village council was arranging to harvest the fields of the poor people, keeping a strict count of the grain yield on the fields of other villagers and taking measures against the grain's going to the support of the bandits. At one of these meetings it was decided to take away the rye from the families of the bandits and put it into the common storehouse. Nine homesteads were found to be bandit hideouts and their harvests were confiscated, and the two homesteads which were held suspect had their crops withheld until a decision could be reached. In the case of three other homesteads also connected with the robbers in some way the council was very careful in weighing the consequences of its decision. In one of these families there was a small daughter. The council gave the child a guardian and an allotment of the grain and the balance was given to the general fund. In the other two homesteads the fathers had joined Antonov while their sons, soldiers in the Red Army, had remained in the village. The council decided to take the harvest only of those who had deserted.

The last flickers of the uprising were put out in the autumn of 1921 and the Tambov province resumed normal life. There had been a reorganization of the village council in Viriatino the previous June, and the revised body started to bring order into the economic life of the village. A month later the people elected a committee to organize the village "co-op." The peasants began preparing to enlarge their planting. The village council, taking into consideration the number of horses available for work, helped the families which did not own a horse. Business picked up in Sosnovka in the bazaar. And so a new period started, known in history as that of the New Economic Policy (N.E.P.).[4]

During the time of confusion and disorder many fields had not been tilled at all and were now covered with weeds. The clearing of this neglected land sapped much of the peasants' strength. There was little livestock and therefore no fertilizer. At that time the peasants did not have time to think about applying newer, more productive methods of cultivating the fields. They were in a hurry to sow as much as they could with as little loss as possible. It is true that some of the affluent peasants were trying to introduce new improved methods of working the land and employed simple machinery; but lack of horses, the forced rotation of crops, and the fact that the tillable land was scattered prevented improvements. The village agricultural organizations were not yet well organized and could not help the population. As a result the harvest of the first N.E.P. years in Tambovsk were pretty small, and in some other districts from 1924 to 1925 the peasants had practically no harvest because of catastrophic crop failures. Mass hunger was threatening. In May 1925 there were 7920 hungry people, and by May 1926 this number was

---

[4] *N.E.P.*—New Economic Policy introduced by the Soviet government after the Civil War permitted small producers to sell their surplus products in the open market at State-regulated prices (Tr.).

raised to 15,384. It became necessary for the government to provide food and to organize grain distribution. A special fund of forty pounds of seed a month for each consumer was set up for those families which remained without grain.

At this time the son of a progressive peasant having graduated from an agricultural technical school in 1924 returned to the village and experimented with the growing of winter wheat. The young agriculturalist convinced his father that wheat should be sown in parallel rows on one acre. The peasants were skeptical of this idea. The sowing was done on a well-prepared soil and on a few separate plots. The seeds were planted in long rows instead of by the traditional scattering method. In the autumn when shoots began to grow these rows promised a good harvest and were conspicuously healthier than the other plots. In December and January, however, when there were heavy rains, sheets of ice formed. No precautions were taken to prevent the process and the shoots died beneath the surface for lack of air. Rye, however, which had been sown by the traditional method, spent the winter very well and ripened. The ice had frozen over the rows which were lower than the land surface but had not covered all the land. Since there was no continuous sheet of ice, these seeds had not suffocated. In addition, the winter rye was acclimated to this particular locality. The fiasco discouraged for a time any further attempts at sowing in rows and only reinforced the peasant's conviction that wheat could not be planted in Viriatino. The young agriculturalist could not stand being laughed at and went to Donbass in search of work.

In the autumn of 1922 there was a renewal of migrations to the mines. During the first years after the end of the Civil War when the mines which were half-destroyed and flooded were being restored, mining had been seasonal. But when the mines at Donbass began working at full capacity it became necessary to prevent migration back to the villages in the summer. Measures were taken to retain the number of workers; wages were raised, a six-hour working day was established, new dormitories were built, construction was undertaken for new housing for workers and their families, a regular vacation was introduced, and so on. These social measures created such good working conditions that the Donbass mines attracted more workers. The peasant migratory workers who had not broken with the land, and considered agriculture to be their primary occupation but looked to the mines for supplementary income, were hard put to make a choice, thus creating a situation which at first glance seems strange in those villages which provided the workers for the mines.

During the first years of N.E.P. the stream of migrant miners became larger, but diminished in 1926–27. By the end of the 1920s there was a gradual cutback in the traditional migration of seasonal workers from many villages, including Viriatino. The ties of these villages with the Donbass were changed, however, rather than cut. There was an increase in the number of workers every year who went off to the mines, and became full-time miners, as opposed to migrant workers. After a few years at the Donbass they were sometimes joined by their families. Meanwhile the process of agricultural improvement was slowly but surely progressing; the amount of tilled land and livestock was increased, and private and cooperative trade developed. The revitalized economic life of the village was accompanied by a temporary increase in its bourgeoisie. Food taxes were levied in proportion to the economic situation of the peasants' homesteads. Those who had been better off previously had more livestock and, as a rule, better agricultural implements than the numerous poor people. Therefore their farms were more productive. The practice of leasing land and hiring farmhands was started again, at first secretly and then openly. A considerable amount of surplus grain was brought into the market. As these homesteads became wealthier they began to exploit their poorer neighbors. Kulaks were reborn.

In the first years of the N.E.P., the kulak homesteads gathered strength in Viriatino. Approximately ten families in the village were engaged in trade, and joined the forces of the kulaks, acquiring threshing machines, seeding machines, and separators. The kulak leaseholders took over the mill again. They also took over the local markets. In 1925 at the Sosnovka county meeting the deputies said that the Sosnovka market was leased out to a few rich people, apparently former traders (there had been many in Sosnovka before the revolution). These men decided the price of space at the market and when the peasants refused to pay for the space they took away their coats, gloves, and parts of their harnesses.

New economic policies of the Soviet government helped to develop national agriculture and industrial growth of the land, but renewed capitalistic elements took advantage of the new agricultural conditions to become dangerous for socialist economics. In 1928, despite the fact that there was a large amount of grain available, the urban centers were running the risk of food shortages. The village rich who hoarded large stores of grain did not sell it to the government or to the co-ops, but tried to increase the prices for the individual buyer and a tense situation developed.

It became impossible to regulate the growth of capitalistic elements in the village simply by imposing taxes. It was necessary to supply socialist industry with raw materials and to stock the administrative and cultural centers with grain to create a basic food supply which would provide for the whole population without deprivation. The peasant's small homestead with its low technical productivity and economic instability nourished capitalistic elements in its midst. The party decided on the course of mass collectivization of the peasant households and the liquidation of the capitalistic elements in the village.

Nine peasant households in Viriatino formed a society in early 1929 for the purpose of working the land together. This society did not exist for long, and was dissolved when the harvest was gathered. This experiment showed that such small groups were not economical and that it was necessary to create larger organizations, based on a different principle, in order to communize the main sources of production.

In August 1930, 460 peasant homesteads (out of 492 existing in the village) united into a collective farm which was named "Lenin's Way." In 1931, twenty more homesteads joined the collective farm, while six households of craftsmen remained private. The remaining five households were recognized as kulaks, who were exiled from the village, and their land became part of the communal fund. In all, the "Lenin's Way" farm collectivized the basic means of production of 481 collective households and owned 4261 hectares (one hectare equals 100 acres) of land, which at the time made it one of the largest collective farm areas in the Tambov region.

Collectivization in Viriatino was accomplished only as a result of severe class struggle, however. As soon as meetings began on the question of communal farms, the kulaks would set fire to the participants' property, usually to a threshing barn or a shed. Fearing to come out into the open, the kulak men conducted their anticollective farm agitation through their wives, sisters, and mothers. At the meetings all of the women of Viriatino at first opposed the organization of collective farms and simply yelled, "We don't want to," to the call to join in the collectivization. But after an explanatory period the mood in the village changed, and even the most active former foes of the collective farm voted to join it.

Joining the kolkhoz (collective farm) did not necessarily convert the peasant into real collectivists. Many were unwilling to take care of "somebody else's" farm. There was danger that the communized livestock would be worse taken care of than those in the private households. The working cattle were, in fact, overexerted and began to die. The enemies of the kolkhoz took advantage of this situation to establish an anticollectivization mood in the community. They persuaded the peasants that horses were henceforth useless, as the tractor, or "steel horse," would soon replace them. Many of the peasants were thus convinced that the horse's day was done, a way of thinking that proved to be both wrong and harmful. The kolkhoz officials tried a new approach. In order to save the horses and cattle they appointed the former owners of each animal to take care of it. Then each peasant caring for his "own horse" did not overburden it and each fed it from his own private store if there was a lack of provisions in the kolkhoz. This continued for several years until collectivization was accepted. The kulak agitation that had aimed at the abolition of horses failed and the kolkhoz, "Lenin's Way," turned out to be one of the best in the Tambov province.

In the Sosnov region there was still especially strong kulak anticollectivist agitation in the summer of 1933. (Viriatino had been included in the Sosnov county in 1924 when the borders of districts were reassigned.) The peasants began to pillage the kolkhoz property, including cattle and harnesses. Peasants began to fear going out to work in the kolkhoz fields because they were often attacked, and the fields were allowed to lie fallow. The harvest was on the verge of perishing. The party organization of "Lenin's Way" turned for help to the activists of the neighboring village, Malopupsk. A group of Communists, for the most part composed of women and girls, came to their aid. The group was forced to live for two weeks in the fields because of the unrest in the village, working all day without rest until the job of salvaging the harvest was done. (In 1933–35 the kolkhozes neighboring to Viriatino had bad harvests and were left seedless and without cattle.

Then, at the request of the Party Organization of "Lenin's Way," the Viriatino peasants helped their neighbors' fields.)

The kolkhoz decided in 1932 to renew the hitherto unsuccessful experiment with winter wheat growing. This was arranged on twenty-hectare plots. The wheat harvest that year was greater than that of rye. In 1933, one hundred hectares were sown. The wheat harvest proved to be greater than rye by 57 percent, and in 1935 winter wheat gave 19.9 centners (hundredweights) per hectare, while rye gave only 9.9. It was thus finally proven that wheat could be successfully and profitably grown in Viriatino.

In 1935 Viriatino's kolkhoz owned 4281 hectares of land. "Lenin's Way" expanded and strengthened each year until the attack on the Soviets by Nazi Germany which effectively put an end to its growth. Hundreds of horses and machines had to be given to the war effort. Most of the men went to the front, leaving only women, children, and old men in Viriatino. All the work on the fields and farms rested on their shoulders. The women worked heroically and were helped by youths but the amount of work to be done was beyond their strength. All production decreased by 50 percent. "Lenin's Way" became one of the most unproductive kolkhozes in the Sosnovka district. The new and inexperienced officials of the farm were partly to blame for this decrease because they allowed too much personal rather than communal work to be done, and work discipline was poor. But even in this sorry state, the kolkhoz helped the families of the soldiers bear the burden of the war. At the end of World War II when the men returned to Viriatino the kolkhoz was restored to normal. It took much work and almost three years to strengthen the collective's objectives, restore productivity and discipline, and raise the standard of living.

The Contemporary Kolkhoz or "Lenin's Way"

The economic life of the kolkhoz determines the entire life of Viriatino as a whole.

The collective farm community on January 1, 1957, consisted of 1128 persons divided into 428 families. Of these, 172 men and 312 women were actively engaged in work there. There are 4476 hectares of land belonging to the kolkhoz. Some 2237 hectares are reserved for planting crops, 598 for meadowland, and 625 for forests. There is a certain amount of clay soil from which bricks can be made and of peat available for fuel. The farm economy is specifically oriented, for the most part, toward cattle-breeding and grain crops.

Soon after World War II the collective farm began building electric power stations. The first built in 1947 was a hydroelectric power station (50 kilowatts) constructed on the Chelnovaya River. The current was used in all phases of farm work as well as for electrifying kolkhoz, administrative, and cultural buildings. The second power station, an auxiliary unit (only 10 kilowatts) built on the Pishlyaika River, provided current for a mill. In addition there are four diesel motors in Viriatino and a total of twenty-three electric motors. The Chelnovaya River does not have enough water to provide uninterrupted electric power to the plant built on its banks, so the kolkhoz is not adequately provided with electricity. Another power plant (100 kilowatts) will be built in the near future.

The kolkhoz has seven trucks, one a specially equipped vehicle for carrying grain or distillery refuse, and there is one car. There are also eighty-nine horses and until recently there were 125 draft oxen; there is currently no need for them and all oxen were sold in 1954–55.

The complex and diversified economy of the kolkhoz requires the services of specialists. Almost all branches of agriculture are mechanized. The Kulevatov Machine and Tractor Station supplies the kolkhoz with tractors, combines, plows, etc., and helps by making available the services of its staff specialists. The Station also helps the kolkhoz in the process of agricultural mechanization. The kolkhoz also has its own agricultural machinery and equipment and other equipment for the auxiliary workshops. Maintenance of the equipment is seen to by the specialists who are members of the kolkhoz.

The major divisions of cultivation are field crops, orchards, and forests. In 1946, 2666 hectares of arable land were accessed to the kolkhoz. Some of it was of a very low yield, however, and was therefore reclassified and transferred to other uses, the more fertile for common pasturage and the less for forestry. Therefore the amount of arable land belonging to the kolkhoz was reduced to 2237 hectares, but forest land increased to 625 hectares. The planting of more trees had a favorable effect on the fertility of the other land as the young forests protect the fertile fields from dry winds and sand drifts and help to accumulate snow on them.

There are 396 hectares of meadowland belonging to the kolkhoz. Some 248 of these comprise good meadow and 148, waterless valleys. There is a very low yield of productivity from the meadows, however, which are partly formed by mounds and hillocks and are covered by bushes which make mechanized mowing very difficult.

There is a variety of soil types; a rather small area of black earth; sandy soil; and podsol, a white, ashy soil. Most of the land must be properly manured and fertilized yearly to increase fertility.

In 1947 some changes were introduced into the system of crop rotation. All the land was divided into two portions, one for fodder and the other for regular cultivation. In addition, 54.6 hectares of arable land was left fallow. All the land allotted for regular cultivation was divided into ten parts and the land reserved for fodder into seven.

The system of rotation worked as follows: the first field was fallow, the second planted with rye and grass, the third with one-year grass, the fourth with two-year grass, the fifth with spring wheat, the sixth with interfield crops, the seventh with mixed spring crops, the eighth left fallow, the ninth with winter crops, and the tenth with oats. But this plan could not be strictly adhered to because of a shortage of seed.

The kolkhoz tried to carry out the following rotation in raising fodder: in the first field, oats and perennial grass; in the second and third, grass for silage; in the fourth, grass for mowing; in the fifth, spring wheat; in the sixth, a combination of vetch and oats; and in the seventh, a fodder root crop for silage.

Most of the arable land is planted every year with cereal grains and bean-pod. In 1954 these crops accounted for 84 percent of all arable land; in 1955, 76.6 percent; in 1956, 73 percent; only 6.2 percent of all arable land is used for potato and vegetable growing. Fodder root crops in 1954 accounted for 6 percent of land use; in 1955, 11.6 percent; in 1956, 15.4 percent (which also included corn); industrial crops consisting of mahorka (a local variety of tobacco), hemp, flax, and sunflowers accounted for 4 percent of arable land cultivation in 1954; in 1955, 5.6 percent; in 1956, 5 percent.

Rye is one of the most important crops; this is a traditional crop in Viriatino and 40 percent of the arable land used for regular crop cultivation is planted with it. The yield is not very high but it is stable. About 14 percent of arable land was planted with oats, and 8 percent with millet. For several successive seasons the winter wheat crop was destroyed by frost, and so the kolkhoz stopped planting it, and substituted millet which had a higher yield when the fields were properly cultivated and fertilized. A combination of spring and winter crops was introduced in 1947 to ensure a good harvest in at least one area, should the other fail.

As already noted, State-owned machine and tractor stations have had a decisive influence on the kolkhoz economy. They helped to develop the main branches of agriculture by assisting in the process of mechanization and providing all kinds of assistance to the kolkhozes. Until 1954 the Kulevatov Machine and Tractor Station's work was not as helpful as it should have been because of a shortage of tractors and other agricultural machinery. The station was not able to carry out repairs in many cases because of the lack of adequate facilities and qualified personnel. Repair work was very often hasty and ineffectual. Deadlines were often not met. In the effort to complete its work the kolkhoz was obliged to use very primitive equipment. The harvest was very time-consuming and costly because conditions were so bad. In addition there was an unusually high charge for the services of the Machine and Tractor Station but the situation began to improve after the Plenary meeting of the Communist Party of the USSR in September 1953. Better equipped repair shops for farm machinery were built for the Station, which also bought some new tractors, combines, and trucks, and highly qualified personnel were added to the staff. The Station's charges were also reduced after this Plenary meeting, thereby creating an easier economic situation for the collective farm. The Kulevatov Station has continued to do all kinds of work for the kolkhoz. After 1956 the collective farm began to use modernized methods of cultivation, including the improvement of soil composition, fertilization, and proper crop rotation.

The collective farm first tried to grow corn in 1955. Unfortunately the farmers had no previous experience with this crop and it was not very successful. In 1956 special teams were organized to study corn growing; seeds were very carefully selected but in spite of these special efforts the results were still not promising for the future.

More effort is spent on the mahorka crop than on any other, especially during the harvest. Second in this respect is the potato crop, which constitutes the main vegetable on the collective farm. During the last several years the amount of land allotted to potato growing increased from fifty to one hundred hectares, but this amount was still less than that under cultivation with the same crop in 1934–36 (270–97 hectares). Almost all members of the collective farm plant potatoes on their individual allotments; this accounts for 120 hectares of land, and explains why the collective farmers are not interested in increasing the general land allotment under potatoes for the collective. It is usual to reserve the least fertile land for the potato crop. The average yield is eight tons of potatoes per hectare.

Until recently other kinds of vegetables were planted only very sparingly. For example, one hectare was set aside for cucumbers, and one and a half for cabbage (the latter was raised only to fulfill the state quota plan as there was no market available for this crop). But when wholesale prices were fixed at a higher rate in 1954, the cultivation of potatoes and other vegetables became more profitable. There were no irrigated vegetable fields in Viriatino. An unsuccessful attempt was made to cultivate melons but it was found that the average temperature was too low. The vegetable fields which were planted on lowlands and not irrigated, however, were very profitable. In 1956 the collective farm decided to increase the amount of land planted with cabbage to five hectares. The yield was 181.5 tons per hectare. One hectare was planted with tomatoes, yielding 18.7 tons. All these vegetables were sold in part to the State and in part at city markets.

Orchards play a far more important role in the total collective farm economy. Ninety-one and a half hectares were devoted to gardening in 1956. The collective farm owns its own nursery and each family cares for an orchard, consisting mostly of apple trees. There are approximately twelve trees per family. Gardening accounted for five thousand rubles of profit in 1955.

Forestry also occupies an important place in the farm economy. Indiscriminate tree felling toward the end of the nineteenth century resulted in soil erosion which changed the fields, and the peasants were unable to do anything to stop the process of decay. By 1955 the collective farm had successfully planted 625 hectares with trees, creating forests that ranged in age from one to thirty-five years, and these efforts were beginning to show a profit.

The second most important division of the collective farm economy is the raising of livestock and dairy farming. The farm now has twenty new cattle barns which were built during the first years of collectivization, gradually replacing the original ones. They are well-equipped brick structures, provided with electricity and piped-in water. A dairy farm, sheep fold, stud farm, and pig farm occupy a separate, lightly wooded area surrounded by a green fence. The process of making silage is mechanized, and the fodder is stored in fourteen special silos, the total capacity of which is 1550 tons. The dairy farm is also equipped for churning butter. This aspect of farming looks very promising for the future.

Although all the oxen were sold in 1954 because they had been supplanted by machines, the number of cattle owned by the collective farm was increased by 65 percent or 150 head. The productivity of the herds (meat, milk, young, etc.) increased too. In 1952 the farm averaged 1560 liters of milk per cow, although in 1953 and 1954 the average yield was sharply reduced because of diseases and shortage of fodder. In 1955 the yield increased to 1734 liters. This occurred despite poor work organization. The milkmaids did not feed the cows themselves or even supervise their feeding; this was done by another group, usually men who otherwise had nothing to do with this area of farming, inasmuch as it was heavy work. No solution has yet been found to this problem because the milkmaids insist that they are too busy to take on any extra work. One possible solution would be to encourage interest on the part of those who feed the cows by paying them for each liter of milk. At any rate the situation is in the process of improving. By 1956 the collective farm was already averaging 2294 liters of milk per cow.

Sheep raising is still in the experimental stage. Efforts were made to improve the strain of the stock through breeding. In 1951 the collective farm bought some rams from Michurinsk, but the resulting improvement in the strain was very slight since local conditions were unfavorable. The only result was an increase in the number of sheep from 150 to 688. Shearing takes place twice a year.

Until 1955 the collective farm raised and sold young pigs to the member farmers; it was unable to keep the pigs and raise them because of the shortage of fodder. In 1952, 94 percent of all the pigs sold were less than two months old; in 1953, 91 percent; in 1954, 84 percent; in 1955, 92 percent; and in 1956, 77 percent. At the beginning of 1956 the farm decided to keep ninety-seven pigs and fatten them for market. In 1952 the average litter consisted of ten pigs; in 1953, thirteen; and in 1955, fifteen.

There is a horse farm on the kolkhoz, but it is not large and its only purpose is to supply work horses to the collective. The horses are stabled during the winter and let out to pasture during the spring and summer. The cattle are also pastured during the summer. A camp has been constructed near the place where the animals are pastured to provide living quarters for the dairymaids and herders. It is equipped with a kitchen and an enclosure for the animals; when the animals are kept in more remote pastures, temporary huts are built and food is cooked over fires.

Poultry is a comparatively new branch of the collective farm economy, and in this area there is an evident lack of well-trained personnel and equipment. A brooder house was built in 1939, but it was very dark and not properly ventilated. There was an epidemic of liver tuberculosis among the hens and almost half the ducks died because of a shortage of water. The geese also had a high death rate. The situation is improving now and a new brooder house was built in 1955. The collective farm has no incubators. They buy chickens at a hatchery and have gradually been improving the strain of poultry. About 30 percent of the flock is used for meat. Since the hens which are poorer layers are eliminated in this fashion, the general productivity of the flock has increased. In 1953 the annual average of eggs per hen was 31; in 1954, 40; in 1955, 67; in 1956, 101.

Beekeeping is not a major part of the collective farm's economy. In 1957 there were 138 hives where bees were kept for pollination. During the summer the hives were removed to fields and orchards. Some member farmers raise their own bees, but more as a hobby than for economic reasons.

The collective farm makes its own bricks and the factory was mechanized in 1952. Its capacity is 350,000 bricks per year. Many auxiliary buildings such as a silo, a clubhouse (capacity four hundred), a garage, and a carpentry workshop were built with them. Bricks were being used to build private houses for the collective farmers since 1957. The production of bricks cannot be increased because there is not sufficient electric power.

The farm has several smithies, a carpentry workshop, a harness shop, a mill, a sawmill (capacity three hundred cubic meters of wood a year), a small shop for making rope, and a buttery—all of which help to save money. All these workshops are mechanized and run by electric power from the farm's own station, except the buttery which has its own diesel motor.

Organization and management plays a major part in collective farm work. The farm is organized in the following way. A kolkhoz management board is elected by the collective farmers for a two-year term of office.[5] The board is responsible for planning all phases of work and production. Most of the farmers are divided into five territorial "brigades."[6] Each of these five brigades works a particular plot of land which, together with certain buildings (stables, barns, etc.) and equipment, is permanently assigned to it. Within each brigade a special team is appointed to cultivate maize. Those merely residing on the territory of the brigade are also considered members as well as those people actually engaged in work. The average number of people in a brigade is 110–20, of which seventy to seventy-five are usually engaged in the cultivation of field crops, and about twenty-five in cattle breeding and other areas of the collective farm's work. In 1955, for example, one of the five brigades had a total number of 113, of which forty-four men and sixty-four women were able to work. Seventy-six people cultivated the fields, ten were carpenters, two were drivers, three smiths, four dairy workers, and three construction workers. Fifteen people who were either older or incapacitated helped out when they could during the hay-mowing season.

All types of work (plowing, sowing, harvesting, and so on) must be done by the brigade. If it is unable to keep up with the field work in emergencies or when meeting deadlines, a small number of workers can be sent for, usually from other areas of farming, to help out for a short period.

Every evening the foremen of the brigades and other

[5] Chairmen of the collective farm either are elected from the local kolkhoz or are recommended by the administration; in either case, however, the chairman must be approved by the general meeting (Tr.).

[6] *Brigades*—The peasants work chiefly in brigades. The number of people in a brigade varies, depending on the size of the collective and the work performed. Each brigade is led by a brigadier who does the planning and the supervision and is responsible for the satisfactory performance of the brigade (Tr.).

managers meet in the kolkhoz management office to plan the work for the next day.

Fifty people on the farm were working as cattle breeders and beekeepers in 1956. Almost all of them had worked for over a year in their respective divisions. Cattle breeding is especially time-consuming and difficult to combine with a normal household routine because of the irregular hours involved. Therefore the majority of people working in that branch of production are men, single women, or widows with grown-up children. The earnings in cattle breeding are relatively high and the simple system of keeping accounts for each individual farmer stimulates the more ambitious workers. (Not only is the working time taken into consideration, but also the final results of an individual farmer's work, i.e., the quantity or quality of milk.) For this reason, cattle breeding is the most popular job and collective farmers working in this area are likely to continue in it for ten to fifteen years or more.

Specialized brigades also exist. The construction brigade consists of two teams of workers—bricklayers (one highly experienced master, three regular bricklayers and ten auxiliary women workers) and carpenters (ten to fifteen men). In cases of emergency the team of carpenters can be reinforced by workers from the field-crop cultivation brigades. This usually happens when there is a lighter work-load in the latter division.

The cultivation of field crops is the most important work done on the collective farm, and so most of the farmers are engaged in it. It is, of course, seasonal, since most of the work-load falls during the spring and summer months and fall and winter are slack periods. In the spring and summer, especially during June, July, and August, everybody is required to contribute his share, not merely those who are able-bodied and would as a rule be working, but the elderly and incapacitated and those who are generally not available for other reasons. There are fewer people working in the fields in September because many of the women begin cultivating their family allotments. The only work they do then on the kolkhoz is digging potatoes, and this only through the first two weeks of October when they stop working for the collective altogether and devote all their time to their individual plots of land. The seasonal nature of their principal occupation creates some special problems for the collective farmers. How can enough work be made available so that all persons can find employment at all times of the year? One solution would be to establish a processing plant on the farm to make fruit preserves, milk and cheese products, and to can vegetables and meat.

A certain number of workdays per year is required of each member of the collective who is able to work.[7] According to the 1942 ruling of the Council of Ministers of the USSR and the Central Committee of the Communist Party, the minimum number of workdays required on collective farms in the Tambov province was one hundred and twenty. In 1954 this figure was changed at the general meeting of collective farmers; it remained the same for women with several children, but became two hundred for men and one hundred fifty for women with no children.

Most of the men try to give as much time as they can to work on the kolkhoz, and the average number of working days is gradually increasing from year to year. In 1952 the average number of workdays for an able-bodied worker was 172; in 1953, 189; in 1954, 224; in 1955, 269. It should be stressed that the increase in the average number of days worked was directly proportionate to an in-

[7] Workdays—The individual peasant on a collective farm receives a share of the profit of the collective. Shares are measured in terms of so-called "workdays." Under a law of 1948 there are nine different labor day rates ranging from half a workday for the least skilled work, to two and a half workdays for the most skilled and most difficult. A minimum number of workdays must be earned by each member of the collective (Tr.).

crease in payment. On the other hand there were many members of the collective who worked less than the average number of days for a variety of reasons. These included not only women with large families of children, but the wives of men who were receiving good salaries. Toward the end of 1955 there were ten women able to work who did not. This problem was taken up in the general meeting of collective farmers and solved by hiking the salaries for less popular types of work, and stimulating interest in general. The management made long-term credit loans available in 1955 to those farmers who worked harder so they could build houses and buy cattle. These loans in 1956 totaled ten thousand rubles.

In 1954 the total income of the collective farm amounted to over a million rubles. Parallel to the increase in total income was an increase in the average incomes of the individual workers. In the very difficult years immediately after the war, 1947–51, the farmers were paid for the most part in grain (three and a half to six kilograms for one day of work). The cash payment evolved only very gradually, from eleven to twenty-five kopeks a workday. However the development of trade and an increase in the wholesale price of grain made payment on a cash basis more economically feasible for the collective farm. By 1952 the cash payment for one workday amounted to one ruble and twenty-one kopeks. It was also decided to fix the amount of grain payment at three and a half kilograms for one workday; this amount was found to be entirely adequate to supply all the wants of a family if each able-bodied worker in it worked the minimum number of days required. The management hopes to increase the amount of cash payment while maintaining the fixed payment of grain. A new practice was initiated in 1956. Each collective farmer was given an advance in cash at the end of each month, to be adjusted at the year's end according to the total income of the collective farm in proportion to the total number of days worked. This system encouraged the farmers to work harder and also influenced young people to remain on the farm instead of looking for jobs in the city. Many who left the kolkhoz are now trying to re-establish their membership in the community.

In 1955 the collective farm participated in the all-union agricultural exhibition and received a medal for its achievements. It was also given a truck as a prize and a number of the farmers received personal recognition and were awarded medals. In 1956 the farm became a permanent member of the exhibition. In that year the prize awarded it was a library, and its chairman received a silver medal.

The following is an extract from the charter of the new collective which was approved by the general meeting of its members on April 20, 1956.

CHARTER OF THE *"PUT' LENINA (LENIN'S WAY)"* AGRICULTURAL ARTEL
Sosnov district, Tambov Province

I. Objectives and purposes

1. The farm workers of the village of Viriatino in the Sosnov district have voluntarily united themselves into an agricultural collective by jointly owning the means of production and by organizing their labor on a joint basis in order to achieve a higher rate of productivity and thereby ensure a better life for themselves. The collective farm approach, the socialist approach, is the only correct one for farm workers. The members of the artel pledge themselves to strengthen their artel, to work conscientiously, to share the collective farm income derived from their labor, to safeguard public property, to comply with all the decisions of the Soviet State and thereby to make their collective farm economically strong and prosperous for all the members.

II. The land

2. The land occupied by the artel (like all other land in the USSR) is State property belonging to the entire people. In accordance with the laws of the Soviet State, it has been assigned to the artel for an unlimited period and may not be bought, sold, or leased by the collective.

Small plots of the collectivized land shall be allocated for personal use to each household on the collective farm for orchard or garden. The amount of personal land allocated by the collective to a household for personal use may vary from 0.15 to 0.4 hectares, depending on the amount of labor which able-bodied members of the family contribute to the common work of the artel and on the amount of land at the disposal of the collective farmers. It shall be allocated as follows:

(*a*) households whose members actively participate in the common work of the artel and who work the required minimum number of working days for members of households with two to three or more able-bodied members, or the required minimum number of working days for a single able-bodied member of a household with more than two non-able-bodied family dependents, shall be allotted up to 0.4 hectares of personal land;

(*b*) households whose able-bodied members regularly fail without valid reason to work the required minimum number of days, or where able-bodied members have of their own choice left the collective farm to earn money elsewhere and have left non-able-bodied members of their family on the collective farm shall be allotted from 0.15 to 0.25 hectares depending on the amount of labor contributed by the remaining able-bodied members of the family working on the collective farm and on the amount of labor contributed to the collective farm by other members of the family when they were still able-bodied;

(*c*) households consisting of families of two shall be allotted 0.15 to 0.25 hectares of personal land.

The amount of personal land to be allotted to each household shall be determined by the management board of the collective farm, and later confirmed by the general meeting of collective farmers.

Households consisting of tractor drivers and other members

of tractor teams living on the collective farm shall be allocated personal land in the amounts specified for members of the collective farm itself . . .

III. The means of production

4. All draft animals, agricultural implements (plows, seed drills, harrows, threshing machines, mowers, etc.), seed stocks, fodder in the amounts required for feeding the collectivized livestock, the farm buildings required for the common work of the artel, and all subsidiary enterprises shall be deemed to be the fixed assets of the collective farm.

The management board of the farm shall in case of need assign a certain number of horses from the pool of collectivized draft animals to serve the personal needs of members of the artel in return for payment at rates to be fixed by the management board. For journeys to the hospital, for the transport of products and animal fodder due in return for days worked, and for the delivery of building materials for the repair of buildings damaged by fire, draft animals shall be provided free of charge. For the transport of fuel and the cultivation of personal land draft animals shall be provided free of charge only to households in which all able-bodied members are working the required minimum number of working days. For households in which the able-bodied members have failed without valid reason to work the required minimum number of days during the previous years, draft animals shall be provided in return for payment at rates to be fixed by the management board of the collective farm.

5. Each household on the collective farm may personally own one cow and up to two calves, one sow with litter, up to ten sheep and goats (counted together), an unlimited amount of poultry, and up to ten beehives.

IV. The work of the artel and its management board

6. The management board and all members of the artel pledge themselves:

(*a*) to increase the yield of the collective farm land by introducing and observing the principles of correct rotation of crops, deep plowing, weed-killing, the extension and improvement of land cultivation, careful interrow cultivation at the appropriate time, the use of manure and mineral fertilizers, pest control, careful harvesting of crops at the appropriate time without wastage, forestry conservation, and the planting of forest shelter belts;

(*b*) to select the best seeds for sowing, to protect them with all possible care from pilfering and spoiling, to store them in clean, well-ventilated premises, and to expand the production of high-grade crops;

(*c*) to use to the fullest extent possible, and on a communal basis, all available draft animals, equipment, implements, seeds, and other means of production belonging to the artel, and to ensure proper care of the collectivized livestock (so that the livestock on the collective farm are in good condition);

(*d*) to increase the number and improve the strain and productivity of livestock on dairy farms; to provide fellow members who work conscientiously for the artel with assistance in obtaining a cow, sheep, and goats; to ensure that livestock on dairy farms and livestock belonging to members of the artel are served by pedigreed sires of improved strain and to observe the established principles of livestock breeding and veterinary science;

(*e*) to increase the production of fodder, to improve the quality of pasture and grasslands, to help members of the artel who have been contributing conscientiously to the common work of the collective farm by enabling them to use the collective farm pasture lands and, when possible, by providing them with fodder for the livestock personally owned by them, in return for days worked;

(*f*) to develop all other branches of agricultural production and domestic industry in accordance with the conditions prevailing on the collective farm, to clean all existing ponds and keep them in good condition and to make new ponds and breed fish in them;

(*g*) to build farm and community buildings on a collectivized basis;

(*h*) to improve the skills of members of the artel and to help the collective farmers by training them to be foremen, tractor drivers, combine harvester operators, truck drivers, veterinary assistants and orderlies, stable-men, swineherds, cowboys, and specialists in other fields;

(*i*) to raise the cultural level of members of the artel, to introduce newspapers and books, radio, and moving pictures, to provide bathhouses and barber shops, to tidy the streets and to plant trees of different varieties—particularly fruit trees— along them and to help collective farmers in improving and decorating their dwellings;

(*j*) to employ more women in the common work of the collective farm and encourage them to take a larger part in social life, to promote competent and experienced women members of the artel to responsible positions and to free them as far as possible from domestic work by organizing kindergartens and children's playgrounds . . .

VII. Labor: organization, remuneration and discipline

14. The agricultural work of the artel shall be carried out on a piece work basis. The management board of the artel shall prepare, and the general meeting shall approve, output norms for agricultural work of all kinds and working day valuations for each task.

Output norms attainable by a conscientious collective farm worker shall be established for each operation, due regard being paid to the condition of the livestock, machinery, and soil . . . Not less than once a week the foreman shall record the amount of work done by each member of the artel, and shall transmit these records to the management board of the collective farm for subsequent processing. Once every month the management board shall display a list of members of the artel, showing the number of working days each has worked during the past month.

15. Elderly people who have worked on the collective farm without interruption for a period of twenty-five years (including periods of military service and periods of training in the skills needed by the collective farm or at specialized agricultural training institutes) and who are not able to take part in the common work, and also invalids who have been injured in the course of their work on the collective farm, shall, if the general meeting of collective farmers so decides, be entitled to a personal pension equal to what they would receive for working twenty-five to fifty percent of the average annual number of days worked by them during the last twenty-five years of their active participation in the work of the collective farm, depending on the economic situation of the farm and having regard to the pensioner's past attitude to the common work of the artel.

Elderly men, seventy or more, and women sixty-five or over, who are still taking an active part in the work of the artel shall be entitled to an additional payment, equal to twenty-five percent more than the standard remuneration based on the minimum number of working days for the current year.

Persons who have been temporarily disabled in the course of their work on the collective farm shall, if the management board so decides, be entitled to an additional payment equal to twenty-five to fifty percent of their average monthly earnings during the last months of their active participation in the work of the collective farm.

16. Members of the collective farm who have fulfilled the output norms and have worked for a total of not less than three hundred working days in one calendar year shall be entitled, if the management board so decides, to paid holidays with an additional payment equal to their average monthly earnings over the last eleven calendar months, and collective farmers who have excelled at work shall be sent to rest homes or spas with their accommodation paid for by the collective farm and shall be entitled to an additional payment equal to their average monthly earnings during the current year. Accommodation in rest homes and spas shall be paid for if the member of the collective farm has worked on the collective farm for a period of not less than ten years without interruption and without any blemish on his record.

17. If as a result of commendable work a crop-farming team obtains from the land assigned to it a yield higher than the average yield for the collective farm or if as a result of improved working methods a livestock-farming team increases the yield of milk and the average fatness of its cattle and loses none of its calves, the management board of the artel shall award to all members of the team or section, or to the individual collective farmers concerned, a bonus amounting to twenty-five percent of the value of the output achieved over and above the planned figure. This bonus shall be distributed to members of the team, dairy farm, or section, or to individuals responsible for achievements of this kind in proportion to the number of working days worked.

If a subsidiary enterprise surpasses its target figures, or if construction work is completed before the specified time limit, a special reward may be paid if the management board of the collective farm so decides, within the limits of income and expenditure estimates for the current year or at the contractually established rates. Persons who have especially distinguished themselves at their work shall, if the management board so decides, be awarded bonuses in cash or kind. Their names shall be displayed on the board of honor and they shall be publicly thanked.

18. The income of the artel shall be distributed among its members exclusively on the basis of the number of working days worked by each member and of the additional allowances granted for old age, temporary disability, or leave.

19. Cash advances shall be made to members of the artel once every month throughout the year in amounts up to fifty percent of the sum planned for the remuneration of labor in the production plan. Advances in kind shall be made to the members of the artel from the time when threshing begins, in the amount of four kilograms of grain for each day worked.

20. All members of the collective farm undertake to work the following number of days during the year: able-bodied men— not less than two hundred days; women—not less than one hundred fifty days.

VIII. Management of the artel's affairs

22. The affairs of the artel shall be managed by a general meeting of its members and, in the intervals between the meetings, by a management board elected by the general meeting.

23. The general meeting is the highest organ of the artel . . .

24. The general meeting of members of the artel shall elect a management board consisting of seven members for a period of two years, to administer the affairs of the artel. The management board is the executive organ of the artel, and is responsible to the General Assembly for the work of the artel and for the fulfillment of its obligations to the State.

26. Foremen and managers of livestock farms shall be appointed by the management board for a period of not less than two years.

A Collective Farmer's Family Budget

The economic life in the village of Viriatino is not limited, of course, to the collective economy.[8] A particular piece of land is also allotted to each family in the community.[9] Almost every family owns a certain amount of livestock; most have a cow, one or two pigs, some sheep, and poultry. Those who live in Viriatino but are not members of the kolkhoz also have small vegetable gardens and some livestock and poultry. The average size of a piece of land allotted to a family which belongs to the kolkhoz is about 0.4 hectare. A family that does not belong receives on the average of 0.15 to 0.25 hectare.

The crops planted are usually potatoes, cucumbers, cabbages, carrots, onions, and tomatoes. Some families, especially those of widows and those in which there are many children, plant a portion of their land with millet,

[8] The main sources which the authors of this book use to explain the economics of the kolkhoz household were an investigation of twenty-four budgets of kolkhoz families, and three budgets of local intelligentsia. The studies showed that in order to clarify the characteristic standards of living of the families, the budget for one year is not enough. In most of the kolkhoz homesteads, the grain was carried over from one year to another. In those households where there are many working members, the sale of surplus grain enabled them to build new houses, buy furniture, and so on.

[9] *Private plot*—Under the Soviet law, a small plot of land is allotted to each peasant household for the family use. The plot is given only to those households whose members belong to the collective farm since all village land is given by the State to the collective in perpetuity. In addition to the allotted plot of land, the size of which depends on the type of collective farm, the household may own one cow, two calves, one sow and sucklings, ten sheep and goats, twenty beehives, and unlimited numbers of chickens and rabbits (Tr.).

retaining some for personal use but selling most of it as produce. The chaff is used for fodder. Some families periodically plant hemp which is used for making homespun cloth for bedding and also for making storage sacks. A number of families cultivate mahorka, home-grown tobacco, which is especially profitable because the government pays a good price for a kilogram of first quality. Some members of the kolkhoz also sell mahorka in local markets.

As a rule all members of a family, including teenagers, work the family plot, but the bulk of the work is done by the women because the men work on the collective farm itself. The management of the kolkhoz provides all the necessary equipment for farming the allotted land, and the families rent it. Each family owns the simplest kind of equipment, which they replace regularly as it wears out. Because of recent changes in the tax legislation on agriculture there is a certain tendency among the families to increase fruit growing. The Viriatino farmers take pride in growing fruit trees, and most cultivate apple trees, having properly studied books on the subject.

It has become increasingly difficult for a single family to keep cows because of the short supply of fodder. Until recently the collective farm did not provide the necessary amount of fodder to individual families for maintaining livestock. The farmers who take in the hay get only ten to twenty percent of the total harvest and so two families will very often share ownership of a single cow. In most cases these are families related by blood or marriage; they alternate pasturing and feeding the animal from week to week and its milk goes to whichever family happens to be caring for it. Almost every family keeps a pig. Baby pigs are bought in the spring, usually from the collective farm, and are kept and fattened for from eight to nine months or until they weigh from 220 to 330 pounds. The meat is usually kept and eaten by the family, although some of the more prosperous households will sell part of it in the local markets. Almost every family owns sheep and uses the wool for making felt boots, stockings, gloves, and shawls; if a family has three or more sheep some of the wool is marketed. The offspring are usually sold by the poorer families and slaughtered for food by the more prosperous ones.

Obtaining fuel is a rather difficult problem for the collective farmers. A certain amount of peat is available on the land belonging to the collective farm, and according to an agreement between the farmers and the collective farm, any farmer may keep half of all the peat he gathers; the other half goes to the farm. If a farmer wishes to keep all the peat he gathers, he must pay for the half which would ordinarily go to the farm. The price is 6.2 rubles per ton. A certain amount of firewood is usually burned in winter time.

A family's income is derived from two main sources, wages paid in cash or kind by the collective farm and gains from the individual plot of land. In some families a salary received for work outside the farm also contributes a major portion to their total income. There are also cases in which the head of the family works permanently in industry, or works only seasonally on the farm and at other times of the year in some other capacity outside of Viriatino. Very often a girl will have a job off the farm for part of the year to earn extra money.[10] The ratio of people who are able to work to those who are entirely dependent is also significant. If the number of family members able to work is at least equal to the number of dependents, a suitable standard of living is ensured. Most of the women who do not work the required minimum of workdays for the collective farm come from the more prosperous families.

Those families without able-bodied men are presented

[10] A family census taken in Viriatino in 1953 shows that almost 22 percent of the population of the village were living and working outside of Viriatino, sending part of their earnings to parents, brothers, sisters, and some other relatives.

with special difficulties as there is no one available for doing heavy work and repairs around the house. The woman
who is the head of the family must either ask a relative to
help her or pay a hired worker. It should be emphasized,
however, that if the woman is a war widow the income
she earns by working on the collective farm together with
the pension paid her by the State is sufficient to enable
her to maintain a moderately high standard of living. In
1953 there were 456 families in Viriatino, 248 headed by
men and 208 by women. Twenty percent (208 families)
had no adult men.

Families can be divided into three major groups: (1)
the ordinary collective farm families which can be further
broken down to (*a*) those working exclusively in field-
crop cultivation; (*b*) those working exclusively with livestock; and (*c*) those working in both areas; (2) the families
of the collective farm specialists and managers; (3) the
families in which some members receive a salary for work
done outside the kolkhoz. Taking into consideration the
ratio between those who are able to work and those who
are dependent, each group mentioned above can be further
subdivided into the following variants:

A. families in which the number of persons able to work
   is at least equal to the number of dependents;
B. families in which the number of dependents is greater
   than the number of persons able to work; and
C. families in which the only adult member is a widow.

Let us first consider the typical budget of an ordinary collective farm family (Group 1).

There are 276 such families in the village. Within this
group 189 families (or 68.5 percent) represent variant A,
i.e., the families with a favorable correlation of working
members and dependents. Variant B, in which group the
number of people able to work is less than the number
of dependents, is represented by 46 families, or 16.6 percent. Families in which the only person able to work is a

widowed mother, variant C, includes 41 families, or 14.9 percent of Group 1.

Variant A. The majority of the families included in variant A (67.4 percent) are engaged in field-crop cultivation. The rest (32.6 percent) combine that type of work with work in other areas of the collective farm economy, livestock breeding and construction, for instance. It should be pointed out that these families are the more prosperous ones. The budget of E. A. Diakov's family is a typical example of the group working in field-crop cultivation. The ratio of able-bodied workers to dependents is 2:2. In 1954–55 when data was gathered the family consisted of four persons, two aged parents, their daughter-in-law (the widow of their son who had been killed in the war), and their granddaughter, a fifteen-year-old high-school student. Both E. A. Diakov, the head of the family, and his daughter-in-law work in field-crop cultivation. In 1954 they accumulated 534 workdays between them and according to standard calculations received 1.87 tons of edible grain and 293.7 rubles in cash. In addition the daughter-in-law receives 132.0 rubles in government pension as a soldier's widow with one child. The family needs at least 1.10 tons of grain annually (a certain amount of grain for cattle is included). They do not sell any grain although the yearly surplus is about one ton. They have a well-tended garden in which potatoes and other kinds of vegetables are raised for market, and they own a cow, a heifer, two sheep with lambs, and about ten hens. Every year a pig is raised for slaughter and is usually killed when its weight reaches 245–290 pounds. Thus the family is well provided with food, including meat, butter, and milk. The only products it has to buy are sugar, groats, and fine flour. Clothing expenses are not high as the adults buy clothes only for work. The daughter-in-law used to provide both her own and her daughter's clothing out of her pension, which, as a matter of fact, is not taken into account in intrafamily calculations. In 1955 her father-in-law gave her a considerable sum of money to be used for clothing for herself and her daughter.

Variant B. As had already been noted, the number of persons able to work here is less than the number of dependents. Fifty percent of the families included are engaged in cattle breeding or construction work, both of which pay better than average, or else combine one of these with field-crop cultivation. The main worker, not necessarily the only one in the family, is the head. The mother who has to look after children accumulates a small number of workdays as a rule, usually below the established minimum. Large families are not only well supplied with bread but in addition have other stored supplies. All collective farm families have sufficient quantities of all the products they need if they plan carefully. Since the cash payment per workday was increased (1954 and 1955) the financial position of each family has improved. The budget for A. B. Makarov's family, which can be considered a typical example of Group 1, variant B, was carefully analyzed. The family consists of six persons, husband, wife, and four children (the older children attend school). The main worker is the head of the family who works during the summer as an accountant in charge of a team of tractor workers and in winter in the cattle yard. Because of poor health his wife earns only a few workdays each year.

In 1953 the family accumulated 502 workdays and received 1.36 tons of grain (the amount they need annually is 1.10 tons). They also received 133 rubles in cash (80.7 rubles were paid for work on the tractor team). Thus, the sources of income for the family were cash in payment for workdays, the father's pension (he is a disabled veteran), state allowance for the fourth child, and income from household plot husbandry. In 1954–55 the financial situation of the family improved. In 1954 they accumulated 540 workdays and received 1.89 tons of grain and 352.4 rubles in cash; in 1955 they accumulated 647 workdays and were paid 2.26 tons of grain and 626.9 rubles in cash. In addition they received 64.0 rubles in allowances from the state.

The family plot of land (four hundred square meters) is usually planted with potatoes, vegetables, millet, and mahorka. Fifteen apple trees were planted in 1955. The family also owns a cow, three sheep, and ten hens, and every year it raises a pig. In the summer the staple foods are dairy products, vegetables, and eggs.

The greater portion of the family's expenses is for clothing, especially for the children, and the requirements as to quality are growing stricter. In 1954 the mother went to Moscow twice to buy better winter coats for the two older children. Considerable sums of money were also spent for educational purposes, i.e., about 100 rubles a year on the two older children attending Kulevatovo High School (tuition is 30 rubles a year; lodging, 4 rubles a month; pocket money, 0.5 ruble a week). The average ration of food sent to the children each week was two to four pounds of meat, two to four pounds of groats, about half a pound of butter and the same of sugar, thirteen to seventeen pounds of bread, and nine to thirteen pounds of potatoes.

Group 2 is composed of families of collective farm specialists and managers. It has a higher proportion of families falling under variant B (33.3 percent) than do the other groups. This fact can be easily explained. The salary of a specialist or manager is higher than that of the average collective farmer and he is better able to support a large family and so the living standards for the family of a specialist or manager are much higher than those of a collective farmer's family. Consequently more money is spent on building, home alterations, furniture, clothing, etc.

The family of M. P. Mishin, a collective farm electrician, may serve as a typical example. The family consists of three persons, husband, wife, and a six-year-old son.

Over several years they were able to save enough from Mishin's salary to cover the costs of the purchase of a house, alterations, interior decoration, and modern furniture. Each year they spent considerable sums on better clothing and footwear.

Another example of budgeting in this group is the family of G. G. Matrochin, a collective farm carpenter. This was the last example of an extended family in Viriatino. In 1952 it consisted of eight persons, two old parents and two sons with their wives and children. There were five working members, two of them well-paid specialists (the elder daughter-in-law, a collective farm bookkeeper; and a younger son, a veterinarian), and three dependents (two small children and the mother of one of the daughters-in-law). A traditional pattern of life prevailed in this family. The younger generation did not interfere in the housekeeping since the older father managed all family affairs and decided how to spend the money earned by all the members.

In 1952 the family accumulated 1974 workdays and received 7.70 tons of grain, approximately the same amount that had been received in 1950. Since they needed only one to two tons of grain a year the surplus was very large (worth about five and a half to six thousand rubles). In addition to the grain the family earned 454 rubles in cash in 1952. They had a standard size vegetable garden (four thousand square meters) which was generally planted with potatoes. Income was entirely adequate for an acceptable standard of living. The family did not take advantage of its material opportunities, however, since their style of living was limited by the traditions of an extended family.

They had no food problems. Throughout the year (with the exception of summer) the family was provided with meat and there were no limitations on milk, sour cream, cheese, etc. Very little had to be purchased, for example, sugar, fish, fruit, and candies for the children. They did not, however, invest any money in improving their house, which consisted of two large rooms—one of them serving as a kitchen and also as a bedroom for the older parents, and the other, called a gornitcha, providing living quarters for the two young married couples.

In 1954 the family income rose again; they earned 6.45 tons of grain and 1014.4 rubles in cash. In 1953–54 two grandsons were born, one to each of the married sons. As a result the extended family separated and the older son and his family settled in a new house. Some grain was sold (3.2 tons) and the money was spent for the purchase of the house. Besides this they received 4.7 tons of grain, a cow with a calf, one sheep, and some hens, as well as an individual plot of land (four thousand square meters). In 1955 the young and now independent family accumulated 1294 workdays, 4.5 tons of grain, and 1365 rubles in cash. All of this is equivalent to 2588 rubles.

Group 3, which includes some salaried workers, is composed of families with a so-called "mixed budget." Among the thirty-six families in Group 3, thirty-two constitute variant A and only four constitute variant B. Analysis of these families is interesting because it shows that the cash salaries received by some of their members has a favorable effect on all aspects of their mode of life.

The family of a collective farm carpenter, P. E. Putchkov, is a typical example in this respect. It includes five persons, Putchkov, his wife, a son by his first marriage (a schoolboy), and Putchkov's elderly parents. Putchkov's father works in forestry and is considered the head of the family, Putchkov works himself as does his wife, a collective farmer. In 1953 the family worked 532 days for the kolkhoz and earned 103.7 rubles in cash. Putchkov also earns an extra income (about 300 rubles a year) as a qualified carpenter making window frames and furniture for sale. A certain income is provided from their collective farm holdings as well (about 140 rubles in 1953). This family has much more money at its disposal than the average Viriatino family. The portion of the family income received in cash is 61.2 percent, while the figure for the majority of families in Viriatino is 15 to 20 percent in cash. This influences all aspects of the family's mode of life—from the appearance of the house and furnishings to the quality of the food they eat.

Some families are in a rather exceptional situation inasmuch as they are becoming oriented toward city life. The next two examples are typical.

E. Neverov, a former miner by trade, worked in a coal mine in the Donbass in winter time and on the collective farm during the summer. His family, a wife and three children, lived in Viriatino all year round. The annual number of workdays accumulated by the family had been decreasing. In 1951 they worked 334 days; in 1952, 192. The main source of income for this family was the salary earned by its head. In the spring of 1953 they left Viriatino and settled in the Donbass for good. The family of P. Diakov, also a mine worker, followed much the same pattern for a time. The head of the family worked as a miner in the winter and on the collective farm during the summer. In 1952 he earned 783.9 rubles for four months of work during the winter, 400 of which he sent to his family. His income for four summer months was 208.5 rubles. Thus his real income was 608.5 rubles a year. The figures for 1953 were 365 rubles in salary, 70 rubles of which he sent to the family and 179 rubles earned on the collective farm. In 1954 and 1955 he worked on the collective farm throughout the year. His net income for 1954 was 404 rubles and for 1955, 510 rubles, only 98 rubles less than his earnings in 1952, his most successful year in which he combined work on the collective farm with work in the Donbass.

In 1955–56 there was no one in Viriatino who preferred to work away from the community, even during the winter.

The economic position of families headed by women has some special features. Of 208 such families in Viriatino, forty-one include no male members who are able to work.

Of these forty-one, fifteen are permanently supported by members of the family who live and work outside the community (usually older children). The women who work in the cattle and dairy industry earn more than those who are engaged in field-crop cultivation. A. M. Kalmikova, a dairy maid, for example, accumulated 508 workdays in 1955 comparable to 1016 rubles in cash. E. M. Starodubova, a herdswoman, accumulated 581 workdays equal to 1162 rubles. But only women who have a mother free to look after the children and do all the necessary housework are able to work with livestock because of the irregular time schedule involved. A predominant number of women who are heads of families therefore work in field-crop cultivation, usually accumulating from 150 to 160 workdays a year, which means they receive about 0.9 ton of grain plus a certain amount of money. This is quite adequate for two people (usually a mother and child). A household plot usually provides the family with other food products. Only 58.2 percent of the families headed by women own a cow, however, since keeping a cow is difficult for a woman without the help of someone else (usually relatives).

A. D. Kusovova's husband was killed in the war in 1941, leaving her a widow with three children ranging in age from four to twelve. Prior to the war this family had been prosperous; they had a large store of grain, a cow, and sheep, all of which helped to tide them over the difficult war years. By intensive work on the collective farm and with the help of her government pension, A. D. Kusovova was able to raise and educate all three of her children. The family currently consists of the mother and two daughters, as the son went to Moscow to work in a factory after being demobilized in 1954. The widow and her daughters continued to work on the kolkhoz in field-crop cultivation. Year by year their economic situation has improved. In 1953 the family accumulated 408 workdays and received

1.0 tons of grain and 79.5 rubles in cash; in 1954, 413 workdays, 1.4 tons of grain and 235 rubles in cash; in 1955, 502 workdays, 1.7 tons of grain, and 401.6 rubles in cash. The family land allotment (four thousand square meters) is used to grow potatoes, vegetables, and mahorka for sale. They own a cow, a sheep with lambs, and a pig. Food is no problem. Clothes are a major item of expense in the family's budget, however, since there are two young girls in the family.

An analysis of family budgets typical of Viriatino's collective farmers leads to two conclusions. A fixed payment based on the number of days worked guarantees the farmers an adequate amount of food and also allows them to store supplies. They are able to improve their living conditions with the income derived from the sale of produce at market.

After a fixed payment was established for a single day's work in terms of grain (7.7 pounds), the cash payment was tripled. This cash increase was progressively reflected in all aspects of the collective farmer's life. Gradually the farmers began to raise their standards in housing, clothing, food, etc. There is evidence of a tendency among them to vary the use of their individual allotments of land. Millet is gradually disappearing, and in 1955 the number of fruit trees noticeably increased. A smaller part of the yield from the allotment is reserved for sale in local markets; more of the garden produce is being used instead to improve the diet at home. On the other hand, the higher-income families prefer to sell the produce from their allotments and buy what were long considered typical "city" products with the proceeds; these include wool and silk clothing, sewing machines, and furniture. But even for this type of family the land allotment remains a secondary source of income, and the economic position of the family is directly proportionate to the annual number of days worked on the collective farm.

CHAPTER VIII

THE CONTEMPORARY ARCHITECTURE
OF VIRIATINO

The years of Soviet rule produced great changes in the outward appearance of Viriatino and in the nature of its buildings. Of the 406 dwelling houses now in the village, 170 (41.87 percent) were built after the October Revolution.

A well-built wooden house will stand for forty to fifty years, but the usable life of a brick house is considerably longer—over one hundred years. As the village had many brick buildings that were built before the Revolution there was no need to replace these with new ones; they needed only to be modernized. Nevertheless, the construction of new housing was begun immediately after the Revolution. The redistribution of land on a new basis, the large families dividing into smaller groups, and the married children receiving their own farms meant that a greater number of households came into being in the village. The formation of the new peasant households led to the rapid growth of the village and to a development of the outskirts. On the former landlords' properties where there had previously been mansions and service buildings there was now a new street called Vyselka (Vyselka are literally "people who have left their homesteads"). Here the newly divided families were settled. The street extended from Sosnovskaya Street, ran in a northwest direction, and turned at a right angle toward the Chelnovaya River. It was built so that houses stood only on the right side so that all the houses could face the river, and the vegetable gardens behind them could extend all the way down to the Pishlyaïka River. The barns were built directly across the street. At the street's end where the river no longer permitted the houses to be built in one line, a second row of dwellings was built on the left side of the street. At the same time the very end of Pesok Street was developed and had fifteen houses constructed upon it.

In the beginning of the 1920s sixty wooden and twenty brick houses were built in the village, eliminating the poor shacks of prerevolutionary times. The return to the use of wood is understandable; in the years immediately after the Revolution it was primarily only the poor who were building new houses, and bricks were completely beyond their means. Lumber, however, was offered to them and to the veterans of the Red Army at reduced prices. The considerable difficulty in obtaining both iron and brick made wooden houses more feasible.

During the years of the Civil War when Antonov's bands were in control of the Tambov province, houses were built in haste and their construction differed in no way from the wooden houses built in the nineteenth century. They all had log foundations and straw roofs, and consisted usually of one room with a tile or wicker hallway. The stove stood in its traditional place although the sleeping berths and the built-in benches were no longer present. As the peasants' way of life gradually changed and the population became more educated there were changes in the traditional layout of houses.

Improvements in the construction of dwellings started after the end of the Civil War when national economic reconstruction was begun. The peasant farms and households were quickly restored. The food allotment system enabled the peasants of Viriatino to sell their surplus grain. This money was used to buy cattle, build dwellings, and take care of other necessities.

During the N.E.P. years steel began to be used as roofing material. Clay and straw roofs and five-walled houses were very popular. Five-walled huts were rare until 1917. The living space in them consisted of a kitchen and a chamber. The plans of these huts were like those of the brick cottages built in the 1900s, with the exception that the wooden huts had only a backyard entrance. In nearly all five-walled huts, as in the brick cottages, the stove stood in the corner by the door on the outside wall, with its opening facing the street. In order to build the chamber in the brick houses the stove was moved toward the door. In the 1920s the dominant type of dwelling house came to be one in which the stove was placed in the corner by the door, with its opening toward the side wall. This made it possible to more fully utilize the limited living space. This type of interior plan is prevalent in Viriatino today.

In the living chamber of the wooden dwelling, a tiled stove (Dutch style) was placed opposite the middle of the rear wall. It faced the backyard and there were sleeping areas on either side. A popular practice was to close off the beds with curtains or screens. This use of curtains was new and indicated a desire for a separate place to sleep with the illusion of a separate bedroom.

A considerable improvement in the furnishings of houses began in the second half of the 1920s. More emphasis was placed on cleanliness; the walls and floors of the wooden dwellings were washed more frequently and the walls of the brick cottages were whitewashed two or three times a year. Tables were always covered with tablecloths; oilcloth became very popular. It became a widespread practice to hang curtains at windows; cotton curtains were often hung in front of the opening to the tile stove and in front of the smoke pipe, and sometimes on doors. Walls were papered, or decorated with posters and pictures depicting the civil war. Photographs were starting to become popular as wall decorations. The influence of the urban

bourgeoisie which had made itself felt at the beginning of
the twentieth century turned out, however, to be one of the
most tenacious survivals of capitalism, and the living room
was usually coarsely and tastelessly decorated.

At the same time the wooden homes were being built,
the old brick houses underwent inner reconstruction.
Families that were growing and splitting up divided these
buildings into two or three isolated parts. With the re-
habilitation of the national economy in the second half
of the 1920s, construction of brick dwellings again became possible, and twenty were built. The housing resources of the village pretty much took care of all the needs
of the population at this time, and new dwellings (either
brick or wood) were built only by those peasants whose
homes had fallen into decay. Usually two or three households that planned to build brick dwellings would unite
to buy the furnace, build a brick shed, make the bricks
for their buildings, and sell what was left over. There were,
however, only two peasant families in Viriatino who made
selling bricks their livelihood.

The new brick dwellings were an improvement on the
old ones. In the years after the Revolution there were
many bricklayers in Viriatino from Sosnov, who apparently
were familiar with urban brick construction methods since
the walls of the new buildings in Viriatino were put together in a more attractive fashion with the bricks with
the narrow side facing out. Windows became rectangular
and much larger and the ceilings were built much higher.
The rafters were not placed directly on the walls as in the
old dwellings but were attached to beams (which were
vertically placed over the walls so that the rafters extended
beyond them). There were iron or board partitions separating the living chamber from the kitchen. A Russian
stove was usually placed in the kitchen in the corner by
the entrance with its opening to the lateral wall. The roofs
were made steeper and were covered with iron.

Contemporary Viriatino — Kolkhoz Construction

Basic changes in the dwellings and in the external appearance of the village took place only after the collectivization of agriculture, when the needs of the kolkhoz required new structures. New large-scale developments have included the erection of large farm buildings, the creation of a village center to house administrative and cultural agencies, and the building of a hydroelectric station and a water tower, all of which have virtually transformed the appearance of Viriatino.

A large building was built in 1957 for the kolkhoz management and for the village soviet. A handsome two-story brick building that was to serve as the kolkhoz club and which gave the village its final architectural touch was also constructed, using a design the kolkhoz brigade had worked out themselves. On the first floor of the club there was built an auditorium capable of seating three hundred people, a library, a reading room, a day nursery, and a room to be used for table games. Provision was made on the second floor for a sitting room, a classroom, a radio relay center, and a film booth. The square in front of the club came to be a favorite hangout for the young people.

Behind the club, on the territory of the new kolkhoz park, the log buildings of the elementary and junior high schools were raised. Not far from the elementary school, in what was once a private home, the post office was located. At the fork of the Upper and Lower Lanes, a large brick building was constructed to house a village cooperative.

The new farm buildings of the kolkhoz were brought out to the northern outskirts and situated on both sides of Sosnovskaya Street. The central cattle farm was made to occupy a substantial grassy territory, which was protected by a fence. In the course of a few postwar years the former clay buildings of the kolkhoz were replaced by well-built brick barns, constructed according to a standard design; these included marvelously equipped cow-sheds, calf-sheds, stables, pigsties, sheep pens, and feeding kitchens. Towering silos were erected next to the cattle barns. Plans for the future include a comfortable hostel, to be built on the central site of the kolkhoz to accommodate all the farm workers when they are on call for night or emergency duty. In 1957 the brick works with their drying sheds and hay storage were moved from Sosnovskaya Street, opposite the proposed hostel, and poultry barns were set up in place of the drying sheds.

The enormous water tower was built in 1952. The two kolkhoz hydroelectric stations were located on Pishlyaika and Chelnovaya rivers, one next to the cattle barns and the other farther away from the village, next to the water mill. To the south of Kulevatovskaya Street (on Sand Street) on what used to be fallow land the industrial workshops, otherwise known as "garages," have been built. The repair shops and warehouses storing farm inventory which are clay-covered wooden buildings have been made to form a closed rectangle. Separate buildings have been constructed for the blacksmith shop, the steamroom for the wheel rims, the guard booth, the creamery (constructed of brick), sheds for drying mahorka, and stands for cutting large logs. The whole "garage" area has been enclosed by a wooden fence.

Much attention has also been given to the organization of public services and amenities in Viriatino in the last few years, and electric lighting has also helped to transform completely the outward appearance of the village. The storage sheds that used to stand in the middle of the street have been moved to the kolkhoz farmsteads so that the streets could be widened and planted with trees and shrubs. Oreshnik Street and Polyana Street, both central routes, were reconstructed in this manner. In recent years it has been forbidden to build houses lengthwise along the street as a fire precaution, and most of the houses have been built with their narrow side to the street so that there is plenty of space between them.

Almost all of the houses have a front garden in which lilacs, acacia, willows, birches, and cherry trees are grown. In recent years there has been a marked interest in cultivation of flowers; hollyhocks, dahlias, and asters are grown in the front gardens. The trees in these gardens both protect the homes from dust and beautify the street.

Not far from the old village cemetery, about two kilometers southeast of the village, an area was chosen for the new cemetery. It was cleared and planted with trees.

A firehouse and tower were built close to the village soviet on Oreshnik Street in 1935. The fire-fighting equipment in the beginning consisted only of two hand pumps and three barrels and hooks but the kolkhoz obtained a motor pump in 1951. Lately, however, the management of the kolkhoz has tended to pay less attention to fire prevention measures; watchmen who are not always familiar with the equipment are appointed instead of trained firemen. The village is well supplied with water, however, as there are many wells in the streets and in the yards of the villagers. An artesian well was drilled in 1955 and water pipes were laid. In 1958 the populace of Viriatino was supplied by seven water hydrants. Plans for the future have stipulated that every street have its own water supply.

Eighty-five wooden residential buildings in all were constructed in the village after the collectivization of agriculture. Those built in the first years were not distinguishable in design, construction technique, or general appearance from the residential buildings constructed just after the Revolution. Residential construction in the first years of collectivization moved along at a very slow tempo, for the full-scale construction of public utility buildings of the kolkhoz employed all of the construction force of the village. The brick works was bogged down with orders from the kolkhoz builders, thus making the use of wood in the construction of residential buildings a necessity.

But great booms and changes in the planning and construction of residential buildings began in the second half of the 1930s and especially after the Second World War (there were only seven houses built during the war). Crowded living conditions could not have been solely responsible for the erection of new houses, since, for the last decade at least, Viriatino's population has remained unchanged since the birth rate has been offset by the outpouring of workers into industry. It was, simply, a rising standard of living that made better housing conditions possible. The consumer budgets of the village populace show that most people had the necessary financial resources to build new houses or to modernize their old ones.

In the long run it has been the great strength of the kolkhoz system that made it possible to improve their living conditions. This fact is mirrored in the nature of residential building today. Each builder strives to choose the best construction for his house, make the house attractive, and furnish it according to his tastes and needs. This is why it has been so important to study the construction and design of new houses in Viriatino; the findings are often indicative of the level of the standard of living and yield facts about the particular cultural needs of the villagers.

As a result of the above-mentioned factors, residential construction has undergone tremendous changes in the last decade. Also, on the whole, the builders have been better qualified. Homes are built by the kolkhoz building brigade, most of whom had experience at the front working on the construction of complicated installations, and had become qualified specialists. Many of the houses having the best architecture, construction, and quality were built in the postwar years by the village carpenter working on his own time after hours.

There have been great changes, too, in the structure of

the foundation for wooden buildings. Many of the houses built in the last twenty years are placed on wooden blocks the same way as before, but the spaces between these blocks are now filled with brick about twenty inches in height. Trade organizations, taking into consideration the needs of the village populace, supplied the village general store with cement and so enabled the people to build their houses on cemented brick pedestals about thirteen to twenty inches high, or at least on cement foundations instead of wooden blocks.

The ceiling beams, as previously, are notched into the penultimate rim, but the structure of the ceiling and roof has been generally perfected. Previously the supporting beams had been scant and wide apart, but under the new system more of them were used and these were placed closer together in order to form a stronger skeleton. The attics in some of the houses have been converted into auxiliary summer lodgings; windows have been installed and floors laid. The attic can then be used for drying grain or for storing fruits and vegetables, and in the summer the young people can sleep in it. For better heating and for easier upkeep inside, the inner walls of some of the wooden houses have been plastered, while the outer ones have been shingled and painted.

A tragedy occurred in May 1953 in the village when a fire destroyed all the buildings that housed the livestock as well as twelve dwelling houses. Five of the houses were brick, but only the walls remained standing. Regional public organizations displayed great concern for the victims and lumber was immediately supplied to those who needed it. The kolkhoz first had to rebuild the barns and utility houses that had burned down, and thus it had difficulty providing those workers whose homes had burned with the necessary carpenters. But by working in the evenings after 7 P.M. and on Sundays the carpenters were able to help in the rebuilding of the homes as well. The entire process of residential rebuilding was undertaken by a building commission in Viriatino in the summer of 1953, and by the fall of 1953 those who were displaced had been resettled into newly built or repaired houses.

Some of the ancient customs are still observed in the construction of houses. The ritual begins with the cutting of the framework, for which a carpenter is hired. Before he hires anyone the owner invites carpenters to visit him, discusses price with them, and then serves refreshments. When a price is settled upon the framework is divided into three parts, and the first layers of logs are placed and notched for setting the floor wood into them. Notches are made on the top logs for ceiling beams. These log frames must dry for two weeks and the foundation is laid during this drying period. The remainder of the logs are fitted into place after that.

The framework is still assembled according to ancient custom, "with helpers." Thirteen to fifteen helpers—family and friends—gather on a Sunday. Of these, three or four are women who spread out moss on the logs. The kolkhoz member Kalmykov, for example, had three women and nine men helpers. The lower logs were put into place before the framework was assembled, and a table covered with a red cloth was placed in the center and a round loaf of bread placed upon it. First everybody kneeled to pray and then at 8 A.M. they began to put together the framework. Money was placed on the moss covering the first layer of logs as a symbol. The framework was assembled by four o'clock in the afternoon, and after that there was a celebration with sounds of gay voices and singing and dancing. Carpenters were hired again to finish off work begun by the others. The cracks between the logs were filled with moss, the roof lathwork was done and then covered, the floors were laid and the windows and doors fitted.

Aside from the construction of new buildings, the collective farmers carried out important work in the modernization of the old brick buildings. Some of these buildings were underpinned with a newly cemented brick foundation, and the old crumbling bricks were replaced by new ones. Inside, the walls were plastered with a mixture of alabaster, sand, and lime in order to prevent their getting wet. For outdoor plastering a mixture of cement, lime, and sand was used. Floors and ceilings in the old houses were relaid; plywood and lined ceilings had become very popular. The roofs were rebuilt in many of the brick houses, the walls covered with wall plates, and roof extensions and cornices installed. "In the old times they did everything without thinking," recounted an old carpenter. A binding of thick steel wire has been used in order to save the brick walls for the last fifteen years. The insides of the brick walls were covered with thin planks in many of the houses as the four-inch layer of air between the brick and the plank protected the inside of the building from dampness. These buildings required less fuel because the air was dry.

A great many changes are taking place in the size of homes and in the design of living quarters. With the growth of prosperity and a raising of the cultural level there are new demands. The collective farmers are no longer satisfied with the old uncomfortably designed interiors and the cramped living quarters.

When the size of the house is increased, the number of square feet or yards allowed per lodger is greater accordingly. The usable living area in the new houses fluctuates between forty-two and fifty-two square yards. The size of a family varies, but usually it is made up of three to six members, meaning about seven to fourteen square yards per person. In order to enlarge the living area in the old houses they often added a wooden three-walled structure to be used as a kitchen. Consequently, the living area in the old houses at the present time is approximately the same as in the newer buildings.

Today, the house of the collective farmer consists of a kitchen and a living chamber. There are four hundred and six houses in Viriatino, but many of these are shared by two or three families, and so there are actually over four hundred and eighty living units. Sixty-six of these buildings consist of one room (with the kitchen not separated). The addition or separation of the kitchen in many other houses has only recently been accomplished. The building of additional kitchens often takes place in conjunction with the dividing up of the old houses among several families.

Usually a young person or a widowed daughter-in-law wants to be detached from an overgrown family. These people cannot always build a separate house and so the living area in the present house has to be reapportioned; this happens very frequently in the old brick buildings. The process of adding a kitchen onto the separated part of the building is then carried on. Formerly it was rare to find a built-on or separate kitchen. In the case of a widow's being left in a two-roomed dwelling (kitchen and living room) with her father-in-law it was quite seldom that she would have a built-on or separated kitchen, even if she wanted one. Over the last few years, however, as shown by an analysis of the consumers' budgets, the economic position of widow has significantly improved. Some of them have the opportunity to spend considerable sums either on major repairs or on building a kitchen.

The interior layouts of the houses in the village are varied. In many of the old buildings the Russian stove was moved several times in the search for a more rational use of the living area.[1] In the brick buildings where two or three families lived together, the placement of the stove had always depended on where the entrance was and also on the position of the house with respect to the street. If the house was situated lengthwise along the street with the entrance

[1] *Russian stoves* are made of bricks covered over with clay. In the front there is a wood-burning range on which the cooking is done. In back of the range is a high bread-oven. It is formed into a broad stairway on the top, the steps of which serve as beds for the children and older people (Tr.).

in the lateral wall, the stove stood in the kitchen, in the back corner in its traditional place, or in the corner by the door, with its opening directed to the lateral wall. If the entrance to the house was located in the back wall, then most often the stove stood in the corner by the door with its opening facing the street.

In the small brick houses which stood with the narrower proportion toward the street and which were not divided among several families, the stove stood in its traditional place until 1917. Now it has been moved to the corner by the door and its opening is directed to the lateral wall. A plank partition separates it from the rest of the kitchen. Changes in the planning of houses and the search for a more comfortable use of the living area were already noticeable in the 1900s, but only within the Soviet were these fully developed.[2]

In the new houses built during the collectivization years and after, in only eight cases (9.4 percent) was the stove found in the traditional place whereas in most cases (more than 50 percent) the stove was placed in the corner by the door and its opening directed toward the lateral wall. It was separated from the rest of the room by a plank partition. This type of interior planning was widely used in the postrevolutionary years because of its convenience and rational use of living space. The placing of the stove by the door in a two-room house allowed a significant amount of space to be allotted to the front (or living) room so that a bedroom could be screened off.

There has been a tendency in the last few years to build many-roomed houses. Curtains are substituted for planks on either side of the Dutch stove partitions in many of the houses. Not infrequently the plank partitions separate a significant area of space, in which is found not only a bed

[2] Collective farms have their own carpenters; if the farm is large enough, the carpenters will constitute a whole brigade. In this case, the carpenters work for the people in their spare time and were paid for it (Tr.).

but also a table with chairs. A window can be put in and in this way a new room serving as the bedroom has been created. The stove in the kitchen is placed in the back corner in some of the houses, with its opening toward the door, and the area in front of the opening of the stove is partitioned off and serves as a place for the preparation of food separate from the area in which the family eats.

A plan for a four-room house is now slowly coming into use consisting of a kitchen, dining room, living room, and bedroom. Many houses in other regions and provinces are being built like this at the present time.

Changes in the interior layout of houses tend to be more elaborate in those families in which one of the members has worked in a factory or in the city, or has served in the Soviet Army or been at the front. Very often the reconstruction of a house will come about as a result of the demands made by young people. New kinds of layouts are also encouraged by the intelligentsia and pensioned service men who stayed to make their homes in the village. A former military doctor's assistant who had been an army major built a house in which the first half consisted of a kitchen, dining room, and a bedroom, and the second half of a reception room and another bedroom.

During the years of the collective farm system several other innovations were made. Electricity changed the entire appearance of the homes; they became cleaner, cosier, and lighter. The floors in the front rooms were often painted with an oil base paint, and the walls were plastered. Furniture also changed. Families that had close ties with the city or with industrial centers acquired urban furniture, wardrobes, cupboards, dressers, sofas and metal beds with wire netting, book stands, and other pieces whose design local carpenters would often copy. Many of the homes, however, still have two or three trunks standing in full view in which the family stores clothes, and dresses and outer clothing are hung on the wall and are covered with a piece of cloth in homes where there are no wardrobes.

The beds usually are found in the kitchen and stand on either side of the Dutch stove behind curtains, screens, or plank partitions. The young people customarily sleep on brightly decorated metal beds, while the old people sleep on wooden beds with plain, unadorned coverings and pillows.

Collective farmers show a great desire to decorate their homes, some of them acquiring reproductions of well-known artists for their walls. Nevertheless, it must be pointed out that the influences of bourgeois tastes, very prevalent here in the beginning of the twentieth century, are still felt. There are many rooms still decorated with postcards, posters, pictures cut out of magazines, artificial flowers, or abominably patterned rugs. This phenomenon is the result of the apathy of artistic and commercial organizations which care little about the assortment of goods sent to the village stores. The markets of Sosnov, Tambov, and Donbass contain an abundance of "artistic" handicrafts, bright rugs of the most incredible colors depicting maidens with wooden faces, swans, storybook castles, etc. All this, for lack of anything better, finds a ready sale and fills the rooms of Viriatino. Nevertheless, the collective farmers of Viriatino by no means lack artistic taste. The marvelous patterned weaving, the beautifully embroidered towels, and the homewoven woolen fabrics all attest to this.

The kitchens in the houses of Viriatino are kept immaculately neat and clean. Almost all of the houses have brick cooking stoves which came into widespread use in the thirties. The Russian stove still continues to have special importance in the heating of homes, however. "Some of us have tried to do without the Russian stove," said one of the collective farmers, "but it didn't work. The livestock makes it impossible to do without it. You have to heat at least three pails of water alone in the winter. This takes a long time on the brick stove and is inconvenient because the steam from the cow's mash goes into the hut while it's being cooked instead of up into the pipe, unlike the Russian stove." The Russian stove is convenient and heats not only the kitchen but also the front room.

With the collectivization of the farms and the resulting end of the economic isolation of the peasant households, the number of outbuildings in each household was cut down. The necessity for keeping working livestock in the back yard ceased and stables became superfluous since they took up a considerable amount of barn space. Fewer cattle sheds were needed and the barns that were used in the past for threshing and storing unthreshed rye, unnecessary in the individual households of the collective farmers, disappeared. Only the storerooms, bathhouses, cellars, hay lofts, and barns for the maintenance of the cows, sheep, pigs, and poultry were kept. There were no great changes in the construction of these buildings. Barns were built as always; poles about four to six inches in diameter under this method are stuck into the ground at a distance of sixteen to eighteen inches from each other, branches woven between them, and then covered with straw. The whole is then covered with a straw roof. Lately these barns have begun to be built with stronger logs placed one upon another and the cracks filled in with moss. Floors and ceilings are now also being added. The bathhouses are still made out of logs, but the heating system has been made cleaner; a chimney has been installed so that the smoke can escape. As previously, the cellars are located in the yard or across from the houses. The cellar walls were formerly made of dirt but are now covered with boards or, more often, cemented. As previously, grain and domestic belongings are stored in the brick storerooms. The locations of the outbuildings remained the same, although less space is taken up since the number of buildings was reduced.

The development of modern living quarters in the village demonstrates how gradually its culture and general everyday life is drawing closer to that of the city. A study of village living quarters shows that the previously existing sharp division between village and city housing is being erased and new transitional forms are being established. The improvements in village housing that have made it more similar to city housing have been in the area of construction methods, carrying over urban building skills, and striving for multiroomed houses and better-furnished interiors. Housing is becoming better suited to the growing cultural needs of the population.

But although certain old housing traditions that no longer fill the needs of the inhabitants are being eliminated, an effort has been made to preserve all those attributes which are valuable and reflect the rural way of life, and those which are determined by climatic conditions have also endured. The homes of Viriatino retain the traditional forms of Russian national architecture; all of the traditions connected with building log cabins remain unchanged. A local custom of building one-story houses on a low foundation does not change even when a storage basement is built under the house. The building of new homes is still hindered by the presence of a large number of living quarters which have accumulated over many decades and which are still considered satisfactory living dwellings. Nevertheless, interior rebuilding and modernization of living quarters have received great attention, a result of the growth of socialist culture in the village.

CHAPTER IX

MODERN DRESS

The contemporary dress of the peasants of Viriatino differs considerably from that of the prerevolutionary period. The years of Soviet rule have done much to rebuild the economy of the village and raise the cultural level of the working peasants. Each year there is a steady growth in the prosperity of the collective farmers, and each year the range of their needs increases. This prosperity cannot help but be reflected in their dress. One feature which distinguishes the contemporary dress of Viriatino from that of the past is the disappearance of the distinctions that denoted social inequalities. These distinctions had been especially visible in the 1900s when the use of factory-made materials for the making of clothes became widespread. The dress of the collective farmers of Viriatino now distinguishes only the various age groups.

The characteristic traits of the dress of the Soviet period did not make themselves immediately apparent. In the first decade after the October Revolution the features peculiar to the previous decade predominated. Domestic spinning and weaving increased in comparison to the prerevolutionary years since there was an overall shortage of manufactured goods in the country. Most families continued to do their own spinning and weaving right up to the organization of the kolkhoz in 1930. The women of Viriatino recall that they had to go back to wearing homespun dresses in the 1920s. Each acquisition of material for clothing in these years was considered a great event in the family. Only a small part of the peasant population, those who had become wealthy during the N.E.P. years, was able to have clothing made of factory-produced material.

The style of dress in the 1920s frequently resembled that of prerevolutionary times, partly because cloth was made at home in traditional ways. Ladies wore long shirts (to the ankle) embroidered at the hem as well as home-spun skirts, jumpers, headdresses, brogues; men wore satin shirts, velveteen pants, coats gathered at the waist, over-coats, patent leather boots, and so on.

The widespread return to homespinning, however, did not always lead to the return to the use of old, traditional patterns. Not only were long shirts with embroidered hems sewn, but also sleeveless shirts, women's jackets, skirts and whole dresses for young girls, teenagers, and children. Old clothing made of woven cloth was recut and resewn according to the new style. Women's jackets and skirts were made from jumpers, short coats were made into jackets; the embroidering was ripped off the long shirts; sleeves were cut off, and so on. Some women remember that while they were still adolescents their shirts were made into sleeveless dresses, and that jumpers began to be converted into skirts after 1921. The men of Viriatino in this period wore belted sateen "Russian" shirts with a side fastening, cotton or wool trousers, laced boots or high shoes, and a coat; an overcoat could be of sheepskin or a short coat. Many still wore uniforms left over from the war. The tall Caucasian sheepskin hats known as papakhas and the Budenovky, a type of conical military hat named after General Budenyi who wore one, were very popular.

In the mid-1920s a ladies' costume consisting of a skirt and blouse of the same material, became very popular. The blouses were belted very low in imitation of the urban styles of that time, the sleeves were long and the skirts straight, gathered, or flared. This costume was worn re-gardless of the coloring (dark or light, solid or multi-colored) all year round and was considered a holiday outfit. Under it an undershirt with short sleeves or with a cutout neck and no sleeves was worn, as was an underskirt of thin wool or calico. It was fashionable for this underskirt (printed or white with lace ruffles) to peek out from under the dress. Hardly any other underclothing was worn, except by young girls who on festive occasions would put on a flat underbodice. A shirt and a linen underskirt were worn to bed; it was considered immodest to sleep in only a shirt. A scarf served as the headdress for women of all ages. As to footwear they made do with what they had: boots, brogues, and laced leather shoes.

The entire aspect of peasant dress in the 1920s continued to carry the stamp of bourgeois taste from which the urban styles of that day had not yet been freed. It was particularly noticeable in women's clothing and was manifested in a predilection for coarse decorations such as belts made of buttons or in a crude combination of colors (black lace on a pink or pale green underskirt), etc. The champion of bourgeois influence in the village was the well-to-do upper crust which had come into being with the establishment of N.E.P.

Further development of peasant dress began in 1930 with the complete collectivization. It is this date that the people of Viriatino consider to be the starting point of fundamental changes in the way of life in the village. Great changes in clothing began to be noticeable, however, only in the second half of the 1930s when, with the improvement of the position of the Lenin's Way collective farm, the standard of living of the farmers rose considerably and their cultural horizon expanded.

The first changes came about in the fabrics used for making clothing. The growing profits of the collective farmers and the development of light industry made possible the minimalization of domestic textile manufacturing. The looms, which are still found in some of the homes in Viriatino, were now used only to weave bedspreads, floorcloths, and sacking. The spinning of wool for knitting was cut down considerably but did not lose its importance. As before, the stockings, socks, and mittens were knitted from wool. During the Second World War knitted woolen head scarves also became popular when there was a shortage of consumer goods. Wool was also used to make felt boots which were ordered from a special shop at the kolkhoz. However the weaving of foot apparel (lapti) from the bark of linden trees, an old tradition which continues up to the present time, was also common although their use is limited because they wear out quickly. Lapti were previously woven in each family; now only three or four old men in the entire village do this.

Everyday and holiday attire for adults is hardly ever made at home any more. The more complicated fashions and the emphasis on being well-dressed make it necessary to turn to the services of a professional tailor. Very little has remained of the old costume, and only a few examples of the old styles can be found in the village. For instance, one sixty-five-year-old peasant woman is saving a long embroidered shirt and brogues for her death; another is keeping a homespun skirt in memory of her mother. Many young girls hold onto the traditional costumes they inherited from their mothers for the traditional celebrations of the New Year and for their weddings. Some old women continue to wear out their old gathered sheepskin overcoats, woven pinafores, and checked cloth underskirts. But only the sheepskin overcoat which is worn for riding or outdoor work in the winter remains in widespread use at the present time.

Clothing like that of the city is taking the place of the traditional costume in Viriatino today. The most popular outfit for men is the traditional Russian blouse with a side closing which is sometimes embroidered, woolen or cotton trousers, and a belt which is worn over the blouse. The older people wear dark-colored shirts and the young, light-colored. On holidays many young people put on ties. Men's suits are generally made of woolen cloth. Many still wear military clothing which dates from World War II; pullovers and sweaters are common in the home. Caps, and hats with earmuffs in the winter, are the normal headgear. Boots and high laced shoes and felt boots in the winter serve as the footwear. Galoshes are worn in bad weather over the high shoes and felt boots.

Women's indoor dress consists of a skirt and jacket. The popularity of such an outfit apparently results from the old Russian tradition of wearing clothing made up of two parts (the long shirt and a homespun skirt or a sarafan). The contemporary skirts and jackets are of many styles. The outfit most frequently seen, however, consists of a gathered or flared skirt and a short overblouse. This costume is most popular among the older generation as it most closely resembles the traditional dress. Only recently (since the 1940s) have one-piece dresses come into use in Viriatino, and these are now very popular among the young people, being considered more festive than a skirt and blouse. As additional indoor attire the women wear knitted cotton and wool blouses and jackets. For work with the livestock and around the house a cotton apron that covers the entire front of the dress from the waist to the hem is worn.

A new item in women's clothing is underwear: undershirts, brassieres, and panties. It is only since the beginning of collectivization that these have come into use. Underwear is usually white or colored cotton, and embroidered or finished off with lace. The undershirt for work is usually made of heavier fabric so that it can fall into place without hampering any movement.

As to hair styles, married women still put their hair into two braids and arrange these in a bun at the back of the head. Young girls also braid their hair, but usually pin their braids up, as this is considered more convenient. Only a few girls and young women cut and curl their hair.

The scarf is the universal headdress for all women. In the summer a thin cotton or silk scarf is worn, and in the winter a warm, often knitted, wool one. One will never see an older woman without a head scarf, summer or winter, indoors or out, holiday or workday. Young girls also wear scarves when they are working and sometimes also at home, but in the summer during the leisure hours they prefer to wear nothing on their heads. Caps and hats are hardly ever worn, although in the fall and winter a warm shawl can be worn over the head and shoulders. The predominance of the head scarf can be explained on the one hand by many centuries of tradition and on the other by the necessities of village life, in which prolonged outdoor work requires constant protection from cold or from the sun.

Women's footwear in Viriatino consists of many kinds of high shoes, sneakers, boots, and galoshes. The high rubber boots, convenient in daily use, were quickly adopted and they replaced leather boots. These are usually worn without shoes so that the heel inside must be filled with a piece of wood. Sneakers also enjoy wide popularity. In the winter all the people of Viriatino, men and women alike, wear felt boots, usually with galoshes. Stockings for the most part are store-bought. Knitted socks and stockings are usually worn in the winter and only under unusual circumstances in the fields in the summer.

Outer clothing is differentiated by the seasons, although not always very clearly. Winter coats of sheepskin, usually of a black raw variety, and quilted jackets, are common. In the spring and fall, lighter clothing of the winter type is worn, especially quilted jackets. These are especially popular among the collective farmers of Viriatino because they are warm, lightweight, and cheap. The farmers, working all day with only short breaks, either outdoors or in unheated or very poorly heated buildings, must wear clothing of this type. Under the circumstances it is natural that this costume is universal and jackets are preferable at all times to long coats, being lighter and more comfortable to work in. A coat is worn only on festive occasions. But the widespread use of short jackets and short coats for everyday wear and the absence of any clear-cut differences between everyday clothing and more festive clothing have brought about the wearing of short coats and jackets even on holidays. This type of attire is becoming habitual, necessary, and fashionable, and has thus become the specific costume of the contemporary village. Aside from the outer apparel already mentioned, raincoats of tarpaulin, rubberized materials, and rubber are also coming into greater and greater use.

In the way one speaks of the clothing of the Viriatino collective farmers one usually means everyday clothing, a category that includes both work and at-home attire. There is also special industrial clothing which is not yet in widespread use in Viriatino and is worn only under special conditions at times when it would be difficult to do without it. The work at livestock farms demands such special clothing, although the only elements already in use are the rubber boots and traditional apron. The lack of attention given to special dress by the directors of the collective farm results in the workers having to use their own old attire. Upon arrival at their jobs, for example, the milkmaids will remove their good scarves and replace them with old ones and put on special old shirts to protect their good ones. The people of Viriatino in their understanding of the elementary rules of sanitation and hygiene see the importance of having a type of apparel which is separate from their everyday clothes. Thus the milkmaids have been demanding special work coats for milking for some time, and some specialized apparel for work can be seen in the fields.

It is generally accepted that lapti slippers are the most comfortable footwear for reaping. They are lightweight, feet do not perspire in them, and they protect the wearer from the prickly stubble. Woolen socks are worn under the lapti instead of rags (as before) to protect the feet from bites of the swarms of midges, horseflies, and mosquitoes. Galoshes and sneakers often replace the home-made lapti. For work at the threshing machine women wear lapti or sneakers and woolen socks, and for other harvesting work galoshes are often worn over woolen stockings and socks. But neither galoshes nor sneakers can be compared to lapti in practicality. A more comfortable, lightweight, or cheaper footwear has not yet been developed, which explains why these traditional slippers of the Russian peasant continue to be used to the present day.

Other kinds of work clothes are simply everyday clothing adapted for different kinds of jobs. Thus for harvesting women wear blouses with long sleeves; wide skirts and head scarves are worn for filling the siloes (a process which is mechanized in Viriatino) and a blouse with short or rolled-up sleeves is often comfortable. The apron is always an integral part of the woman's working costume. Tractor operators wear tarpaulin pants, a field shirt, a quilted cotton jacket, and boots. Cotton pants are worn in the winter under the tarpaulin ones, and a warm jacket or sheepskin coat is worn over the quilted cotton one. No special overalls exist for these jobs.

Most of the Viriatino collective farmers, especially the young people, come to work neat and well dressed. When they come home they change into clean everyday clothing if it has been a dirty job. Different kinds of older costumes were sometimes worn on holidays. A dress that has been worn for festive occasions and has become old and a little shabby, however, will become a work dress. In the old days women had as many as thirty jumpers put away in their trunks for holidays. Today clothing does not lie around in trunks anymore.

The wedding dress of the bride and groom is especially festive. The suit and dress are especially made and beautiful shoes are bought. The only traditional article left in contemporary wedding dress is the bridal scarf. It is curious to note that at one of the weddings in which the bride was bareheaded, a scarf was placed on her head at the time of the ceremony. Ceremonial clothing, which even in prerevolutionary Viriatino was poorly developed, has almost completely lost its ritual character. It is very rare, for example, for a corpse to be dressed in special attire anymore, and even a shroud is not always used. For the most part the deceased are buried in what they wore when alive, if possible in an all-white or dark suit.

Unlike the past, a great deal of attention is now paid to children's clothing. Instead of cast-off clothing and incidental garments, today's children receive clothes which are especially made for them. The smallest wear babies' vests, warm jackets, and crawling pants. As soon as a child can walk, he receives trousers, dresses, high shoes, stockings, etc. Children always have three or four changes of indoor wear, and even the female children of large families have at least two good cotton school dresses. In most cases their clothes are made of inexpensive cotton, but families with larger incomes try to obtain good woolen fabrics, especially jersey, for sweaters, suits, and breeches. Parents are very much concerned with getting good shoes and outer wear. In the streets of Viriatino in the winter one can see a number of children dressed warmly in well-fitting good coats with cotton linings, felt boots with galoshes, hats with earmuffs, and warm scarves. The best and most neatly dressed children are those who attend school.

Girls have clothes aside from the usual clothing which are sewn for their trousseau. Traditionally a trousseau is still prepared for the bride, although it may not be as large as it was in the past. Trousseaus today usually consist of several dresses, underwear, shoes, and stockings but cannot compare with those of the past which were made up of a number of trunks, all stuffed with clothes. There still is the custom of preparing a package for the groom but the contents have changed considerably. Today they consist of a shirt, socks, a towel, a handkerchief, and toilet soap.

In order to get a trousseau together young girls will often leave the collective farm to find seasonal work, in the peat works for example, returning to the village later. But in most cases the trousseau is obtained through collective family means.[1] It may be pointed out here that the clothing budget is agreed on by the adult members of the family, with the needs of the younger members given primary consideration.

In most cases clothing is stored in trunks as before. They are in practically every home, where they are an integral part of the living room furniture. But some families now have wardrobes, which are very much in demand at the present time. The absence of any clear-cut difference between everyday and holiday clothing necessitates that each garment be kept in freshly pressed condition, able to be worn at any time. In former times when clothing was worn only on special occasions, the storage trunk was a suitable receptacle, but it no longer serves its purpose. In many of the houses of Viriatino that have not yet obtained wardrobes one can see dresses and suits hanging on the walls with paper or a piece of cloth covering them.

Clothes of an urban type are the predominant kind worn in Viriatino now. Homespun garments are no longer used. Clothing has become more varied and there is more of it in each family, a result of the close economic and cultural ties between the city and the village. The city itself

[1] The linens which a bride who married in 1954 typically received as a dowry from her parents to take to her new home include one feather bed and three covers for it, four slipcovers embroidered at the edges, one sheet, two blankets, two quilts, two down pillows and four pillowcases, a canopy for the bed, small curtains for the kitchen shelf and for the stove, curtains for the windows, four towels of which two were of the embroidered variety used to drape over icons and photographs hung on the wall; a lace tablecloth for the table under the icons, two plain tablecloths, and an oilcloth for the kitchen table. According to the tradition the girls' family also prepares a "bundle" for the groom.

has, of course, changed. Whereas the villagers who left for the industrial centers used to bring back city bourgeois tastes to the village, now they bring back the styles of the contemporary working class and Soviet intelligentsia.

CHAPTER X

FAMILY STRUCTURE AND FAMILY LIFE

Fundamental changes in the life of the peasants took place after the October Revolution, and during the first years of Soviet power the widespread breaking up of extended families was characteristic in Viriatino. The decree on the redistribution of land and property was primarily responsible for the splintering of families.

Some old residents remarked that the decline or ruin of many of the individual farms during the First World War and the tumult of the Civil War were responsible for sharp conflicts. Added to this was the attitude of some of Viriatino's residents who, after returning home from the Civil War, did not want to go back to the stagnant life of the joint family that they had known.

As a result of the breaking up of Viriatino's families and the movement of nuclear families to the outskirts, a new settlement, Vyselki, was created as early as 1918–21. The results of a questionnaire showed that the number of independent families in Viriatino between 1918 and 1930 increased from 375 to 487, i.e., almost thirty percent.

Only a few large families remained as early as 1918. G. Diakov's family consisting of twenty-two people (four married brothers and their families living together) might be considered one of the few examples. The traditions of extended families lasted even into the thirties, however, since it remained common for aged parents to live with their married sons. Nevertheless, the internal structure of such families was weakened.

The awakening of social consciousness during the Revolution, especially among the young, the gradual involvement of women in public life, and the exposure of the rural population to political views gradually destroyed the isolation of the peasants and introduced new trends and ideas. This awakened consciousness changed the nature of the ties within a family, especially the relationship between generations. It created a more independent position for the younger generation in particular, who began to play a more active role. One example was the weakening in religious commitment. Some accounts of the young people during the first two decades of the Revolution mention the complete break with the traditional ideas about marriage and school. A middle-aged collective farmer related some remarkable facts. Her husband-to-be was a typical representative of the sophisticated young people who belonged to the Young Communist League, and who were thus hostile to religion and traditional family life.

The bride's family would not consent to her marriage with a member of the Young Communist League and the situation was further complicated by the bridegroom's refusal to participate in a religious wedding ceremony. The marriage took place in 1922 only because of the intervention of one of the bride's brothers, also a member of the Young Communist League, and the resolute position taken by the bride herself. The couple reached a compromise; instead of following the usual religious ceremony they walked around the church three times.

Their life together was based on new principles. The husband did his best to make his wife more interested in the new aspects of life and tried to distract her attention from church activities, explaining to her the absurdity of superstitions; he helped her to read books (by reading aloud to her) and took her to movies and meetings of the local branch of the Young Communist League. He insisted on engaging a paid babysitter when their children were born so that he and his wife could attend meetings and parties together. These were completely new trends, and wherever they appeared one saw real evidence of a basic social reorganization of family life.

This fundamental reorganization was closely connected to the change from a traditional peasant farm economy to a collective one. Inequality among the members of a family could exist while the economic basis was still the small, family-owned farm.

The population of Viriatino when comprising 456 families totaled 1547 individuals. Of these, 248 families are headed by a male and 208 by a female. Of those family units composed of two people, forty are headed by a man and sixty-seven by a woman. Those headed by men are comprised of married couples, 64.9 percent of whom have children who live and work outside the home. The families headed by women are in general (88.1 percent) those which have no man at all (widows with children). More than half of them, 54.2 percent, have children living and working outside.

Among the families composed of three people, fifty-three are headed by men and fifty by women. Those families headed by men are, in a predominant number of cases (77.4 percent), married couples with children. More than half of them have children living outside Viriatino. The rest of the families in this group are made up of married couples living with the mother of one of the spouses (six families) and widowers with children. The families headed by a woman in a predominant number of cases (66.0 percent) consist of widows with children; 22.2 percent of them have children living outside. All the other families comprise three generations.

Of the family units consisting of four people, sixty-six are headed by a man and thirty by a woman. The greatest number of those headed by men (74.2 percent) are married couples with children. The rest of the families consist of three generations, an old parent with a married son, his wife, and a grandson (two families); married couples with one child and the mother of one of the spouses (seven families); old parents living with their widowed daughter-in-law and grandson (one family), etc. Fifty percent of the families of four headed by women are composed of widows with children. All the rest consist of three generations: a widow with a married son and his wife and grandchildren (five families); a widow with a married daughter and her husband and grandchildren (one family); a widow with a daughter and grandchildren (four families). In addition to this, two families consist of married couples, but the women are considered heads of the families.

Within the group of families consisting of five people, forty-three are headed by men and seventeen by women. More than half of the families headed by men (55.8 percent) consist of married couples with children. The others comprise three generations, an old parent with a married son, his wife, and their children (eleven families; in one case a widowed daughter-in-law); old married couples with children and a grandchild (two families); married couples with the mother of one of the spouses and their own children (four families); etc. Some 41.2 percent of the families headed by women are those of widows with children. The others include three generations, and are usually the families of widows living with a married son, his wife and grandchildren (six families).

In its structure a modern collective farm family is a small, separate unit. An investigation held in the summer of 1953 showed that in a large number of cases (60.3 percent) a family in Viriatino consisted of two generations, that is, a married couple (or one of the spouses) and their children. A modern family characteristically includes a young married couple living with the parents or a parent of one of the spouses. In the past one of the sons (usually the youngest) supported the parents. There are some families that consist of old parents, a married son, and younger children as well. Now, however, there are only nine such families in Viriatino. Of the total number of Viriatino's families, 20.4 percent consist of three or four generations, and it should be stressed that some old family traditions, and some folk customs, remain only because of the influence of the older generation. In thirteen families a widowed daughter with children lives with her parents, but seldom does a daughter-in-law live with her deceased husband's parents. It has already been pointed out that a daughter-in-law in an extended family is somewhat isolated, and remains an alien to some extent, while on the other hand she usually continues to maintain close relations with her parents, especially with her mother.

Another new phenomenon connected with the so-called *small* family should also be stressed. In a number of cases a young married couple takes in the wife's widowed mother as their dependent. Close ties between old parents (especially widowed mothers) and their married daughter's families are extremely common. Even when both parents (or one parent) and a younger married couple have their own property and houses, the economic ties between them are very close.

A large family of a collective farm stableman serves as a good example of such relations. His mother-in-law, an old widow, has her own house and property and is considered to be an independent housekeeper. During the winter, though, she lives with her married daughter's family, looks after the house, and takes care of her grandchildren. In the summer because of seasonal agricultural work she returns to her own house.

The same situation applies to a collective farm driver. The father of T. M. Kalmikov lives separately from his widowed daughter and her children. What he earns at the kolkhoz, though, he shares with his daughter's family; all products, in fact, both his and those belonging to other members of the family, are shared. Two orchards belonging to the two families are cultivated by both and they own a cow in common. There are a number of such examples which are rather typical of the modern way of life in Viriatino. Generally speaking, the ties between relatives in the village continue to be strong and in an emergency each usually does his best to help the other.

Families in Viriatino were patrilineal and patrilocal as a rule; the institution of a *primak* in which young married couples settled with the wife's family was never very widespread. Primak is a term used for a young husband who is too poor to support his own family and is forced by circumstances to live in the house of his in-laws and work for them. Literally a primak is "one who is adopted by another family." Now the word has practically passed out of use and is unfamiliar to the younger generation. This kind of arrangement also occurred when for some reason the couple was unable to get along with the husband's family and decided to live for a while with the wife's parents until they could afford their own homestead. Such cases can be seen at the present time, but they are relatively rare. At the moment there are four families having primaks, three of them with a widowed mother as head of the household.

Today there is not even a trace of an extended family in Viriatino. The last one (the family of a collective farm carpenter consisting of ten people—two married sons living with their parents) dissolved in the spring of 1955. Economically that family was rather stable and strong and therefore resisted the trend toward disintegration. Now young married couples leave home soon after marriage and settle in another house or go to the city to work in factories or plants. This explains the existence of a number of married couples living in Viriatino without children (8.6 percent of the total number of families) and the so-called "singles."

In describing the structure of families in Viriatino it should be stressed that as a consequence of the Second World War 44.5 percent of the total number are headed by women. The average number of persons in those Viriatino families headed by men is three or four (48 percent of the total number of families with a man at the head) while families headed by women usually consist of two to four persons (70.7 percent of the total number of families in that category). Within the group of families that consist of five or more persons, 33.5 percent are headed by men and only 10.6 percent by women.

In attempting to calculate the average size of the Viriatino family today it is worth while to remember the great exodus of the village population that has taken place. Former residents of Viriatino currently living outside the village constitute 32.7 percent of the total number of the village's working adults. Of these former residents, 66.4 percent work in factories and plants. Before the Revolution the participation of Viriatino peasants in industry was largely limited to seasonal migration. At present, however, the exodus is permanent and the shift from peasantry to the working class is on the rise.

It should be noted, however, that this picture is not totally correct since a certain proportion of young men remain in the Army and the mobility of women has increased. (About thirty percent of Viriatino women live outside the village, either temporarily or permanently.) This mobility which began in the late thirties increased after the Second World War and can help explain the modernity of the girls of today. With very few exceptions, modern young men and women in the country receive a minimum of seven years of education. The greater proportion of them are high school students or graduates. Of the women living outside Viriatino, ten percent are students at universities, pedagogical institutes, and so on. Many opportunities in industry have opened up to the modern Viriatino woman, especially in coal mining, a traditional occupation of many residents of the village.

One of the basic reasons for the decline in the number of women involved in collective production in Viriatino after the war was the sharp decrease in the number of men in the village. Without the possibility of settling down to normal married life in the village, the girls sought their livelihood elsewhere. This migration generally contributed to marriages with outsiders which became a characteristic feature of the contemporary life of the village. This ease of movement to other places was absolutely unknown in the old village where marriages were contracted within the village or at least within a neighboring area.

The socialist economy provided the grounds for establishing new types of relationships within the family. In contrast to the situation existing in the old patriarchal family, the relationships in the contemporary collective farm family are based upon the rules of socialist society and the equal rights of all its adult members.

The head of the peasant family in the past was the oldest male member; in his absence it became the oldest female member (usually the mother and, in rare cases, the grandmother). At the present time this order still prevails in cases where a young married couple lives with parents; in most such situations the head of the family is a member of the older generation, even in cases of extreme old age and loss of ability to work. In families headed by men, the cases in which the head is the eldest in the family comprise 56.1 percent of the total; the cases in which the head is a member of the younger generation (e.g., a married son) comprise 43.9 percent, 92 percent in the presence of an old father.

In contemporary family relationships one must bear in mind in addition that the preservation of the old father's position as the head of the family is frequently merely a formality, done out of respect to the old man. The actual head of the family and the organizer of its economic and agricultural life is still frequently the married son. In one family, for example, while the son is a collective farm activist (a member of the management board), a member of the party, and in fact a middle-aged man, the father, an extremely old man and an invalid, is still considered to be the head of the family. In actuality, however, the son has exercised this responsibility for many years.

Most important is the fact that the position of the head of the family has changed in terms of role, function, and influence. Previously he enjoyed unlimited power, having complete control over the property and work of the other members of the family. Now he is merely the spokesman for the family and for family affairs, and legally responsible to the government for the payment of taxes. He has no special power over the other members. His responsibilities include the general management of the household but he is no longer the sole controller of the family income.

All the family income from fixed wages (received by members of the family working in industry or in cooperative or government enterprises) goes into a joint family budget, along with income from the household's subsidiary farming. Payment in kind for workdays is paid by the collective farm, not to each member of the family separately, but to the family as a unit and is stored in the family storehouse. All this comprises the joint family income which in most families is spent with the mutual agreement of the members, taking into account the needs of both the household as a unit and the individual members. This completely new factor in family relationships is particularly important in the families where a young married couple is living with parents. The old father, nominally the head of the family, does not feel that it is right to make expenditures without consulting with the son or another member of the family who is contributing to the budget. In one case, for example, the head of the family (a man very much of the old tradition) had a married son who worked for many years in the Viriatino general store. He gave all his earnings to his father, who managed the finances. All major undertakings and major expenses for the household were, however, initiated only with the son's knowledge and consent. This has become the rule in the families of Viriatino. The opinions of the older members of the family are respected but the freedom and initiative of the other members are not suppressed, especially those of the younger generation when they explain their needs to their parents.

The essence of contemporary relations between parents and children can be summed up in the principle "everything for the children," as the parents themselves constantly point out when comparing the new order of things with old family customs. This is also clearly shown by the budgetary facts; a large portion of the money spent goes toward covering the needs and the cultural aspirations of the children.

Thus in most contemporary collective farm families the past despotism of the father and husband is completely disappearing, and new relations between parents and children are being established. In some families, however, all attempts to establish the new order in family life are still opposed by the conservative outlook of the older generation which still attempts completely to control the earnings of the young couple. But these families are not stable as a rule, and at the first opportunity the young couple usually moves away from the parents.

The position of women in the family has changed radically. In the first years of the revolution women were legally emancipated and the victory of the collective farm system has made their emancipation a reality. An analysis of the budgets of several collective farm families shows that the earnings of the women make up a considerable proportion of the total. Women who work in the fields accumulate an average of 120–160 workdays; in higher paying work such as transporting hay from the fields or mowing they achieve up to 230 workdays, and the women who work at the livestock farms total at least 340–360 workdays.

The economic independence of women made a new role in the family possible for them. Also of great importance to their new position is the care with which mothers are surrounded in the Soviet state where the government makes laws for the protection of them and their children and provides grants for mothers with many children and aid to mothers who are alone.

At the present time the woman is gaining authority within the family as a housekeeper, child rearer, and the organizer of daily life. It is often difficult to tell which of the parents has more control over the household. A characteristic statement is that made by an elderly woman whose family includes her husband, an unmarried son, and a son with a wife and child: "My husband is the boss, but I dictate to him—'Father, we need such and such.' I know the needs of the family better. I do all the washing and can see better than he who needs what."

Some traditions of the old joint families still exist, most clearly visible in the situation of the widowed daughter-in-law who has remained in the house of her late husband's parents. There are, however, only four such families. Today a widowed daughter-in-law moves away almost immediately, taking her share of the household and her husband's. Usually she goes to the house of her parents if there is no married son. Sometimes if there is space in her father-in-law's house she is given a separate room, but even if she remains with her husband's parents their relationship continues on a new basis. In one such family that we observed there are certain arrangements. The widow is in full control of the pension which she receives for the children, and with it she clothes herself and her children. All her earnings on the collective farm go into the joint family budget controlled by her father-in-law and are used to cover various family expenses. The father-in-law, however, is responsible for letting her know how money is spent because her earnings comprise a major portion of the family income. He keeps a special notebook where he records all expenses. In 1954 when a higher rate of pay for workdays went into effect he gave the widow a large sum of money for her personal use. This is a far cry from the old tyranny of the father-in-law, and the relationship is based on a fair household arrangement.

A young woman with her own earning power on the collective farm today enters a family into which she marries not as a worker into a strange household but as a full member of a collective working team. At the time of the marriage it is agreed that part of the workdays she has accumulated will be transferred to the household of her husband, and she enters his family on an independent footing.

Perhaps a more striking indication of the change in family relationships is the fact that in the contemporary collective farm family the wife of the son is accepted by his parents as a daughter and cared for by the family. This is seen most clearly in the relationship of the mother and daughter-in-law. Certain traditions are still observed in the division of work between the two; the mother always prepares the food while the young daughter-in-law does not go near the stove but helps by bringing water, fuel, and so on. The daughter-in-law usually takes care of the laundry, washes the floors, and does general housecleaning. But the complete domination that the mother formerly exercised has utterly disappeared, not only because of the economic independence of the bride, but because her personal rights are recognized.

Almost all of the young women who have had seven years of education have developed tastes, understandings, and needs different from those of the women of the older generation. Many of the young women learn to enjoy reading in the course of their schooling and do not give it up when they marry. In one example the young daughter-in-law uses every free minute for reading; she reads while knitting and during her holidays. With her husband she goes to the club and to the movies; all of her behavior in the family is uninhibited and is influenced to some extent by her personal interests. Her relationship with her mother-in-law is friendly and is based on mutual help. When the mother-in-law divides the wool for knitting, she usually gives the girl the better wool. The daughter-in-law is an excellent knitter and in the winter months when she is freer of the work of the collective farm she can add to her wardrobe and income in this way. During this time her mother-in-law takes some of the household chores upon herself. During the very busy summer months her mother-in-law frees her completely from any housework. This type of relationship between the two women has become typical of the contemporary collective farm family.

The same kind of mutual respect and mutual aid are characteristic of the collective family in general. While most of the household work falls by its nature to the women, all of the family members will pitch in in cases of very heavy work. Chopping wood for the winter and cutting peat is done by the whole family, for example. The situation is the same for the work in the family garden—all the members are expected to help. The men usually do the plowing and the furrowing while the women and children do the sowing, weeding, and harvesting. Young married couples no longer stick to the strict traditional division of labor. Young husbands often help their wives with weeding and harvesting. When the family includes an old father who is still able to work he usually takes charge of the garden, with occasional help from the other members. There is still some division of labor according to the old traditions, however, as in caring for the livestock, for example. Preparing the feed, milking, and caring for the young calves, suckling pigs, and lambs are done by women, while feeding the livestock (cows and sheep) and caring for them generally are done exclusively by men. The stability of such traditions has had a detrimental effect on the kolkhoz system. For that reason it is important to note that recently they have begun to die out. Not only in the households of widows where the women must do the household chores themselves, but also in normal families, where there are men, the women who are less occupied in the fields (especially in wintertime) will sometimes take care of chores usually left to the men. In this way the wife of the kolkhoz worker does all the work around the house and farm when he is busy at the kolkhoz.

The tenor of home life varies with the seasons. The women of Viriatino who usually work in the fields do very little work on the collective farm in the winter. This is true not only for mothers of families but for younger women as well. The exceptions are usually widowed mothers who are the sole supporters of their families. Some of these women work at the livestock farms, but most work side by side with the men at various seasonal jobs.

Women are mainly occupied with household chores in the winter. Aside from the daily chores—cooking, washing, cleaning, and taking care of children—they spend a great deal of time sewing and mending the work clothes that will be necessary in the hot days of the summer when they will be too busy to sew. Almost every family has a sewing machine, and the mother sews for herself, her husband, and her children—only heavy outer clothing is made by a dressmaker or bought at the store. The wool socks, stockings, gloves, and shawls, without which a peasant family cannot get along, are knitted usually by the younger female members of the family who are frequently excellent at the job. Some of them knit shawls and scarves for sale as well as for the family. The younger generation does not know how to spin and so it is usually done by the older women. If a family has younger children in addition to a married son the mother-in-law will do the spinning only for her husband and her unmarried children; the young bride must go to her own mother for help. In families with a mother and daughter-in-law, the wool is still divided traditionally; the result of the spring shearing is divided equally between the mother and daughter-in-law unless the mother has children other than her married son, in which case she will keep a larger share. The first part of the autumn wool is set aside for the making of felt boots and the rest is divided up in the same manner.

One can find a weaver's loom in the homes now only

infrequently. Although the collective farmers periodically cultivate hemp in their gardens, weaving has very limited place in contemporary life (only bedspreads and the necessary sacking are woven). Only the very old women still know how to weave.

The organization of the family's day is determined by the general work routine. In the winter the household usually rises at 7 A.M. The women in charge of the cooking get up much earlier (at 5 or 6 A.M.) in order to have time to prepare breakfast. The food is prepared in the Russian stove for the whole day. It is still cooked in cast iron and earthenware pots that are adapted to the design of the Russian stove. There are aluminum and enamel pots for food prepared on the other kind of stove. There are metal cans in addition to hold milk. Metal utensils have become a part of the daily life of the village and one can see enameled metal bowls, pots, tubs, teapots, samovars, metal children's wash tubs and troughs everywhere. Water is no longer carried in wooden buckets, although these remain at the wells for drawing up water; metal and often enameled buckets are used. Wooden mortars are still used for grinding grain into flour, but the ancient wooden salt-cellars have been largely replaced by new ones turned on a lathe and lacquered.

The family breakfasts at 7 to 7:30 A.M., after which the members who work at the collective farm go off to work. The children who attend the morning shift at school leave and the other children prepare their lessons. The mother of the family and the young women who have stayed at home attend to the household chores. Dinner is eaten at noon when the children have returned from school and the workers have come home for a break. Supper is usually eaten at 6 or 7 P.M., although in families where tea is taken in the evening, the evening meal is usually later. The whole family tries to come together at mealtimes. If someone has been delayed at work, the rest usually wait for him. Only those members of the family who work at unusual hours eat their meals alone. The workers at the livestock farms fit into this category and usually do not eat at home. Public dining rooms, men's halls, have not yet been established and this is reflected in the eating habits of many of the collective farmers. The pig tenders, for example, complain that they are busy from dawn until dusk at the pig farm and often do not have enough time even to have breakfast. They put some bread into their pockets in the morning and eat only that during the day.

The table at which the family eats is usually covered with an oil-cloth. There is no absolute seating plan for the table, and everybody sits at the place where he is used to sitting. News and family matters are discussed at the table. Food is served by the older woman, and she also cuts the meat and bread; but often some other member of the family helps her. Some old customs are maintained by some even today, however; for example, all the adults eat from one bowl, although there are enough porcelain and earthenware dishes and plates (deep and shallow) for individual serving. It is considered a great improvement when children are taught to eat from their own separate plates, and this is now done in many families. Eating bowls are usually metal and sometimes cast iron although wooden bowls are still found. Spoons are usually the wooden kind bought at the bazaar. "Everything in the old way because of the old people," say the collective farmers.

Food during the winter usually consists of grain and farinaceous foods, dishes cooked with wheat, potatoes, pickled cucumbers, sauerkraut, and vegetable oils. Animal products usually include pork, salt, and fresh ham, lard, and beef. Closer on to spring, veal, rendered lard, and butter in very small quantities are eaten.

In the summer the day is organized around the work on the collective farm in which all the able members of the family take part. Household chores are reduced to a minimum at this time. In families where there are no old people, the mother has to prepare the day's food in the morning before going off to work. In all other household chores she is aided by the children; the older girls take care of the cleaning and caring for the younger children, while the older boys look after the livestock, prepare the feed, and clean the shed. The children usually do as much as they can in the vegetable garden.

In the summer it is generally impossible for the family to come together for their meals as they are occupied at different hours, and so they eat separately. Regular meals are kept only for the children.

Milk and milk products, fresh vegetables and greens and sometimes fresh fish make up the bulk of summer food. Eggs are a great boost to family nutrition in the summer. Most households no longer sell eggs as they used to, but more often buy additional ones.

In the summer any one of the regular meals may be replaced by a quick snack—milk and bread, cooked eggs, eggs fried in lard or butter, lard with bread and onions, just plain bread with onions, or fresh or salted cucumbers. Bread, eggs, pies, lard, and always milk are taken out to the fields.

Bread and grain products make up the greater part of the diet in Viriatino. This remains traditional and widespread in the Southern Russian provinces (Tambov, Ryazan, Kursk, Voronezh, and others) regardless of the fact that the food of the Viriatino peasants have undergone significant changes during the years of Soviet rule. Many of the old traditional dishes have disappeared completely.

Unlike the past, the peasants of Viriatino now demand not only rye bread but also wheat bread, as it is grown on the collective farm. The use of vegetables, especially tomatoes, has increased. The calorie count of the food has risen because of the increase in the amount of highly nourishing foods, meat, eggs, animal fats, and milk, although these are far from equally available to each family.

The use of sugar and sweets has grown immeasurably; tea with sugar or candies is drunk by every family.

Yet, it must be stressed that, aside from some few innovations, cooking in Viriatino continues to preserve the traditional ways. Innovations in nutrition make their way very slowly and with great difficulty.

Significant changes have come about in the cultural life of the family, and these have had an effect in turn on its material and spiritual life.

To see the paths along which the family and family life are being rebuilt, it is most interesting to study the different generations. The contemporary collective farm family is far from uniform in the education of its members or in their overall culture. This is particularly true among the women. Many of the women of Viriatino who are over fifty-five are illiterate or only semiliterate. This is the terrible heritage of the past which we cannot overlook. The overall majority of younger women, however, have at least seven years of education.

It takes more than raising the literacy level and educating the population, however, to transform the mode of life. One can see in the stories of many of the older women of the village how life under the collective farm system and the general uplift of culture in the village molded their social consciousness and formed new outlooks on life, on the future of their children and their upbringing.

An important figure in this respect is the collective farm worker, T. M. Kalmikova (born in 1903), a widow of a soldier killed at the front. When she lost her husband during the war she was able to continue her children's education through her own hard work on the collective farm. One of her sons is an officer, two are continuing their studies in colleges, and the fourth is finishing school. The Makarov family is very similar. E. A. Makarova is a woman no longer young (born in 1908) and is almost illiterate. In her youth she was unable to attend school.

There were many children in the family and as she was the oldest she had to care for the younger ones. She learned to read and write under Soviet rule. Lively and full of initiative, she did not miss one cultural event; she went to all the productions at the local club, to the movies, and greedily absorbed all the new trends of life. These character traits (her inquisitiveness, curiosity, liveliness) remain with her to the present. She takes the most active interest in the lives of her children. She enjoys listening to the radio, especially to music, but also to lectures on childbearing (the program *Soviet Mother*). All this plus the constant contact with the school her children attend, gave her a firm understanding of how to bring them up. She raises her children carefully and knowingly—combining their school activities with duties at home, necessary rest, and so on. She is always able to find funds in the small family budget for a movie for the children or for necessary newspapers for them.

The growing intellectual stratum among the peasantry has had an enormous effect in bringing about changes in the family and family life. It is composed for the most part of the educated youths, or those members of peasant families who received at least a secondary education and now work in the cities or industrial centers. (The continuing ties of Viriatino with the Donbass have to some extent influenced some of the young people to enter professions in mining engineering.) The young people who study and work in the cities and industrial centers, and still maintain very close and active ties with the families in the village, exert an enormous influence on the material and spiritual aspects of family life and on its inner structure of family life.

The great changes that have come about in the last few years in the cleanliness of houses and in the clothing are related to the rising standards of living, combined with the new tastes and cultural needs. Let us examine some of the material advances that have changed the habits of the family. To begin with, one must notice the good sanitary condition of the houses and the higher standards of personal hygiene. As a result of the observance of hygienic requirements in the village and the regular use of insecticides, insect parasites, which were previously the scourge of the village, have been almost completely eliminated. The homes are kept clean and the floors are washed twice a week. There are over eighty steam baths in Viriatino, and these are used not only by their owners but by all the neighbors as well. The family bathes twice a month in the winter, and the bedclothes are changed at this same time. Twice a year, before Easter and the Saint's Day feast, the slipcovers are washed. Hair and personal underwear are washed weekly, daily in the summer while work in the field is in progress. The beds are always kept clean. Before the Revolution only married couples used beds but now the whole family has them. It is especially important to note the change for the children since before the Revolution they usually slept in rows on the floor on straw mattresses covered with sacking. The younger generation has introduced the custom of using sheets, although the older people as a rule continue to use homespun cloth.

Pressing and ironing clothes, previously unknown in the village, has become customary. Because of this the traditional method of storing clothes in trunks is no longer satisfactory, especially for the younger members of the family. The village strongly feels the need for wardrobes, which are still very scarce in Viriatino.

One should also note, however, that several features of the old way of life still exist. In most families, for example, calves, suckling pigs, and lambs are kept in a closed off corner in the kitchen in the wintertime. (The people are beginning to realize the disadvantages of this practice, however, and the growing tendency is to eliminate it.) The custom of eating out of one bowl has also remained. These customs will finally disappear when the older generation of the village has died off. The difference in cultural habits of the different generations was well expressed by one of the village inhabitants. To the question of why the custom of eating out of one bowl has lasted so long he answered: "When Mother dies, then we will each eat off separate plates. We growl at Mother for her old habits, but when my sister (a college student) comes home from the city she growls at us for our old habits. This is no good and that is no good, and how can you live this way?"

One of the clearest indications of cultural growth is the change in the character of leisure pastimes. Listening to the radio has become a firmly entrenched village habit. Concerts of folk songs are especially popular, but so are lectures on farming and childbearing. Other popular pastimes are attending a club, seeing the movies, and reading newspapers and books. These pastimes are, of course, not participated in equally by the older and younger members of the family. One of the reasons why this is so is that parents will usually put their children's interests before their own, allowing such expenses for the children but considering them luxuries for themselves.

But it is customary for the younger and older generation to exchange and share their views, knowledge, and experiences. It is traditional to read books and newspapers aloud and to tell about school experiences and films seen. Many children who have received an education have taught reading to their parents. One can hardly find a family that does not make some use of the village library. Books are rarely bought, however; the exceptions are children's books, though, now very much in demand.

In no other area have the effects of socialist culture on the collective farm family been as evident as in the methods of bringing up preschool and school children. This applies to physical training as well as to the spiritual aspect of the child and his character.

The use of untrained midwives has only recently disappeared from Viriatino. Babies of up to a year are now under the supervision of a trained nurse who consults with a doctor. Instructions in the care of babies are given to in-experienced mothers.

Various superstitions connected with babies and pregnancy have also recently disappeared, though some of them are still alive. It has been observed that women, and especially young ones, are reluctant to report their pregnancy to the nurse, and this of course hinders medical aid. Older women are reluctant to give birth in a regular bed; they prefer the child's birth in the steam-bath room or on the floor on a pile of straw. Fortunately the attitudes of the family toward a woman's pregnancy have changed a great deal. Husbands are careful not to impose heavy loads on their wives during pregnancy and shortly thereafter.

Young mothers feed the babies as instructed, according to a timetable; but often they encounter strong opposition from their mothers or mothers-in-law who were brought up to nurse the baby on demand. The baby is wet-nursed for a whole year, and sometimes longer, but at the age of four to six months the baby receives additional food in the form of cream of wheat or some other kind of porridge cooked with milk. The old custom of masticating a cookie and feeding it to the baby still persists.

At present, the prevailing type of cradle is a rocker or one suspended from the ceiling which can be rocked like a hammock. The babies are kept clean, and special linen is now used for the crib. Diapers are also in use. Until the age of four months the babies wear little dresses regardless of sex, but the boys are put in pants after this time. Children are given a great deal of attention, and given both homemade and store-bought toys.

According to observers, the village children are as well developed as city children, and no difference in mental or physical development can be detected. Due to the influence of the city, birthdays are now remembered and gifts are given to the children. An evergreen tree is brought to the house for the New Year and adorned with sweets and toys.

Strict discipline in upbringing is still considered necessary, however, for the well-being of the children. Most people in the village refrain from physical punishment, although they strictly supervise children's activities. Whenever necessary the older children may be explained the reasons for a decision made by their elders, but the decisions are not changed to appease them. They are assigned light domestic work and varied chores in order to have them help with the housework and to develop the child's sense of responsibility to his family. The people of Viriatino feel that the crucial age is between five and seven and that at this time the children should receive strict instructions as to their behavior; otherwise they feel the children will become spoiled and it will be difficult to manage them later.

Youngsters do not swear or use obscenities in front of their parents, but they do it on the street when they get together. At school, the teachers try to eliminate this rough language without much success.[1]

Whenever the children are left in the care of old people, the task of modern upbringing is quite difficult. While the old peasants were very demanding with regard to their own children, they are completely helpless with their grandchildren and cannot bring themselves to reprimand them or to punish them. This is considered very bad for the children who then have tantrums at the slightest contradiction. In addition to love for their grandchildren, the old folks are probably afraid of gossip among the neighbors, and wish to avoid misunderstandings with their sons and daughters. They are also afraid of the responsibility for the welfare of the children.

In the 1930s the kolkhoz organized a kindergarten for the children of its members. The kindergarten occupies two floors in a separate part of the kolkhoz club and has a

---

[1] Swearing is a long standing habit among the Russians, both young and old, and this was also true before the Revolution. They admire proficiency and sophisticated use of vocabulary in swearing. Elaborate expressions are called "three-story swearing."

dining room, sleeping quarters, and a playroom. The rooms are kept clean and the furniture is child-size. But each mother is required to supply bedding and linen for the small beds.

The children are fed three times a day. The kolkhoz provides flour, buckwheat grain, milk, and apples to the kindergarten. There is a definite schedule; outdoor activities alternate with sleeping periods. Before retiring for the night the children wash their feet, and before eating they wash their faces and hands. In good weather they may play in the kolkhoz park where group games are planned for them and books read. Unfortunately the kindergarten has few toys; those few are made by local carpenters and there are no plastic or rubber ones. The personnel consists of the teacher who also doubles as the administrator and the cook. The village nurse provides medical attention.

It is important to note that in the contemporary kolkhoz family the parents are making serious attempts to keep abreast of the children's studies at school and to make sure that they do their homework. An attempt is also made to develop cleanliness and tidiness in dress.

Most families allow children to go to the movies on Sundays. The boys, however, often congregate near the movie house during the week and try to slip in, regardless of what picture is playing.

Special attention is given to the older students who attend the full ten years of school at Kulevatovo. No matter how difficult conditions at home may be, the families always carefully put aside provisions to support students who attend this school.

Family Customs and Rituals

As has already been mentioned in connection with the increased mobility that followed the Revolution, young men and women who worked outside the village would often marry while away although they seem to prefer marrying their co-villagers. Men marry later now than they did before the Revolution, generally after they have completed their army service and are between twenty-one and twenty-five. The young women marry earlier, between eighteen and twenty, except those who want to continue their educations. Marriages tend to be based on mutual sympathy and agreement; they seldom come about as a result of a prolonged friendship. A girl will very rarely wait for her young man to finish his military service, no matter how friendly they have been before he leaves; she is afraid that when he comes back he will not want her anymore. When they have finished their term of service the young men look for wives slightly younger than themselves because they consider the girls their own age too old.

A young man, as an example of this, having finished his army service worked for a year in the Don Basin. He decided to marry a girl from his own village. The girl he had liked before going into the Army had married someone else. A second girl turned him down because she wanted to continue her education. Then he met a third girl and sat next to her at the club three days in a row and then proposed. She accepted and they got married. "We don't ask for great friendship," remarked one of the young farmers. "You find a girl you like and marry her."

Traditional marriage customs are generally observed. Of eleven marriages in 1954, only one was not traditional. In this case the two young people met outside the village, reached an understanding and then, having informed their families of their intentions, consented only to a small evening party for their relatives and some of the usual partying. Generally speaking, parents do not bring pressure on their children and where the family does attempt to interfere, the young couple will generally assert their independence. Here, for example, is a conversation which took place between one mother, her son, and the prospective bride. The bridegroom's family was making preparations for the forthcoming marriage but the parents of the young couple had not met as yet to discuss the marriage contract and conditions. The mother was just about to leave to visit the bride's parents and arrange for the match when her son came in with his fiancée. "Will you give us your consent?" the son asked. "But," replied the mother, "we haven't reached any agreement with the bride's family yet. Who wants a marriage contract anyhow?" Masha, the bride, said, "You can decide as you please but our minds are made up." The son added, "Well, Mother, as you wish; I'm going to marry her." In another family the mother objected to her younger daughter's marriage because her older sister was still single. The girl went ahead with her plans just the same.

The marriage ritual as it is now performed in Viriatino derives from customs which were established long before the Revolution. Although the decision to marry is made by the young people, the traditional meeting between the two sets of parents to make the betrothal official is still considered essential. The bridegroom's mother goes by herself or with a close relative and the matchmaker to call on the family of the bride. Food and drinks are not offered during this meeting. The bride and groom's parents then decide on the amount of money to be spent, the dates to be set, the guests to be invited, etc. An agreement is also reached on the amount of flour the bride will be expected to add to her new family's supply (the average person is estimated to consume forty pounds of flour per month). No discussion is necessary to fix the dowry as it is adjusted according to the bride's means, but a rather detailed list is drawn up of the linen and bedding the bride will bring with her. A young girl makes up her dowry over a period of years. Mothers are especially eager to help their daughters by saving wherever they can so as not to be "criticized by other people." At present only relatives and very close friends of both families are invited to the wedding, but the ritual of the toasting proceeds according to the old ceremonial forms.

Several days after the ceremonial toasting the young couple will register with the civil authorities and then proceed to the bridegroom's house, where they are entertained with food and drink. Only members of the groom's family are present. This is the first time the bride enters her husband's house as his wife.

It is becoming more and more accepted for the act of registration to provide by itself the necessary step for a marriage to be formally recognized by society. Many young people consider themselves married after the registration, but the young woman continues to live with her parents. It is often said by the villagers that the traditional wedding ceremony is necessary before the young woman can move into her husband's house.

The wedding currently takes place in the course of two days' festivities. On the evening before the wedding the bride's "bed-bundle" is brought to her husband's house; this is usually done in the late afternoon. A trunk containing the bride's dowry is placed in the far right-hand corner of the bridal chamber; a featherbed, a pillow, and two bundles, one of them containing gifts for the groom, are placed on top of it, and, in keeping with the old tradition, a broom decorated with multicolored rags is placed on top of everything. The matchmaker and close female relatives who are guests of the groom bring a bottle of vodka and a loaf of bread. They then carry on a mock auction of the bride with the bride's girl friends in which the groom is forced to state a price for his new wife. The money he agrees to pay is then spent on refreshments for all the girls.

When they arrive with her "bed-bundle" the bride's relatives give the bedroom and all the rest of the house a thorough cleaning, decorating it with items that form part of the dowry (they hang curtains, decorate the far corner of the bridal chamber, etc.), after which they are fed and entertained. Songs and dancing last late into the night.

The wedding itself includes all the moments of the traditional ceremony; the parents give their blessing, the bride's seat beside the groom is ransomed, the mother-in-law unveils the bride and then dances with the veil. The wedding feast begins in the bride's house and then moves to the bridegroom's. The bridegroom's youngest brother leads the bridal procession to the bridegroom's house with a hen in his hand according to tradition. The bridal procession is met at the gate by parents holding a loaf of bread and a bottle of vodka. The party usually lasts through the following day.

The staunchest advocates of all these traditions are the older people, especially the women, and most of the young people would gladly do without them, but a compromise is usually reached. For example, a marriage took place in 1952 between a young man from the district whose ties with the village were already considered loosened and a young girl from Viriatino. The young couple wanted to limit the celebrations to the bridegroom's house. But because of the pressure from the bride's family, the marriage was celebrated with all the traditional rituals (except for the "gilding" and breaking of the pots).

In the last few years there has been a noticeable tendency to shorten the marriage ceremony and to eliminate those portions which put the young bride and groom in a ridiculous or awkward position. The initiative for this change has come from the more progressive and educated elements of the young people who usually work in industry. In one kolkhoz family the daughter married a local young man who worked in a factory in Moscow. He was a member of (the Young Communist League) and the girl was one of the most talented young members of the community (she had worked for a while in industry too). The wedding took place in Viriatino and the young people gave an evening party after the registration. Several other kolkhoz farmers also decided on a simple "evening party" in place of the traditional ceremonies.

The basic reconstruction of family life among the former peasants began with the introduction of collective farming in the early thirties, but that did not mean an immediate end to all forms of religious observance. The effects in adult education together with the tremendous progress of the Soviet schools for children hastened the formation of an atheistic outlook among the village youth, but this process still did not affect the older generation which was in the main responsible for preservation of traditional forms. In 1933 the village church was closed in accordance with the wishes of the bulk of the Viriatino population. The older people were dissatisfied and since they were afraid that all traces of religion would disappear from daily life they strenuously opposed the efforts of the younger people to do away with particular rituals. This is the chief reason why vestiges of certain rituals continue to survive in Viriatino families to this day, especially in the celebration of religious holidays and in connection with the major events in the life of a family: birth, death, and marriage.

Some of these customs and rites have almost entirely lost their significance and continue to be observed only as a matter of habit. Others, especially those connected with the above-mentioned events, continue for the most part to preserve some element of religious belief. The lack of new forms to solemnize these major events accounts in part for the tenacity of the old customs, and it explains, for example, the continued vitality of the traditional marriage ceremony. Moral pressure of the community as a whole also has a bearing; in frequent instances where there is no inner conviction as to the meaning of a particular custom it will be retained because the people are afraid of what their relatives, neighbors, and fellow villagers will say. The attitude toward icons will serve as a good example of the effect of such moral pressure because with few exceptions they are in all of the houses in the village. But this in no way indicates strong religious feelings. One of the main reasons these icons are still kept is because the people are afraid to defy convention. There are still icons in the house of one of the older collective farmers, a man with a thoroughly communistic outlook. "I keep them to humor the wife," he said. "She says, 'I don't want people coming to visit and find no icons in our house.'" One old woman explained, "Nobody in our house prays. I've forgotten how myself. But all the same we keep the icons. An empty corner without icons doesn't look right." A typical incident occurred in the home of another collective farmer; a confirmed atheist had asked his wife more than once to remove the icons but she resolutely refused and yet when her husband took them down without telling her, she noticed it two weeks later.

The same holds true with regard to religious holidays. The most frequently celebrated in Viriatino today are Christmas, Epiphany, Easter, Troitsa (a movable holiday, fifty days after Easter Sunday), and also the local Saint's Day, St. Michael's. But if all these holidays involved a whole complex of customs related to the general culture of family life before the Revolution, today their very essence, and most importantly, the role they play in family life have entirely changed. The women, especially the young ones, usually have to rely on the older women in the community who are better informed about the Church calendar to sort out one holiday and its meaning from another. This meaning, in addition, is variously understood by the members of different generations. Only the older generation in the family, especially the women, invest them with religious significance.

The men and younger people are coming more and more to regard Church holidays as days of rest and gaiety. One collective farmer defined this attitude very well when he said: "Faith is obsolete. We spend holidays eating and resting from work. In our family the holidays are observed mostly by Father."

Even so, religious holidays remain an essential feature of family life. In families where there are old people, important annual holidays are celebrated no less than two days in a row, and St. Michael's Day, up to three. Young families rarely take off more than a day, although they too regard the holidays as special occasions. They will prepare more elaborate meals, leave off the regular housework, and pay calls on relatives. The house is cleaned beforehand, white curtains are hung, a fresh coverlet is put on the bed, and the entranceway is decorated. On the evening before a holiday the whole family takes a steam bath.

Specific ritual observance during the different holidays is almost entirely obliterated, but a few elements of religious significance are still preserved to a greater or lesser degree depending on the family. The head of the household, for example, will signal the beginning of a holiday meal in accordance with an old custom whereby he drinks a glass of vodka alone and then fills the glasses of the remaining members of the family in order of age, after which the whole family sits down to eat. Several traditions continue to be preserved in the celebration of Easter. Nobody, for example, fasts any more, but the "breaking of the fast" is observed by beginning the Easter meal with eggs, milk, and cottage cheese, after which everyone sits down to the table.

In some families, especially those of very old people, certain rites in connection with the Epiphany are still performed, particularly the custom of going to the river at midnight to fetch holy water. The family begins the holiday meal by drinking it. The old people sprinkle it around the house and in the cattle yard. In other families there is no trip to the river, but water is taken from the well for the same purpose, as it is thought that all water is sanctified on Epiphany night. This ritual is no longer practiced in the families of the younger people, nor are crosses placed by children (in those families where this custom still prevails it is done by adults) on the gates, window screens, and the doors of the barn and storehouse. These are long outmoded and scarcely practiced.

Many religious rites would seem at first glance to have entirely disappeared, but their influence is still felt. Weddings do not take place during Lent, for example. A "toasting day" can occur, as they did at an earlier time, but no singing is allowed as it is considered sinful during Lent. In one kolkhoz family a widow was hurrying the wedding preparations because the bridegroom was going into the Army and the bride was afraid that if the wedding didn't take place before he left, she couldn't move into his house until his military service was over. Nonetheless, the wedding was postponed until after Lent. The same holds true in regard to the prohibitions on work at holiday time or during holidays. Old people consider work sinful at such times, and the members of the younger generation, especially the women, respect this custom. Where direct influence of the older generation is lacking, the religious rites and traditions have, for the most part, considerably weakened. The kolkhoz farmers themselves are frequently aware of this tendency. A villager named Makarova began to neglect the observance of traditional rites as did the rest of her family when her household split up in 1947. In her own words she began to forget the holidays, and although there were icons in the house nobody in the family prayed. "Children cannot be forced to pray," she said. "Their life is different from ours."

Among those religious customs which continue in practice but lack true significance are those connected with the birth of children. Almost all of the children are baptized. "The old customs will go away by themselves, but in the meantime we are going to baptize our children," said one young couple. Baptism is not obligatory on the second or third day after birth as it used to be, but can occur whenever circumstances warrant, in some instances when the child is already half-grown. But the christening (actually a joint celebration of the birth and christening) occurs immediately after the mother has left the hospital or several days after the birth of the child if it took place at home, regardless of whether the child had been baptized or not. The christening party is traditional in form. A godmother and godfather is chosen usually from among the younger generation. A special dinner takes place to which relatives bring refreshments. They are seated around the table according to the degree of the relationship, the godfather and godmother at the head together with the closest relatives. At the end of the meal the guests present their gifts to the child by laying them on two plates set out for this purpose. Money is put on one plate, and gifts on the other. The evening is finished off with harmonica playing, dancing, and singing. The absence of a number of elements which were once considered essential—the role of the midwife, the ban on the mother's presence, and, most importantly, the baptism of the child as the necessary condition to the party—makes this gathering an ordinary family celebration to mark the birth and naming of a newborn child. It is accepted by literally everyone.

In the majority of families those religious customs connected with the burial of the dead are strictly maintained; burials are traditionally Christian. In the period of 1952–56 there were only three civil burials. In all other instances a religious ritual is observed including a reading of scripture over the dead and those parts of the service which do not require the presence of a priest. There are funeral suppers after the service and on the ninth day and fortieth days following.

Prayers for the dead were discontinued after the church was closed, and only the very oldest women continue to observe certain rites connected with a whole cycle of ancient notions about life after death. One social activist worker noticed how, on a recent Saturday before Shrovetide, old housewives put the first of a freshly baked batch of pancakes beneath the icon. The purpose of this pancake is to remind the living of their dead relative. The members of the family are to remember him while eating the food. This custom is only found among older people; the middle generation, not to mention the younger, do not pay any attention to such practices, and, indeed, for the most part, have never even heard of them.

The instances in which certain traces of outworn customs survive in village life indicate the marked influence which the old religious ideology continues to exercise on certain portions of the population, thereby helping to impede the socialist reconstruction of village life. A thorough study of all facets of these folk customs would contribute substantially to the work of the party organization and the Soviet agencies in the cultural reconstruction of the village.

CHAPTER XI

SOCIAL LIFE OF THE VILLAGE

The victory of the October Revolution had far-reaching effects on the social stratification of the Russian village. Many people who had previously had no hope of advancement gradually became skilled workers, specialists, managers, and public figures, and this process was accelerated by close ties between the members of the Viriatino community and the working class outside.

It has already been pointed out that some of the poor peasants in Viriatino supported their families by working during the winter months in factories, mines, or at odd jobs. These were the very men who were to introduce proletarian ideology to the village. They, along with soldiers returning home after the war, played a decisive role in collectivizing the peasants and organizing the farm "Lenin's Way," and many became members of the Communist Party. V. M. Kabanov organized Viriatino's first "Committee of Poor Peasants" (Kombed).

In the 1920s no local Communist Party organization existed in the village. There were only two registered party members who formed the nucleus for all political activity in Viriatino. Interestingly enough, all the members of the "Committee of Poor Peasants" considered themselves Communists, although they were never officially members of the Party and had gone through none of the qualifying procedures to become eligible for membership. The two pioneer Communists and the group that formed around them became the first adult study group in Viriatino and were the first to organize cultural and educational life in the village.

One of them, S. S. Kalmikov, grew up in an extended family of relatively affluent peasants. His father worked in the mines for thirty years. After three years of elementary school, the son also became a miner at the age of fifteen. In 1918, having married in the meantime, he began to attend a local school for adults. He fought in the Civil War and returned to Viriatino in 1921. Three years later he was elected a deputy of the village soviet and also participated in an amateur theatrical group in the community. Later he took an active part in collectivization and was elected the first Chairman of the collective farm.

In the early 1920s one of the major problems in Viriatino (and throughout the country) was getting women involved in community life. The thirty-four members of the village soviet included not one woman. It was only in 1925 that two women, a young peasant, Zhiriakova, and an elderly widow by the name of Starodubova were elected. Toward the end of the decade two more poor peasant women, Saiapina and Diakova, were likewise voted members of the village soviet. Saiapina was one of six children born to a poor family; her parents were illiterate and she had not gone to school since her father died when she was very young. She started work when she was an adolescent, working during the winter as a housemaid for the local priest and the teachers and during the summer hiring herself out as a day laborer. In 1925 her mother hoping to better her condition forced her to marry a tailor; the marriage did not succeed, however, and after two years Saiapina parted from her husband. She subsequently attended classes for illiterate adults, went to meetings, and gradually became involved in political work. She was elected to the village soviet in 1929. During the period of collectivization she joined other activists in recruiting peasants for the kolkhoz. In recalling those times, Saiapina said that she herself had visited at least eighty households.

There were no more than five or six such activists at that time and all were either widows or unmarried. The only married woman who became active in political life was Yermakova who was not a native of Viriatino. Before her marriage she had lived in another village working as a housemaid; her husband was an agricultural laborer. After their marriage they came to Viriatino and Yermakova became one of the organizers of the Committee of Poor Peasants, taking an active part in local struggles with the kulaks. Later she worked for a few years in the People's Court.

Gradually the wives of some activists became involved in the political life of the village. Thus Burkina, a member of the kolkhoz, recalls that in the late twenties, under the influence of her husband, she began to take part in meetings, was elected a woman's delegate, and took part in the district convention of women activists. Those women activists are now elderly but they remember that their political work took place under difficult conditions because of the strength of traditional attitudes toward women. It was especially hard for young women to liberate themselves from the dominance of the patriarchal family. But gradually the number of women in political life increased, and during the years of collectivization girls constituted about half the membership of the Young Communist League.

All of the village activists had to struggle against not only the political and cultural backwardness of the peasantry, but also the resistance of their own families. Some wives opposed their husbands' devoting time to politics on the grounds that it was detrimental to the well-being of their own households and families. In addition, many activists themselves were not free of the old attitudes. Because of these conflicts the activists had less influence in their own families than outside the home.

The progressive young people were also instrumental in initiating changes. The important role of the Young Communist League should be emphasized. One of the most pressing problems with which the group had to deal with has already been pointed out—the authority of tradition and the resistance to change. Very gradually, however, changes were brought about, and toward the end of the twenties girls began to take part in group activities. The Young Communist League played a considerable part in raising the level of education for the young generation far above that of the rest of the population of Viriatino. This factor was a decisive one in the process of cultural change.

The village soviet forms the nucleus of all social life in the community and constitutes the main source of Soviet power. It decides such issues as the type and amount of taxes, electoral procedures, welfare policies, and general methods of improving living conditions in the village. The Chairman of the collective farm makes regular reports to the plenary meeting of the village soviet about the progress of work on the farm. The village soviet also supervises cultural and educational activities (clubs, schools, libraries, etc.) in the village. Many economic and cultural problems are discussed and decided at the joint meetings it holds with the management of the collective farm. Almost all the members of the village soviet are charged with problems in specific areas. A group of the members, for example, may act jointly with the local physician on medical questions or questions of hygiene. Sometimes disputes will arise between families about boundaries and the like, and in such cases members of the soviet try to work out solutions. Sometimes they are asked to settle disputes within a family.

The soviet also organizes political activities in the village. One rather large committee is responsible for the political education of the village population. This group includes Communists, members of the Young Communist League, and non-party members. To simplify organization the entire village is divided into groups of ten houses and one person is held responsible for each group.

Two of the most important events in village life are the local and the state-wide elections. Campaigns start well in advance of the voting. During the local campaign the members of the soviet must report on their achievements while in office. A number of meetings are called to nominate candidates. Election day is a holiday and the atmosphere is very festive. Voting takes place in the high school and the older people consider it their right of seniority to cast first vote. Everyone remains at school after voting and there is some kind of social function, perhaps a movie or a concert.

A brief look at the life histories of members of the village soviet makes clear the backgrounds and experiences of local activists. S. Ozhogin, for example, was born in Viriatino in 1907 and had finished only three years of grade school when the October Revolution broke out. When the school was reopened in Viriatino after the Revolution he was to begin again in the first grade. But he was drafted into the Army instead and following the Civil War was sent to study animal farming. In 1935 he was elected Chairman of the collective farm. Three years later he was sent to the Riazan agricultural technical school. But again war broke out—the Second World War—and he fought again. After returning home he was again elected Chairman of the collective farm.

E. Starodubova is another example of the more active type of person. Her family was one of the first to become a member of the kolkhoz, and she has been working for fifteen years in the livestock division of the farm. Before the Second World War her husband was a member of the managing board of the collective farm and also worked in the livestock division but was killed during the war. Starodubova was then sent to take agricultural courses and became a well-trained specialist. She still continues to study, however, and has been attending a three-year seminar on cattle breeding given by the regional veterinarian. In 1951 she was elected to the village soviet and in 1953 to the managing board of the farm as well.

V. Kalmikova, born in 1921, is a representative of the

younger generation and studied accounting. As a member of the Young Communist League she took an active part in community social activities. She was elected a member of the village soviet and served on the jury of the People's Court. Just before the Second World War she finished a course in mechanics without giving up any of her numerous jobs, but she had no opportunity to begin working as a tractor driver because she entered the Army shortly after the war broke out. It was during her military service that she became a member of the Communist Party. After the war she returned to Viriatino and worked as a bookkeeper. She was elected secretary of the local party organization and a member of the village soviet. After graduating from the district party school she was invited to work on the Sosnovsky District Committee of the Communist Party of the USSR. She is currently a professional party worker.

Peasant women made up the most conservative group among the rural population and were initially very reluctant to join the collective farm. They later realized the advantages of participation, however, since work offered them economic independence and gave them a sense of importance within the family group. Thus many young women who had to stop working on the farm because of family complications were eager to return to their jobs as soon as possible.

The most socially active element of the population in Viriatino consists for the most part of teachers and the intelligentsia. The teachers were among the first to welcome the Revolution. They participated in the new social life of the village from the outset and contributed to the development of the new culture. The first school for adults was opened with the help of a teacher, D. Popov. Toward the end of the twenties another teacher, Bobrov, became a member of the Commission for Eliminating Illiteracy. A. Nagornova, also a teacher, worked with women. Many teachers served as lecturers and propagandists. Even now the collective farmers remember these teachers with gratitude. For example, S. Kolnikov, recalling these teachers, said, "They were enthusiasts."

The teachers worked very hard to organize and strengthen the collective farm community. In many instances they accomplished more in this respect than did imported specialists, for they commanded the trust and respect of the people. They were personally acquainted with many of the inhabitants of Viriatino, understood the problems of rural life, and were able to find ways to influence the peasants. Although they were not themselves members of the collective farm they took part in many discussions at the plenary meetings of the farmers, were active in volunteer work squads, and contributed a great deal in terms of moral support. Every week they would organize discussion groups in the village club and were also very active participants in the amateur dramatic groups.

Most of the teachers belonged to the generation of the intelligentsia which began its activities long before the Revolution. Some of them settled in Viriatino permanently. Now the village has a rather large group of educated people consisting of ten teachers, an agronomist, a physician, librarians, the postmaster, and other state employees, in addition to modern specialists such as radio-technicians and electricians. These people were born either in Viriatino or in the surrounding neighborhood.

The present generation of high school teachers is better trained and educated than those of the older generation. In the twenties and even in the thirties there were no teachers who had advanced degrees. Of the ten teachers now in Viriatino two have university degrees, three are taking university correspondence courses, and two are preparing to enter the university. During the summer these teachers spend a considerable portion of their time and money on trips to Tambov, Moscow, and other large cities so that they can become well informed about cultural developments. On their return to Viriatino they are active as lecturers and will speak to the community several times a month on topics of scientific, political, literary, and agricultural interest. They are highly respected in the village and are welcome visitors in the people's homes. Very often they are consulted on personal problems. Many of their former pupils maintain contact with them and when they return to the village for a visit they drop in at the school. The teachers themselves form a closely knit group often passing weekends together, meeting at private parties and literary discussions, and always spending holidays and special occasions such as New Year's Eve in each other's company.

The influence of the teachers in such matters as speech, deportment, dress, and so on is very far-reaching and they teach as much by example and practice as they do through formal instruction. The collective farmers look up to them and try to emulate their behavior.

Radical changes in village life were reflected in the development of new customs which have acquired a certain authority. The public celebration of two Soviet holidays, May 1 and November 7, has come to occupy a central place in the village calendar. At one time, only the more activist part of the population and the schoolchildren participated, but now the whole village is involved. On the evening before the holiday the people gather in the clubhouse and hear a speech outlining the achievements of the previous year, after which there is a concert or a dance. Over the holidays the villagers meet in each other's homes in small groups; this is itself an innovation in social life since before the Revolution such parties included only relatives. Young people have their own gatherings.

Over the last several years, holidays that were previously considered typical only of city life such as New Year's Eve have begun to be observed in the village. In many families the houses are decorated with evergreens. The new celebrations and holidays have gradually come to replace the old religious festivals.

Certain old customs have been retained, however. A second New Year's Eve, fixed according to the old calendar, is celebrated thirteen days after the official one. On this day a certain ritual is performed; a group of mummers made up mostly of single women between the ages of thirty and forty-five dress up in costume and, dividing themselves into the traditional roles of grandfather and grandmother, master and mistress, gypsies, etc., go from house to house, entertaining with traditional songs and dances. In return they are given small amounts of money with which they give a party of their own on the following day, inviting the families they have visited. Young people do not take part in this amusement since it is considered an offshoot of amateur theatricals. The custom has long since lost its religious and ritual significance and remains merely as a secular entertainment.

Christmas, Easter, and the day of the patron saint of the village are still celebrated as religious holidays, however.

The young generation fully accepts the new ways but also retains some of the old. For example, according to one social convention still observed, a young girl's reputation is damaged if she crosses the threshold of her boy friend's house. After she is married, a girl no longer takes part in the social activities of the young people; she will attend social functions at the club, but as a rule she does not dance. Nor does she join in the activities of the dramatic group and will often stop going to meetings of the Young Communist League. This can be partially explained by the shift of her interests to family matters, but also she runs a risk of being condemned by public opinion if she associates with unmarried men.

Relations between the younger and older generations in the village are characterized by the marked respect of young people for their parents and grandparents. This is an example of the favorable influence of old family traditions. At times awkward situations result, however; a girl well trained for leadership may refuse to take a position which will put her in authority over a woman of her mother's generation, for example.

Viriatino has very few cases of juvenile delinquency or of serious disputes between neighbors. But there is still one very ugly phenomenon; the villagers tend to use foul language, not intending to be insulting or outrageous, but as a matter of course.

CHAPTER XII

CULTURAL REVOLUTION IN
THE VILLAGE

At the close of the Revolution almost the entire population of the village was illiterate. This was one of the factors that hindered the people's active participation in the building of a new life. The elimination of illiteracy became one of the most important goals of the new society and the major precondition of the cultural revolution. The Soviet government's decree on the elimination of illiteracy made it obligatory for all teachers and literate people to help, without pay, in teaching the illiterate to read and write. All the political work of the Communist Party was closely allied to this major effort.

An evening school for adults was organized in Viriatino toward the end of 1918. D. Popov was its only teacher. He had thirty students ranging in age from twenty to thirty, of whom only three were women. Most of the students had completed two or three grades of the village or parochial school, but the majority were completely illiterate. The evening school was named the "Village University," and the students were taught Russian, mathematics, geography, and history. Every day the teacher read newspapers to them and conducted political discussions. They studied then under very difficult conditions; there was no heat in the classrooms and they had no supplies such as books and pens and pencils. But in spite of the hardships, the young peasants worked willingly; they understood that in the new social order there was no place for illiteracy.

An all-out campaign against illiteracy was not to begin

in Viriatino, however, until 1920. Up to 1921 there were 529 completely illiterate persons in the village, 463 of them women between thirty and fifty years old. Two hundred and ninety-eight persons (only forty-two of them men) were exempted from attending school because of advanced age, illness, etc. Studies were cut short in the spring of 1921 because of kulak rioting, but they were resumed in 1922.

The village's educational system for adults was highly organized; all illiterate persons were divided into groups and every teacher or educated activist was made responsible for the studies of one group. The teachers visited the peasants in their homes, and spoke at parents' meetings in the school about the need for literacy. They contacted illiterate married women who had begun school but had subsequently dropped out, sometimes because of family circumstances and domestic responsibilities (frequently because they had the time-consuming responsibility of making cloth), but more often because of the prevailing prejudices against the education of women. The same difficulties were encountered in the attempt to educate young girls. Teachers tried to arouse interest in them by reading interesting books aloud which were then discussed during evening social gatherings. The effort to eliminate illiteracy in Viriatino reached its peak in the thirties. By then even middle-aged women who had previously refused to be taught became interested in studying and asked to be enlisted in the classes. The new forms of collective organization of labor played a decisive part in the elimination of illiteracy since the peasants came to understand that an elementary knowledge of reading and writing was essential to their work. They were not even able to calculate the number of workdays they had earned without such elementary instruction. Only people who were educated to some degree were eligible for work as team leaders and supervisors.

In 1934 there were 183 students enrolled in the school

for adults, most of whom were women under fifty. The program of study continued through three winter terms during which they learned to read and write. There were no special classrooms and the groups would meet irregularly in the houses of the students. If a woman had many children, a teacher would come to her house. The teachers encouraged teenage students to help their parents. Those who had started studying in the 1920s and 1930s and whose education had been interrupted were given refresher courses. The District Department of Education registered all illiterate and near illiterate persons. As recently as 1954 the teachers in Viriatino were giving individual instruction to thirteen women collective farmers (thirty-five to fifty years old).

All these activities had one very interesting result: the peasants in Viriatino became more willing to send their children to school. Even in the 1918–19 academic year there were 237 children in the first four grades of school, a fifty-eight percent increase over the same grades in 1916.

After the Revolution the Church was separated from the State and religious instruction was abolished. This measure was resented in some villages. In Viriatino there were villagers opposed to antireligious education, and some of them did not allow their children to attend school at all.

Some new subjects, history, geography, and social science, were introduced into the primary school curriculum. The teachers tried to inculcate a Communist approach in the pupils, to encourage respect for public property, to accustom them to the idea of working in a collective, and to inspire an interest in newspapers and books.

Through its students the school began to affect family life. Certain elementary notions of hygiene became acceptable because of its influence. Conversely, parents tried to help the school in any way they could; they did all the repair work needed in the schoolhouse, for example. All classes stopped as soon as spring work began in the fields before the Revolution, but now most families are anxious for their children to complete the regular school year. A certain backwardness persisted, however, since some families still refused to send young girls to school, and so they remained illiterate throughout the twenties.

When the laws on compulsory education were adopted parents were no longer able to keep their children from going to school and by 1934 all the school-age children in Viriatino were enrolled. In 1930 the primary school was reorganized and a fifth grade was added; in 1933 it was extended through the seventh grade. By 1953 only twenty-one percent of the village population consisted of illiterate or near illiterate persons, most of whom were old villagers born in the nineteenth century, and primarily women.

During the Second World War a number of young men and girls were unable to finish the seven years of grade school. Today Viriatino has a night school, and in 1955 all the young men between fifteen and twenty-five who had received an inadequate education were attending it.

At the present time there are plans to build a much-needed high school in Viriatino. Since 1950 about half the young people in the village have been continuing their studies at the Kulevatovo High School; in 1954 there were forty-three students (ten boys and thirty-three girls) from Viriatino enrolled there. Most of them lived in dormitories, but some rented rooms locally. There are two dormitories on the premises, one for boys and the other for girls. The rather large rooms are furnished with beds and a table which is used for eating meals and for doing homework in the evening. There are no closets; clothes are kept in chests beside the beds or simply hung on the walls. Each student has a separate night table.

The students spend the weekends in Viriatino and take food from home for the following school week (bread, potatoes, butter, etc.). Each dormitory is equipped with kitchen utensils and a large stove. A female staff member (who has the status of an instructor rather than that of a cook) helps the students prepare meals. Usually students eat together in groups of four and five. Housemothers are responsible for discipline, room inspection, and especially the supervision of homework. Boarding school conditions are thought to exercise a favorable influence on the student, teaching him how to plan his time and how to live successfully in a collective.

In addition to its academic curricula the school introduced vocational training so that those who did not continue their education after high school would have an opportunity to learn some skill such as carpentry or blacksmithing. This training is included in every student's education and is required even of those who will continue studying in other areas. Much of the furniture in the dormitories and classrooms (chairs, benches, rostrums, etc.) is made by the students. The older students have an opportunity to study meteorology since the school offers a particularly good program in this area and has equipment for making the sort of meteorological observations that can be of help to the collective farm. As a result the students come to feel that their studies can lead to concrete contributions to the work of the collective.

Certain hobby groups under the auspices of a local branch of the Young Communist League and the "Pioneer Organization" are popular among students. Among these are chess groups, singing and dancing groups, a physics study group, and a literary society. These amateur activities are of considerable interest to the collective farmers.

The Collective Farm Specialists and
Viriatino Intelligentsia

The diversified work of a collective farm requires many specialists. A tremendous effort has been made by the government to train tens of thousands of agronomists, veterinarians, stockbreeders, etc. Many specialized training programs and schools have been established, and the young generation has been offered unprecedented opportunities for training that could not even have been dreamt of in the old Russian villages.

During the first ten years after the kolkhoz "Lenin's Way" was organized (1930–40), fifteen members of the community became tractor drivers and mechanics. The first tractor mechanics, S. Neverov and D. Nagornov, were middle-aged. During World War II, twenty-two more were trained as tractor mechanics, four of them women.

All the main categories of collective farm work are headed by experienced and specially trained managers, all either born in the village or at least long-time residents. The manager of the dairy farm and sheep farm is P. Makarov, a graduate of a special school. The farm veterinarian, A. Matrochin, is likewise a trained professional. I. Sukhov was trained as a forester, and O. Matrochina a bookkeeper. O. Matrochina's assistants, A. Neverova and E. Diakova, also graduated from a special training school.

In the interests of progress and the modernization of machinery, a high level of education and professionalism is expected of all the collective farm personnel. During the winter all team and brigade leaders attend weekly courses in agriculture, thus combining theoretical studies with the discussion of practical problems that arise in the course of work. Ten members of the community graduated from such courses in 1954–55. In 1955 several farmers were proposed for special study in electronics, mechanics, and beekeeping. Correspondence courses are also very popular with collective farmers, especially with the younger generation.

Until recently there was a tendency to leave the village and work in the factories or plants of nearby cities. This was especially true of young people as a result of two factors: first, their desire to obtain special skills and to take advantage of city life, and second, the inadequate organization of work on the collective farm and the inadequate salary system. Young men returning from the army were unable to receive any special training on the collective farm and therefore they too were attracted to the cities. The situation, however, has been improved as a result of new legislation in 1955. The demand for technicians, mechanics, and others has increased and with it the desire of the young men to remain in the village.

A completely new phenomenon in Viriatino is the emergence of a well-educated rural intelligentsia. Before the Revolution there was hardly any opportunity for a peasant to receive a higher education; now it had become the rule more often than the exception.

I. Malakhov is an example. He is the son of one of the most active organizers of the Viriatino Kombed. His father completed only three grades of grammar school in Viriatino, but Malakhov and his brothers and sisters have all had a university education. Their family was large. Ivan, the oldest son, finished primary school in 1927. He was one of the most advanced students in his class and his teacher, insisting that his education be continued, enrolled him as a matter of course in the Sosnovka High School. The Malakhovs, however, were in difficult position financially at the time, and his mother told him, "You know, Vanya, you need clothes to go to school and money for room and board, but I cannot give them to you." Ivan, therefore, had to remain at home to help his mother while his father worked temporarily in the Donbass during the winter. But in 1930 when the fifth grade was established in the Viriatino school, he was able to continue his studies while working as a postman in the village, accumulating twenty workdays a month. During the summer he was a nightwatchman in charge of horses. Despite his efforts he was unable to complete high school.

In 1932, however, Ivan Malakhov enrolled in a special course for teachers, and, after completing it, began to teach and to prepare to enter Rabfak.[1] After finishing the three-year program he enrolled in the Voronezh Veterinary Institute. During the few years that followed his graduation, while working, he wrote a Ph.D. thesis which he successfully defended for his degree. His older sister's education was also frequently interrupted and irregular, but in spite of the difficulties she became a teacher. The younger brothers and sisters did not encounter the same problems. In the 1930s the economic situation of the collective farm improved and the family was able to finance the children's education. In 1955 one of the younger Malakhovs graduated from the institute as a chemical engineer and started postgraduate courses. Another son was studying mining engineering and the youngest graduated from high school.

By the end of the thirties the number of educated persons in Viriatino had considerably increased. Between 1930 and 1950 eighty residents of the village received college or university degrees. The men usually became engineers or career army officers. Those who chose the civil branch of service usually became mining specialists because of the long association between Viriatino and mining. Women were most interested in becoming doctors, teachers, or agricultural specialists. It is worth remarking that fifty percent of all those who received a higher education were women.

It is useful to trace the relationship between those residents of Viriatino who left the village (to work in the city, to serve in the Army, or to attend schools of higher education) and those who remained. Almost all of those who left kept in close touch with their relatives and friends. In 1953, 421 persons, forty-four percent of whom were women, lived away from the community. Twenty-

[1] *Rabfak* is an abbreviation of Worker's Faculty, a three-year training course. No previous education is required and there is no entry examination (Tr.).

five were students, and 343 worked in industry or government institutions or were in the military service. Most of them were young or middle-aged. Forty-four percent of the group that left had already had at least seven years of education.

It is important for these people to retain their old ties because they exercise an extremely favorable influence on those who remain in the village and are continuously helpful to their relatives. They express concern for their younger brothers and sisters, taking an interest in their affairs and trying to influence them constructively, as well as offering their families financial assistance. When they come back to visit they show a marked interest in the schoolwork, successes, and personal problems of the younger children. They are able to give their relatives and friends the benefit of their enlarged experience and to introduce new ideas and habits into the old milieu, to the extent of bringing about changes in such apparently minor matters as food, clothing, and furnishings. The inhabitants of Viriatino are very proud of those relatives who have left the village and always welcome their visits. If someone is expected home the family will make preparations for his arrival, cleaning and cooking as for a holiday occasion.[2]

Cultural Life in the Village

In 1918 the first cultural circle, consisting of forty-five persons, was organized for the purpose of making a library, a club, and an evening school for adults available to the community. The following year the village club was opened and the best building in Viriatino was selected for

[2] Every month some 1000 letters, 30 telegrams, 70 parcels, and 30 money orders were sent from Viriatino to Tambov, Moscow, Stalino, Novo Sibirsk, Central Asia, Sakhalin and Kamchatka; in return, an average of 1200 letters, 50 telegrams, 60 parcels, and 100 money orders were sent from these points to Viriatino.

its use. A library opened in 1920. An idea of its activities can be gained from looking over its reports. One of them, covering a period of only three months, October–December 1925, states that there were nine discussions on current events, fifteen lectures, and thirty-nine evenings on which newspapers were read aloud; twenty villagers organized a special group to study political events; and an average of twenty-five persons made use of the library services every day.

The amateur dramatic group occupied a central place in cultural activities, although it was hampered by having no permanent building or headquarters so that finding a place to stage its productions was often difficult. Performances were given in the neighboring villages of Sosnovka, Kulevatovo, and Griaznoe. There were also exchange performances with similar groups in nearby villages. The decade that began in 1930 was the dramatic group's most prosperous period. The average age of the participants was twenty-three. At first women would not join; it was only toward the end of the twenties that some women became interested, and most of these were the sisters of young men who were already active in the group. In spite of all attempts to woo them, the women refused to take part in performances. They would consent only to make costumes and to rewrite some of the roles. In many instances the women's roles were taken by young men.

Girls and young women were at first also reluctant to attend club meetings. The teacher, M. Popova, relates that sometimes a group of young girls would stand around outside the clubhouse trying to get up enough courage to go in. Young girls and boys usually went about in separate groups and were reluctant to mix at dances and other social occasions. There were very few young women among those who went to the club, and these who did were almost always widows of poor peasants. Gradually, however, the situation changed and toward the end of the twenties parents no longer objected to their daughters' taking part in club activities. The club offered the young people an opportunity to meet and to spend time in a social atmosphere. Parties of a sort previously unknown in the village were particularly effective in this respect. On these occasions young people began to learn modern dances and ballroom dancing. Middle-aged people attended the club activities infrequently and when they did, it was usually because there was some scheduled event such as a play, a movie, or a lecture.

The music repertory was changed in the choral group. Years ago only folk songs had been sung but now revolutionary songs and new Soviet songs were added to enrich the repertory. In the 1920s "chastushki"—limericks—came into vogue. Many of the chastushki were derived from conventional songs rewritten to refer to topical events.

Certain traditional types of entertainment were retained for a while. If the club was closed or nothing was scheduled, young people would gather in the street outside and sing songs or play games of traditional kind. But gradually, as club activities became more regular, these impromptu gatherings were given up.

Chess became very popular after the Second World War because many people had learned how to play in the Army. Some of the villagers developed a strong aptitude for this game. A collective farmer, I. Neverov, won the district championship in 1953. Young people in Viriatino also take a keen interest in sports such as skiing, volleyball, football, and track, but because of the lack of equipment not many became experts.

Antireligious propaganda is considered a very important feature of cultural development in the village. The teachers frequently lecture on this subject in the club, taking great care to see that their instruction is not offensive. Interest in these lectures is widespread; those dealing with moral issues have recently been prominent. Two hundred and fifty villagers attended a lecture on social conduct, and there were also large turnouts for lectures on such topics as "The Moral Make-up of Soviet Youth," and "The History of the Komsomol." (There are also many lectures on strictly agricultural topics.)

Cultural life in Viriatino has a seasonal rhythm. Cultural activity is better organized during the winter when the people are free to meet; in the summer when everybody is needed to work in the fields there is a slowdown in activities. The average number of people who use the library, for example, is greatly reduced during the summer. The teachers and lecturers have to go to the fields to reach their audience.

Growth of the Cultural Needs of the Kolkhoz People

One of the marks of expanded cultural interests is the large number of villagers who subscribe to newspapers, magazines, and brochures. Immediately after the Revolution there were very few people who read or subscribed to publications of this type, but by the thirties a newspaper was no longer a rarity. Currently about half of the families in the village subscribe to newspapers and magazines, the most popular of which are *Pravda, Izvestia, Selskoe Kosiastvo* (an agricultural periodical), and two local newspapers, *Tambovskaya Pravda* and *Put' Octyabria.* Men frequently stop by the library in the evening to look through recent issues of newspapers and magazines. Some school children subscribe to *Pionerskaya Pravda,* and two other magazines, *Ogonyok* and *Krestianka,* are very popular with women. Women rarely read newspapers, however, although they do listen to news reports on the radio every day.

The collective farmers' library was opened in 1953, at which time it contained 2584 books. As of January 1956 there were 479 books on agriculture, 993 on political topics, 235 on technical subjects, 1622 works of fiction and literature, and 528 children's books in the library. Four months after it opened, 382 villagers (166 collective farmers, 170 school children, and 26 other people) had taken out membership. By January 1956 this number had increased to 457. Many collective farmers who are not members get books from the school library through their children. Many families, especially those which include children, have started book collections of their own.

Before the Revolution there existed a didactic type of literature compiled from folk, literary, and journalistic sources especially for peasants which was crude and moralizing in tone, but such books are no longer read. Volumes that popularize science (astronomy, physics, and so on) are very popular with elderly men in Viriatino. A completely new phenomenon in the village is the interest in books for preschool children. Such books can be found even in families where the parents are illiterate. The tradition of orally recounting the plots of books is also very popular in Viriatino. *Anna Karenina,* for example, is sometimes so narrated.

Films and radio have become normal features of rural life. The men on the collective farm rarely miss a film shown at the club; leaders, managers, and young married men are particularly interested in films. The elderly among the collective farmers, especially the women, attend showings much more rarely, although on holidays almost everybody goes. Special movies for children are particularly popular, even with parents. Very often the plot of a movie is retold orally after it has been shown.

Every family has a radio set or a loudspeaker. The value of the radio for illiterates is inestimable because it is used to transmit all kinds of useful information.

Broadcasts of music are popular with everyone. The radio is practically the only source of musical education and the repertory of the chorus has been permanently enriched through this means. Classical music is much less appreciated than popular, and concerts of symphonic and chamber music are not listened to with any interest. The exceptions are two operas, Tchaikovsky's *Evgeni Onegin* and Glinka's *Ivan Susanin*.

In spite of the variety in the cultural needs of the different segments of the rural population there is a constantly growing rapport between city and country. However, the gap is still considerable.

ANCHOR BOOKS

HISTORY

FROM THE STONE AGE TO CHRISTIANITY—W. F. Albright, A100

GATEWAY TO HISTORY—Allan Nevins, New, revised edition, A314

HISTORY BEGINS AT SUMER—Samuel Noah Kramer, A175

A HISTORY OF BOLSHEVISM—From Marx to the First Five Years' Plan, Arthur Rosenberg; translated from the German by Ian F. D. Morrow, A588

HISTORY OF ENGLAND, Vol. I—G. M. Trevelyan, A22a

HISTORY OF ENGLAND, Vol. II—G. M. Trevelyan, A22b

HISTORY OF ENGLAND, Vol. III—G. M. Trevelyan, A22c

A HISTORY OF EUROPE, Vol. 1—Henri Pirenne, A156a

A HISTORY OF EUROPE, Vol. 2—Henri Pirenne, A156b

A HISTORY OF ISLAMIC SPAIN—W. Montgomery Watt and Pierre Cachia, A601

A HISTORY OF THE ITALIAN REPUBLICS—J. C. L. Sismondi; Introduction by Wallace K. Ferguson, A520

A HISTORY OF ROME—Moses Hadas, ed., A78

A HISTORY OF WEST AFRICA—Basil Davidson, A550

HITLER'S SOCIAL REVOLUTION—Class and Status in Nazi Germany, 1933–1939—David Schoenbaum, A590

THE HOUSE OF HABSBURG—Adam Wandruszka, A453

IMPERIALISM AND SOCIAL REFORM: English Social-Imperial Thought, 1895–1914—Bernard Semmel, A618

THE INTELLECTUAL HISTORY OF EUROPE, Vol. I: The Beginnings of Western Civilization to Luther—Friedrich Heer, A610a

THE INTELLECTUAL HISTORY OF EUROPE, Vol. II: The Counter-Reformation to the 20th Century—Friedrich Heer, A610b

JOURNEYS TO ENGLAND AND IRELAND—Alexis de Tocqueville; J. P. Mayer, ed., A611

LABOURING MEN—Studies in the History of Labour—E. J. Hobsbawm, A552

MARTYRDOM AND PERSECUTION IN THE EARLY CHURCH—W. H. C. Frend, A546

MEDIEVAL CITIES—Henri Pirenne, A82

MONT-SAINT-MICHEL AND CHARTRES—Henry Adams, A166

A NEW HISTORY OF THE COLD WAR: Third edition, expanded, of A History of the Cold War—John A. Lukacs, A533

THE OLD REGIME AND THE FRENCH REVOLUTION—Alexis de Tocqueville, A60

THE PATH TO DICTATORSHIP, 1918–1933: Ten Essays by German Historians—trans. by John Conway, with an introduction by Fritz Stern, A547

THE PHILOSOPHY OF HISTORY IN OUR TIME—Hans Meyerhoff, ed., A164

THE POLITICS OF CULTURAL DESPAIR: A Study in the Rise of Germanic Ideology—Fritz Stern, A436

ANCHOR BOOKS

ANCHOR BOOKS

Sociology (*continued*)